Titles in Series:

Why It's OK to Trust Science
Keith M. Parsons

Why It's OK to Be a Sports Fan
Alfred Archer and Jake Wojtowicz

Why It's OK Not to Think for Yourself
Jonathan Matheson

Why It's OK to Own a Gun
Ryan W. Davis

Why It's OK to Mind Your Own Business
Justin Tosi and Brandon Warmke

Why It's OK to Be a Gamer
Sarah Malanowski and Nicholas R. Baima

Why It's OK to Be Fat
Rekha Nath

Why It's OK to Be Amoral
Ronnie de Sousa

Why It's OK to Have Bad Spelling and Grammar
Jessica Flanigan

Selected Forthcoming Titles:

Why It's OK to Be a Socialist
Christine Sypnowich

Why It's OK to Be a Moral Failure
Robert B. Talisse

For further information about this series, please visit: www.routledge.com/Why-Its-OK/book-series/WIOK

JESSICA FLANIGAN

Why It's OK
to Have Bad Spelling and Grammar

NEW YORK AND LONDON

Designed cover image: Mayer_Photography / Getty Images

First published 2025
by Routledge
605 Third Avenue, New York, NY 10158

and by Routledge
4 Park Square, Milton Park, Abingdon, Oxon, OX14 4RN

Routledge is an imprint of the Taylor & Francis Group, an informa business

© 2025 Jessica Flanigan

The right of Jessica Flanigan to be identified as author of this work has been asserted in accordance with sections 77 and 78 of the Copyright, Designs and Patents Act 1988.

All rights reserved. No part of this book may be reprinted or reproduced or utilised in any form or by any electronic, mechanical, or other means, now known or hereafter invented, including photocopying and recording, or in any information storage or retrieval system, without permission in writing from the publishers.

Trademark notice: Product or corporate names may be trademarks or registered trademarks, and are used only for identification and explanation without intent to infringe.

ISBN: 978-0-367-89772-7 (hbk)
ISBN: 978-0-367-33323-2 (pbk)
ISBN: 978-0-429-31919-8 (ebk)

DOI: 10.4324/9780429319198

Typeset in Joanna and Din
by KnowledgeWorks Global Ltd.

Why It's OK to Have Bad Spelling and Grammar

Grammatical errors and orthographic mishaps are often played for laughs, but this subtle sanctioning by the sticklerocracy can have real social consequences too. Attention to prescriptive spelling and grammar rules is insidious and harmful.

As Jessica Flanigan argues in *Why It's OK to Have Bad Spelling and Grammar*, grammarianism often maintains hierarchies, entrenches the advantages of privileged groups, and imposes arbitrary barriers to knowledge production and innovation. For example, the stigmatization of bad spelling and grammar disadvantages linguistic minorities, non-native speakers, and people with disabilities. Spelling and grammar norms are also frequently arbitrary and unnecessary. The petty grammandos among us, who cling to pedantic linguistic conventions, are standing in the way of innovative forms of communication and efficient speech, such as the emoji ☺. For these reasons, Flanigan argues that bad spelling and grammar are OK. It's time to break free from the tyranny of the grammilitia in the name of comprehension and creativity. As long as speakers and writers can effectively communicate to charitable listeners and readers, people shouldn't care about bad spelling and grammar.

Jessica Flanigan is the Richard L. Morrill Chair in Ethics and Democratic Values at the University of Richmond, where she teaches Leadership Ethics, Ethical Decision Making in Healthcare, and Critical Thinking. Her research addresses the ethics of public policy, medicine, and business. In *Pharmaceutical Freedom* (2017), she defends rights of self-medication. In *Debating Sex Work* (2019), she defends the decriminalization of sex work.

Why It's OK: The Ethics and Aesthetics of How We Live

ABOUT THE SERIES:

Philosophers often build cogent arguments for unpopular positions. Recent examples include cases against marriage and pregnancy, for treating animals as our equals, and dismissing some popular art as aesthetically inferior. What philosophers have done less often is to offer compelling arguments for widespread and established human behavior, like getting married, having children, eating animals, and going to the movies. But if one role for philosophy is to help us reflect on our lives and build sound justifications for our beliefs and actions, it seems odd that philosophers would neglect arguments for the lifestyles most people—including many philosophers—actually lead. Unfortunately, philosophers' inattention to normalcy has meant that the ways of life that define our modern societies have gone largely without defense, even as whole literatures have emerged to condemn them.

Why It's OK: The Ethics and Aesthetics of How We Live seeks to remedy that. It's a series of books that provides accessible, sound, and often new and creative arguments for widespread ethical and aesthetic values. Made up of short volumes that assume no previous knowledge of philosophy from the reader, the series recognizes that philosophy is just as important for understanding what we already believe as it is for criticizing the status quo. The series isn't meant to make us complacent about what we value; rather, it helps and challenges us to think more deeply about the values that give our daily lives meaning.

Contents

Acknowledgments ix

Introduction 1

Grammarians and Grammar School **1** 9
1.1 Education, Economics, and Citizenship 11
1.2 The Problems with Literacy Instruction 14
1.3 Disability and Disadvantage 18
1.4 Spelling Rituals and Parent Choice 27
1.5 The Style Guide 32
1.6 The Golden Age 37
1.7 Conclusion 40

Spellocratic Sanctioning **2** 49
2.1 Language and Law 51
2.2 The Ethics of Social Sanctions 61
2.3 Advice 75
2.4 Manners 81
2.5 Grammarian Gaslighting 88
2.6 Offense 91
2.7 Conclusion 97

Sticklers and Stigma **3** 103
3.1 Social Egalitarianism 105
3.2 Class 107

	3.3 Gender	114
	3.4 Sexuality and Sexual Identity	119
	3.5 Race, Ethnicity, and Regionalism	124
	3.6 Culture, Language, and Appropriation	130
	3.7 Pronouns and Politics	136
	3.8 Gender, Grammar, and Politics	146
	3.9 Egalitarian Language Policing	151
	3.10 Conclusion	155

Pedants and Progress — 4 — **167**

	4.1 The Anarchic Origins of Language	169
	4.2 Flexible Language Today	176
	4.3 Linguistic Solidarity	181
	4.4 Linguistic Innovation ¯_(ツ)_/¯	184
	4.5 Linguistic Conservativism	193
	4.6 Conclusion	197

A World Without Word-Warriors — 5 — **203**

	5.1 Dispositions	206
	5.2 Sticklerlessness	210
	5.3 Is this argument self-defeating?	213
	5.4 Poor Spellers Untie!	216
	5.5 Conclusion	220

	Appendix	**223**
	Notes	**227**
	Index	**255**

Acknowledgments

In case you were wondering, spelling is not my strong suit. I do not have a gift for grammar. I've heard countless corrections, tricks, and tips for linguistic compliance. My papers were once covered with red ink, and now the screen lights up like a Christmas tree whenever I type. I've lived my whole life under the tyranny of the grammilitia, learning the ways of the formalists, complying with snoots' corrections, and catering to pedantic preferences. Unlike other aspects of my education, studying sticklerism hasn't made me a better thinker or communicator. Regrettably, I've probably wasted hundreds of hours correcting my speech and prose so that it (mostly) followed nitpickers' petty principle. But these negative experiences with all the quibblers and orthography obsessives out there did prepare me to write this book. So, in a small way, I guess I'm thankful to the haters after all.

I'm far more thankful, however, to Andy Beck. As the editor for this series, Andy has been so supportive and flexible throughout this whole process. Even though he works in the word industry, he was refreshingly open to my case for linguistic rebellion. Andy's comments and advice were always spot on, including his insistence that I proofread the manuscript before publication. I guess you gotta fight the battle before you can act like you won it. Even more importantly, Andy was remarkably supportive as I completed the book amid several unexpected delays. I will forever be grateful for his patience and understanding.

I am also thankful to Greg Robson, Alison Suen, and Matt Strohl, who participated in a manuscript workshop for the book in 2023. Together, these commentators provided feedback on the manuscript that challenged me to make the book more accessible and more philosophically interesting. Several anonymous reviewers wrote excellent comments on the proposal or the draft of this book as well. Ryan Davis and Javier Hidalgo also helpfully commented on several of the arguments that appear in this book.

My four children (and their teachers) also inspired me to stick with this project. I hope that this book can contribute to the fall of the Spellocracy in American education and that parents can one day reclaim their evenings from the specter of the weekly spelling test. I would also like to thank my colleagues at the University of Richmond. I've been surprised to find that the case for anti-grammarianism is one of my most controversial takes! But even the committed conventionalists in my School have remained admirably open to my case for linguistic contrarianism. Many of these colleagues commented on the earliest version of this proposal and I've learned so much from our conversations about the origins of orthography and the cultural significance of language.

And finally, though the irony of this is not lost on me, I would also like to thank Jonathan Merrett for working on the final manuscript. If we have to live in a world of linguistic prescriptivism, I am grateful that there are such talented copyeditors to guide clueless people like me through the gauntlet of conventions and corrections.

Introduction

There is a certain kind of person who takes pleasure in pointing out others' shortcomings, especially when it comes to rules of spelling and grammar. We can call these people spelling sticklers, snoots, pedants, grammandos, grammarians, grammar Nazis, quibblers, the grammalitia, word nerds, nitpickers, disciplinarians, prescriptivists, or linguaphiles. They're the people who create the bots on Reddit that 'helpfully' point out common errors of usage. They're the people who make fun of their political enemies by mocking typos and punctuation errors on social media. They're the people who pride themselves on raising children who win spelling bees. They're the teachers who bust out the red pen and gleefully tear apart the mechanics of an essay like a lion eating an antelope, cheerfully blooding the pages while nevertheless failing to actually engage with whatever their students were trying to say. They're the detail-oriented, organized, hyperconscientious people who pride themselves on their neat handwriting and orderly lines, taking these arbitrary aesthetic signifiers as a proxy for intelligence or moral virtue.

I'm against the sticklers. We've ceded too much of the economy of esteem to these snooty pedants. Radical anti-grammarians should reclaim the linguistic landscape, one typo, and mispronunciation at a time. Teachers, editors, email-readers, tweeters, managers, and anyone else who interacts

DOI: 10.4324/9780429319198-1

with the written or spoken world should mostly abandon their tiresome pastime of correcting poor spelling and grammar. What good is it? Praising someone for their excellent spelling and grammar is the faintest praise I can imagine. Discriminating on the basis of spelling and grammar is almost always a pointless exercise that leaves talent on the table for the sake of … avoiding apostrophe errors? People should abandon linguistic sticklerism because, as I am going to argue, it's not only super-annoying, it's also morally bad and it doesn't help anyone ☹.

Do you think I'm exaggerating the snoots' social tyranny? Here is something that professional stickler Lynne Truss recently wrote in an (impeccably proofread, I'm sure) defense of grammarianism:

> If you still persist in writing, "Good food at it's best", you deserve to be struck by lightning, hacked up on the spot and buried in an unmarked grave.[1]

Is this hyperbole? I mean, probably. But we can't be sure with these folks. Sticklers can be really intense; we've all met next-level pedants like the people Weird Al Yankovic parodies in his genius song "Word Crimes." There, Yankovic sings from the perspective of word-warriors who use think that people with bad grammar sound like uneducated morons the grammar police who hear the word 'literally' used as a figure of speech and respond, "That really makes me want to literally smack a crowbar upside your stupid head."[2]

Because of sticklers like Truss and all the other language police out there, there really are significant penalties for orthographic unorthodoxy. These penalties are typically overlooked as subjects of moral inquiry because they seem low-stakes or trivial. Yet at the same time, there are dozens of books and computer programs and so on and so on that instruct people on how to comply with the spelling rules, grammar conventions, principles of punctuation, and all the other trivial rules that govern our language. Why is it petty to complain about the complainers? They are the ones who are being petty.

I also think word-nerds vastly underrate the harm they impose on everyone else by sticking to their stickler ways. After all, a person's perceived competency with spelling and grammar can affect her wellbeing because it's a real downer to hear people's judgmental little corrections all the time. When children are sorted by their linguistic compliance in school, this system turns some kids into copy-cops and others into orthographic offenders. And the cycle of viciousness continues as grade school grammarians grow up and enter the workforce. And for what? We can understand each other even if some of us break linguistic rules from time to time. It's not morally wrong to spell things in a way that departs from convention. Errors and innovations in language don't hurt anyone. It's not wrong to use slang. It's not wrong to eschew the Oxford comma. It's not wrong to speak with an accent. It's not wrong to know only some parts of a language but to try to speak and write it anyhow. All of these things are OK.

It's OK to have bad spelling and grammar!

In contrast, it's *not* OK to be a stickler about spelling and grammar. I'm not saying that sticklerism is a crime or that doctrinaire social dictators like Truss should be struck by lightning (I would never! If only because lightning is a tricky word to spell). Rather, I'm saying that there are a lot of reasons against living this way, and I'm pleading with the social tyrants among us to please just cool it with the corrections.

People should not interrupt speakers to 'correct' their speech because these little interventions usually serve as an effort to assert social dominance through condescension. People shouldn't uphold a system of sanctioning and stigma that hurts people's feelings and makes them feel inadequate. People with privileged linguistic capacities should not vocally defend norms that perpetuate social inequality and maintain their own position in an unfair social hierarchy. Maybe word nerds think of their linguaphilia as a harmless hobby. Do a crossword puzzle! Making other people feel ashamed because they communicate differently is a bad hobby. Instead, spelling stans should just consider playing Scrabble or Wordle or some other boring game they can keep to themselves. Leave the rest of us out of it.

The case against grammarianism includes four claims, which I will develop in the next four chapters:

- Education would be better without the grammarians.
- It's bad to correct peoples' speech and writing.
- Sticklerism undermines social equality.
- Pedants are the enemies of linguistic innovation.

Together, these four related arguments support the conclusion that everyone should just chill out about how other people speak and write. It's perfectly OK to use non-standard spelling or to violate grammar rules despite what the most uptight 10 percent of listeners and readers say about it. We should all stop living in fear of correction. We should stop catering to the language police. It's time to liberate our language—and ourselves!

The first chapter is about schooling. Most people first encounter linguistic authoritarianism in an educational setting. Throughout history, schools have partly served as a means of preparing children to become compliant and effective citizens and workers. By training students to adhere to prescribed linguistic conventions, educators could accomplish both of these goals. But when we look at the evidence, it's clear that reading and writing instruction in most schools is bafflingly counterproductive if the goal of school is to teach children to read, write, and communicate effectively. Rather, contemporary schooling forces students to comply with a strict set of linguistic rules, to participate in a punishing schedule of weekly spelling testing, and to write rote, boring five-paragraph essays. Not only does this one-size-fits-all fail to promote literacy for many students, but it also rewards students for neuroticism and compliance instead of cultivating more valuable verbal skills like critical thinking and reading comprehension.

The second chapter is about social sanctions. It's probably clear to anyone who's been subject to the enforcement of linguistic norms that these practices are harmful if only because they are really annoying. But it's kind of puzzling why it's so bad for sticklers to uphold these norms in everyday life. One reason is that corrections can be insulting. Sticklers can make people feel ashamed or inadequate. Their little passive-aggressive amendments to people's speech are rarely well-motivated. Instead, they amount to an assertion of dominance, or they provide a signal of their allegedly superior intelligence or education. People also use language as a means of social control. From the simplest standards that specify semicolon usage to large-scale government propaganda, people realize that controlling others' language is an especially effective way to control their behavior and their thoughts. For this reason, linguistic disobedience is not only interesting and innovative, it can also be a form of quiet resistance to some of the subtler forms of social control. For these reasons, the enforcement of linguistic norms is makes people worse off when they weren't liable to be made worse off. This analysis of the wrongfulness of linguistic normativity sheds light on broader debates about the ethics of social life.

In the third chapter, I argue further that linguistic policing is also harmful because it is objectionably inegalitarian. I begin by explaining why people have reasons to uphold norms that help everyone relate as equals, and then I show that linguistic normativity is contrary to this goal. The data bears this out. In general, the harms of correction disproportionately burden people who already occupy a disadvantaged position in society—young people, minority groups, non-native speakers, people with disabilities, and people with lower socioeconomic status.

The fourth chapter is about linguistic innovation. There, I make the positive case for mixing it up and breaking some spelling and speech rules. One defense of language policing stems from a fear of linguistic anarchy. Someone needs to keep the commas and apostrophes in line, the thinking goes, or no one would be able to communicate! The first thing to point out in response to this defense is that there were no language police for most of human history, and people seemed to manage. Linguistic anarchy is the norm. And the second thing to say to this defense is that linguistic anarchism is actually great. Language is always in flux, and that's how languages adapt to the changing needs of the people who use them. It's not socially destructive to violate linguistic rules; it's socially destructive to work so hard to maintain them.

In the concluding chapter, I talk about the broader implications of this argument. Many of the arguments for linguistic transgressiveness are also arguments for other forms of low-stakes non-compliance. Many of the arguments against grammarianism are also arguments against social sanctioning in other contexts. These arguments show that even if social norms are not enforced, the subtle dynamics of correction, blame, exclusion, and sanctioning are nevertheless subjects of justice. The upshot here is that everyone should care a little less about the rules and go a little easier on the people who break them. There's a broader lesson here. If we all stopped looking for flaws and living in fear of correction, we could focus on listening, and the world of words would be so much more fun for everyone.

NOTES

1. Lynne Truss, *Eats, Shoots & Leaves: The Zero Tolerance Approach to Punctuation*, 1st edition (New York: Avery, 2004).
2. Weird Al Yankovic, *Word Crimes*, Mandatory Fun (RCA Records, 2014).

Grammarians and Grammar School

1

People experience the imposition of linguistic normativity from an early age. Schoolchildren encounter the rules of speech and writing as they learn to speak and write. A substantial part of most children's education consists in spelling and grammar instruction that continues well into high school and college. This kind of instruction indoctrinates students into the ideology of sticklerism. Students who are capable of pleasing pedantic instructors are praised while students who may love reading and writing are nevertheless punished for noncompliance.

Educators may defend the decision to teach spelling and grammar on the grounds that students must comply with linguistic rules in order to succeed as adults. Yet this justification overlooks the possibility that competency with spelling and grammar is only necessary because people mistakenly value this competency, likely because their teachers told them that spelling and grammar skills were valuable!

To the extent that schools emphasize compliance with a privileged set of linguistic rules, this approach rewards nondisabled children and children from families whose speech complies with those rules. Not only is schools' current emphasis on linguistic normativity inegalitarian, it's also counterproductive to the more important goal of promoting literacy and a love of reading for children. Spelling and grammar instruction can

DOI: 10.4324/9780429319198-2

be useful, but it can also divert resources from more urgent instructional priorities and disproportionately disadvantage students with learning disabilities. Additionally, the widespread practice of holding weekly spelling tests in Grades 1–5 is a truly unconscionable tax on working families' already scarce time.

The oppressive effects of linguistic normativity don't end with primary school instruction either. Even adult readers and writers can face penalties if they fail to comply with the English teachers' rigid demands for language. Authors publish style guides to remind adult writers of the myriad ways they can fall short of prescriptivists' communicative ideals.

Maybe the worst part of this whole system is the obvious fact that many of the rules we've been taught are so clearly arbitrary and unnecessary. Each generation learns a strict set of linguistic guidelines in school and then some people in that generation appoint themselves the guardians of grammar and determinedly enforce the conventions that happened to be popular when they were in school as if these conventions represented the platonic ideal of the written word. Meanwhile, language slowly changes despite the vigilante efforts of the grammar gang, and it's clear that none of us needed these fusspots in the first place.

There's a better way. In this chapter, I argue that educators should focus on literacy instead of linguistic compliance. At a broad level, this means that educators should care about whether a child can comprehend what she is reading and effectively communicate, and educators should focus very little on matters of style or punctuation. At the specific level, this means that educators should throw out their red pens, weekly spelling tests, and tournament spelling bees. Instead, educators should focus on fostering literacy skills that are practically important for reasons other than social prejudice.

1.1 EDUCATION, ECONOMICS, AND CITIZENSHIP

Philosophers have long argued that education is a subject of justice. We can measure the extent that a society is just, in part, by knowing how people in the society educate their fellow citizens. If justice requires that all people have equal opportunities to succeed, then justice requires an education system that promotes equality of opportunity.[1] If justice requires that everyone have the capacity to participate in society and to meet their basic needs then a just society will have an education system that brings everyone to that level of sufficient capacities.[2] Most philosophers and policy scholars who write about education and justice talk about educational equity broadly. For example, they talk about whether public officials should abolish private schools for the sake of equality. Or, they argue about whether parents should be allowed to choose whether and how to educate their students.[3]

Considerations of justice also apply to the curriculum, even if curricular decisions are not as salient to voters and lawmakers. When philosophers discuss the ethics of the curriculum in public and private schools, they generally focus on civics education. In some instances, philosophers emphasize the importance of education as a way of cultivating civic virtue and promoting democratic institutions.[4] They also complain that education is indoctrinating students into the dominant statist ideology.[5] Or philosophers and politicians alike object to the way that educators teach about race, sexuality, or history.[6] It's clear that curricular choices about how people teach children about patriotism, virtue, history, race, sexuality, or other normatively charged topics can matter for questions of justice. But some of the same moral reasons that should apply to these curricular debates also apply to curricular choices about seemingly neutral topics, such as how schools teach reading and writing. Say that public education is at least partly justified as a way of reducing social and economic disparities among citizens. Could this justification support a prescriptive approach to language instruction?

Here is the case for making language instruction a matter of civics education. Some people think language is a matter of civic virtue because citizens can better communicate if they all speak the same language and use the same conventions. Historically, educators emphasized linguistic competence as a way of promoting democratic solidarity. At the start of the nineteenth century, orthographic enthusiasts believed that the United States should adopt a national language as a way of uniting the country and nation-building.[7] At the time, about a quarter of American citizens did not speak English as a first language, nor did the Native Americans. Other languages were suppressed in the name of national unity.

More recently, the educational theorist E.D. Hirsch argued that schools should teach a common language and a common law, so that all students would have similar opportunities to participate in society regardless of where their parents were from or how they talked at home.[8] This kind of instruction involves encouraging or requiring students to abandon their native languages or regional dialects while in school. Hirsh's ideas were influential in late twentieth-century educational reform movements that eventually led 46 states to adopt unified educational standards in K–12 education.[9]

A problem with adopting a prescriptive approach to language for the sake of promoting civic solidarity is that this approach it can be counterproductive. People who support a pedagogical emphasis on spelling and grammar might say that it's important to cultivate an awareness of convention for the sake of students' economic and social mobility. After all, people who spell or speak in a non-standard way are disadvantaged.[10] But these justifications for emphasizing spelling and grammar might also get the direction of fit wrong. It could be that people only came to value linguistic competency when schools emphasized it, and this emphasis is just the thing that makes spelling and grammar important for economic mobility. I suspect that this is at least part of the story. Spelling and grammar wouldn't be as important if public schools didn't train students to value it. If the education system punishes poor spellers with lower grades, then the system might set up a kind of self-fulfilling prophecy that leads people to infer that spelling and grammar are important for equality because people with different spelling abilities are treated differently by the school system.[11] Civic-minded proponents of spelling and grammar education cannot cite the fact that many people think that these skills are important as a justification for emphasizing spelling and grammar in public schools because people learn that these skills are important in school.

In response to this line of argument, an educational researcher might reply that spelling and grammar probably don't matter for civic solidarity and/or economic inequality either way. Very few innovations in education effectively reduce social and economic inequalities between schools or between students.[12] This is a plausible claim. I haven't found any evidence that prescriptive language instruction affects national pride or democratic participation either way. But if prescriptive language instruction doesn't widen or narrow opportunity gaps and doesn't matter for civic participation either way, there are still other pedagogical reasons to resist it. For one thing, prescriptive language instruction is super boring. If a curricular reform made learning more pleasant, inclusive, or easier for students, then it would be worth trying, even if it didn't' reduce achievement gaps between students and schools. Also, as I argue in the next section, prescriptive language instruction might also get in the way of educational approaches that promote literacy.

1.2 THE PROBLEMS WITH LITERACY INSTRUCTION

Spelling and grammar instruction in schools is included within the broader category of literacy instruction, which also includes teaching children how to read and write. But it's not clear that prescriptive language instruction really is helping little kids learn to read and write. It's also not clear whether prescriptive language instruction is helping teachers identify children who are at risk for illiteracy. Rather, when teachers grade children's spelling, their evaluations reflect all sorts of things that are not literacy. Spelling grades might reflect conscientiousness, parental investment, or overall intelligence and fail to identify markers of literacy or illiteracy. We can all remember encountering poor spellers with messy handwriting who were penalized for their seeming lack of intelligence or virtue even if they were also active readers with excellent comprehension abilities. Teachers have very good reason to value reading comprehension and written communication. Prescriptive language instruction can distract teachers from this goal though, because a child who is a terrible speller with very poor grammar may nevertheless be able to comprehend and communicate effectively whereas a perfectly compliant speller might struggle to know what she's reading. So, there's a misfit between spelling and grammar instruction and the reading and writing skills that really matter.

Children are wasting hours and hours of their childhoods on useless spelling and grammar tasks. The emphasis on compliance with linguistic rules in education is misguided for four reasons. First, teaching students to read and write is not the same thing as teaching students to obey specific spelling and grammar rules. Even for students who do not face any distinctive challenges in mastering principles of spelling and grammar, this approach to literacy education distracts from more effective ways of teaching students how to read and write.[13] Second, emphasizing spelling and grammar in public schools can be counterproductive when it comes to teaching reading and writing to students with disabilities—especially dyslexic children. Third, spelling and grammar education can be harmful to students who are non-native speakers and students with non-standard dialects. In these cases, spelling and grammar education can exacerbate disparities rather than reducing them. And fourth, spelling and grammar instruction sets people up to mistakenly value spelling and grammar for the rest of their lives, thereby further perpetuating the wasteful and destructive practice of language policing.

Begin with the claim that spelling and grammar instruction is pedagogically bad for students, as a general matter. Again, I am not suggesting here that *literacy* instruction is bad for students. Literacy instruction is extremely important and good. Obviously, it's valuable for a child to learn how to read and write in school. Yet there are only so many hours in the school day, and among those hours, teachers can only devote a few hours to literacy instruction.

Do teachers who focus on spelling and grammar use their class time to foster literacy? Probably not! There isn't any high-quality evidence that spelling drills and grammar exercises help students learn to read and write beyond the general benefits of exposing students to the written word.[14] But there is evidence that other kinds of reading and writing instruction can promote literacy. The field of education research is flawed because educational entrepreneurs who develop and sell curricula, consultants, and schoolteachers do not consistently implement this research. But it's not like researchers are totally in the dark about what works when it comes to literacy instruction. The best evidence for reading instruction suggests that a phonics-based approach to literacy is superior to a whole-word approach.[15] For reading comprehension and writing instruction, students often benefit from learning techniques such as argument mapping and from having the opportunity to write and revise many drafts. Teachers should focus more on general conventions and comprehension and less on producing error-free text and speech.

We know what works, but teachers persist in outdated and ineffective strategies for teaching reading and writing.[16] Mark Seidenberg, an educational psychologist who studies literacy instruction, characterizes the problem with reading instruction as a divide between the culture of learning sciences and the culture of education. On his view, educational culture includes teachers and the people who train people. Seidenberg writes,

> When we think about educating kids, we think about education, and so we go to schools of education, we go to the people who train the teachers, and we go to the educational establishment for answers. And my belief is that that's really kind of going back to people who have helped create the problems that we have and really have not been able to deal with them. And one of the reasons is because they really have very little contact with this whole other body of work that says much more about how reading really works, how children learn and develop, and so on.[17]

There is a great deal of inertia in education, and a lot of that inertia involves upholding old standards and approaches to language that do not effectively teach students the reading and writing skills they need. Educational culture upholds linguistic normativity because educators conflate compliance with spelling and grammar rules with literacy, and because spelling drills and sentence diagrams are the way they've always done it.

Seidenberg also argues that educators have long attributed their inability to promote literacy to students' experiences of poverty and other social disadvantages rather than taking responsibility for their failure to teach reading effectively. And on this point, there is some evidence in favor of educators' claims that education can only do so much. For example, in recent years several prominent authors have written books that argued, in part, that education doesn't create as much human capital as people generally think and that even the best educators are limited in their ability to close achievement gaps.[18]

I do not dispute these claims. But to say that a more evidence-based curricular approach would have a small effect on balance or that it would be unlikely to close achievement gaps is not to discredit the claim that educators should adopt a more evidence-based approach to the teaching of reading and writing. Effective education is hard enough as it is. People shouldn't make it even more difficult to effectively educate people by throwing up their hands and declaring that it's pointless to invest in changing the status quo. There are only so many hours in a school day. Any hour devoted to instruction that doesn't work takes time away from an approach that might. It'd be one thing if kids spent time in school doing something fun instead of learning how to read and write. But spelling and grammar instruction isn't like art or music or dodgeball on the playground. It's sooooo tedious to learn this stuff, and in the end, it doesn't even help. What a waste ☹.

1.3 DISABILITY AND DISADVANTAGE

It gets worse. When teachers emphasize prescriptive language rules in the classroom, this approach is especially harmful to students with disabilities related to reading and writing, such as dyslexia. (Side note: who thought it was a good idea to spell dyslexia this way?!?) In this section, I make the case that it is counterproductive to focus on spelling and grammar when teaching students with dyslexia. And an unnecessary emphasis on spelling and grammar perpetuates the cycle of stigma against people who struggle to comply with language norms.

For dyslexic students, the main problem with spelling and grammar instruction is that it diverts resources and class time from more effective educational interventions that could help students learn to read and write. Many dyslexic children struggle more than they need to academically because educators persist in emphasizing spelling and grammar rather than literacy. Though educators and psychologists have known about dyslexia for more than a century, the evidence about how to teach students with dyslexia is still extraordinarily poor.[19] That said, educators do know that weekly spelling tests and grammar instruction is counterproductive.[20] The more controversial claim I am making is that emphasizing prescriptive language rules more generally can also be counterproductive for dyslexic kids.

My claim that it is counterproductive to emphasize prescriptive language rules when teaching dyslexic students is controversial because the most prominent approaches to dyslexia education are currently partly in the grip of the ideology of linguistic normativity. To see why, it's first necessary to say a bit more about dyslexia. People with dyslexia have a harder time recognizing words on sight, spelling, and decoding text to find words. The condition is heritable, and it potentially caused by differences in the left temporal lobe of the brain.[21] Dyslexia is not correlated with IQ—it's a learning deficit that is almost entirely limited to a person's reading and writing abilities. If people did not use written language to communicate, then dyslexia would not be a disability at all. Dyslexia is especially challenging for children whose native language is alphabetical because people with dyslexia have a very difficult time forming consistent associations between phonetic symbols and sounds. In contrast, there is some evidence that suggests that dyslexic students might have an easier time learning a logographic writing system such as Chinese.[22] English is especially tricky for dyslexic students, even in contrast to other alphabetic languages, because it is also not consistently phonetic.[23] In this way, dyslexia is similar to deafness.[24] Disability advocates in the deaf community argue that in that many of the burdens associated with deafness are due social norms associated with an oralist culture. If people did not communicate verbally, then deafness would not be as significant of a disadvantage.[25] Deaf advocates then argue that people should therefore provide accommodations for deaf people, such as ASL interpreters or closed captioning, in order to enable their full participation in public spaces.

With the analogy to deafness in mind, consider called out the celebrity chef Jamie Oliver for his poor spelling. Oliver responded, "Get lost you idiot im dyslexic and I cant spell so stick that in your pipe! its better than being smug."[26] When this kind of language policing is aimed at dyslexic people, it is akin to a person mocking or shaming a deaf person for the way they speak. Obviously, it would be hurtful and offensive to make fun of a deaf person who devoted considerable effort learning to communicate verbally despite lacking the feedback system hearing people use to ensure that they pronounce words in the standard way. Yet people pervasively make fun of poor spellers, not knowing whether they are poor spellers due to dyslexia.[27]

Even more frustratingly for people with dyslexia, many dyslexic children suffer even more than they need to, academically and emotionally, because educators persist in emphasizing spelling and grammar rather than literacy. The first drawback of this approach for dyslexic students is that it can make them feel judged or ashamed for falling short of a standard that they should not have been expected to meet. This is not to say that teachers shouldn't expect dyslexic students to learn how to effectively communicate in writing. Rather, I'm saying that teachers should not conflate effective written communication with compliance with spelling and grammar rules, as I argued above.

It is also reasonable to expect teachers to make an extra effort in decoding what their dyslexic students are writing as they develop their writing abilities rather than imposing punitive sanctions on them in the form of low grades or accusations of laziness.[28] Additionally, if teachers can provide evidence-based accommodations to dyslexic students that assist with their spelling, and if these accommodations would improve the clarity of dyslexic students' written communication, then educators should provide them. the most popular method for teaching dyslexic students how to read. This method is called the Orton-Gillingham (OG) approach. It is a phonics-based program that uses decoding activities and multi-sensory learning exercises.[29] (Do we think the same people who decided to spell dyslexia also decided to spell phonics with a 'p'?) National organizations license OG tutors and private schools charge tens of thousands for a learning environment where students can learn from OG instructors. In public schools, educators also train to teach with OG and the schools are often legally required to provide certified OG instructors for students with dyslexia.[30] Despite the popularity of this instructional approach, and despite the fact that this method is the best supported by the evidence, the evidence for OG as a method for promoting literacy for dyslexics is nevertheless frustratingly limited.[31]

I am not questioning whether OG is a good instructional approach for dyslexic students compared to other available approaches. Rather, I bring up OG to question whether the dominant approach to dyslexia instruction needs to cede so much to the legitimacy of language rules in order to teach dyslexic kids to read. The OG approach is phonics-based and it doesn't emphasize compliance with spelling and grammar rules the way that conventional language arts instruction does. But even OG discourages dyslexic students from using assistive technology, such as dictation software or spellcheckers, at least early in their development as readers, on the grounds that it may prevent them from learning how to comply with spelling conventions unassisted.[32] In part, instructors' emphasis on proficiency in visual reading and unassisted handwriting is justified, given that many students will one day be expected to spell without assistance. A pedagogical focus on visual reading and normative writing standards can also be harmful to dyslexic learners insofar as emphasizing these skills distracts from reading comprehension.

Reconsider the analogy to deaf education. Scholars have long debated whether educators should discourage deaf students from learning sign language (manualism) in favor of an educational approach that emphasizes lipreading proficiency (oralism). Oralism is controversial because it shifts the burdens of accommodation from the community to the disabled learner.[33] Deaf students generally prefer manualism.[34] At the same time, manualism is also controversial because hearing members of the community may be reluctant or unable to accommodate deaf people's preference for sign language or captioning in all contexts. Deaf children are likely to encounter situations in their lives where closed captioning is unavailable and speakers do not use sign language. As a middle ground, many deaf students are now trained with an approach known as bimodal bilingualism, which emphasizes competencies in at least one oral language and one sign language.

In contrast, dyslexic people's literacy education is not bimodal in the same way. The current approach to dyslexic education focuses on advancing students' visual reading skills and orthographic abilities. This approach is analogous to oralism. And there is a value to teaching these skills. Dyslexic students will encounter signs or forms that cannot be read aloud to them, and they will sometimes be required to write in a way that an untrained reader can comprehend. These are good reasons to make sure that students can comprehend what they are reading and effectively communicate in writing, but they are not good reasons to refrain from training dyslexic students to use other modes of communication which may be easier and preferable for them. A bimodal approach to dyslexia would also include training in forms of reading and communication that dyslexic students may prefer, such as the use of audio formats for reading and dictation software for writing.

A bimodal approach can avoid some of the risks involved when educators shift the burdens of accommodation from the community to the disabled learner. If educators eschew a bimodal approach when it's available, they can entrench social norms that are more harmful to disabled learners than they are beneficial to other members of the community. Oralism in deaf education can undermine social support for closed captioning or ASL translations, for example.[35] And educators' current emphasis on the dyslexic students' ability to comply with prescriptive rules for written communication, especially instruction in spelling and punctuation, can blind them to the possibility that dyslexic students could also benefit from learning how to use assistive technologies and alternative means of communication, which they might ultimately prefer.

Instructors might resist a less prescriptive approach to literacy instruction because it can sometimes be hard to decode dyslexic students' handwriting. It is reasonable to expect that dyslexic students will eventually learn to communicate effectively, but it is also reasonable to expect teachers to make an extra effort in decoding what their dyslexic students are trying to say as they develop their writing abilities. It's unfair to impose punitive sanctions on dyslexic learners in the form of low grades or accusations of laziness just because they struggle to comply with the dominant communicative conventions.[36] Instead, teachers should provide effective accommodations to dyslexic students that assist with their spelling. If there are effective accommodations would improve the clarity of dyslexic students' written communication, then educators should provide them too.[37]

By analogy, it would be unfair and ineffective for a teacher to hold students with hand tremors or other physical impairments to the same standards of penmanship and neatness as nondisabled students, even if reading disabled students' handwriting took an additional effort. If a teacher could feasibly allow a student with hand tremors to type instead, then typing should be permitted. So too, it is also especially unfair for teachers to require dyslexic students to comply with normative standards of writing, especially when teachers could decode their dyslexic students' writing with additional effort. And if it's feasible for dyslexic students to use dictation software or spell-checking technology, teachers should provide these assistive technologies because they will enable dyslexic students to communicate clearly, which should be the main goal of writing instruction.

Another drawback of a prescriptive approach to language instruction is that it can make dyslexic students feel judged or ashamed for falling short of a standard that they should not have been expected to meet. This is not to say that teachers shouldn't expect dyslexic students to learn how to eventually communicate in writing. Rather, I'm saying that teachers should go easier on students who submit written work that is comprehensible but full of perceived errors. Like deaf people, many of the disadvantages that dyslexic people face are due to arbitrary social norms that put them at a disadvantage, such as conventions related to spelling. In these cases, teachers and readers should often just look the other way, as long as they know what someone is saying, because it's not nice to correct or mock someone for an error that has no bad consequences and which would have been hard for them to avoid.

Think of it this way: the people who mock and shame their fellow citizens for poor spelling do not uphold the values of clear communication—they're just being mean. Almost no one would publicly mock a deaf person for her speech. This would be especially messed up because deaf people who speak aloud clearly devoted considerable effort to learning to communicate verbally despite lacking the feedback system hearing people use to ensure that they pronounce words in the standard way. Yet people make fun of poor spellers all the time, not knowing whether they are poor spellers due to dyslexia. Everyone is so in the grip of linguistic normativity that somehow, we treat making fun of spelling as a fun little social game rather than a blatantly antisocial pattern of behavior, which is how people would view comparable corrections for deaf speakers.[38]

The same arguments about dyslexia also extend to other kids with disabilities who are harmed by language policing in the schools. For example, children who have cognitive or behavioral disorders that are correlated with a lack of impulse control or conscientiousness may transgress linguistic norms more often than neurotypical children.[39] As with dyslexics, when teachers correct how these children use language, they will not change the underlying condition, but they are likely to cause students to feel shame, embarrassment, or distress associated with their inability to comply with linguistic standards.

In addition to disabled children, educators' emphasis on spelling and grammar instruction specifically and prescriptive language rules more generally is also disparately burdensome to students who come from a family background that is less compliant with the dominant linguistic norms. This group can include students whose parents are not native speakers or students whose families speak in a dialect that is stigmatized as sounding low status. I will further discuss the ways that linguistic normativity burdens members of these groups in the next chapter. Let's grant the point for now, just for the sake of my argument about education. Given that the imposition of normative language rules is especially burdensome to non-native speakers and people with non-standard dialects, children from these groups bear especially heavy burdens when their teachers emphasize compliance with prescriptive language rules.

It's especially worrisome that spelling and grammar instruction is particularly burdensome for non-native speakers because members of these groups are likely to be socially or economically disadvantaged outside the school system. Just imagine being a recent immigrant. It's hard enough for all parents to manage their careers and home lives, and it's even harder for parents who are living in a new country where they are unfamiliar with the dominant language. Piling a bunch of unnecessary language arts homework on their kids' plates doesn't help, especially because it will be more challenging for them to help with this kind of homework. In cases like these, the decision to emphasize normative language exacerbates achievement gaps by tying student success to their parents' familiarity with the dominant language.

In response to these arguments, a proponent of spelling and grammar instruction might reply that this kind of instruction is valuable because educators should prepare students to get jobs and work with the public and employers and members of the public value good spelling and grammar. I will address this argument further in the next chapter as it relates to economic opportunity. For now, I will just say that as it relates to education, this response is unpersuasive because it could be that educators are responsible for the fact that employers and the public value good spelling and grammar.

Consider an analogy to make this point. Imagine a society that is predominantly Christian where public elementary school teachers devote an hour of class to teaching catechism. Against this practice, someone might argue that teaching catechism puts non-Christian students at a disadvantage and that it should be abandoned because it's not valuable for all students to know catechism and catechism takes class time away from other, more valuable things students could learn. In response, an educator might claim that she will continue to teach catechism in order to prepare students to get jobs and work with the predominantly Christian public. This response would be unpersuasive to the critic of catechism, because the critic may reasonably claim that the only reason that employers and the public value knowledge of catechism is because educators promoted catechism as a marker of academic ability and status.

Similarly, educators' current emphasis on spelling and grammar instruction sets people up to mistakenly value spelling and grammar for the rest of their lives, thereby further perpetuating the wasteful and destructive practice of language policing. And when the broader culture approaches language and language use in a high-stakes way, where language is a key to social mobility and cultural acceptance, these practices not only divert resources from more valuable educational pursuits, they can also widen existing disparities between the advantaged and the disadvantaged.

1.4 SPELLING RITUALS AND PARENT CHOICE

If spelling and grammar instruction so misguided and counterproductive, then why do educators persist with this approach? Sadly, part of the answer when it comes to spelling instruction is that it's driven by parent's preferences. Though educators' emphasis on spelling and grammar, especially in early grades, can be burdensome to parents, parents also advocate for this kind of instruction because they are also in the grip of the ideology of linguistic normativity.

The standard method of spelling instruction represents this dysfunctional dynamic. For many educators, their approach to

Language Arts instruction involves assigning a weekly word list for students to memorize and testing their skills on Friday. In general, weekly testing is a poor way to teach just about anything; direct instruction that includes rapid feedback, spaced practice, repeated opportunities to transfer and recall knowledge, and mastery learning is a better way to teach spelling (if that's what you're into) just as it is a better way to teach most things.[40] And yet while weekly spelling tests have very little influence on students' overall spelling abilities, but they do reward students who can do well on the test and humiliate students who score poorly.[41]

The weekly spelling test approach therefore results in the familiar phenomenon of "Friday test, Monday miss," where even students who score well do not retain lasting knowledge of how to spell.[42] Instead of glorifying spelling through a weekly testing ritual, recent research suggests that instructors can more effectively promote adequate spelling skills is to focus on reading, not rote memorization.[43] Other education researchers advocate for word study, which focuses on teaching students patterns in language which promotes greater understanding of words, a broader vocabulary, and which may only incidentally improve spelling, though this approach is not as supported by the available evidence.[44]

Despite the evidence against using a weekly spelling test, the practice persists for two reasons. First, it shifts some of the burdens for language instruction from teachers to parents. Educators who fail to follow evidence-based strategies for literacy instruction often attribute children's poor learning outcomes to a lack of parental investment.[45] Of course, it's clearly not feasible for low-income parents who work multiple jobs, or non-native speakers to provide high quality literacy instruction to their children, so weekly spelling test disproportionately shift the 'blame' for poor outcomes to parents who already encounter more parenting challenges.

The second reason that weekly spelling test persist is that pushy parents like it this way. Some parents would prefer that their children's schools engage in a useless practice of periodic humiliation for no reason other than an unthinking commitment to this messed up tradition. For example, when some Houston area schools tried to abandon spelling tests, parents protested, and the plan was cancelled.[46] "I always had spelling tests. My wife had spelling tests. Our whole generation had spelling tests," said a parent in the district, as if that observation was on equal footing with a decade of educational research.[47] Another district in the area did eliminate required weekly spelling tests, but some schools continued to distribute weekly lists and conduct tests "mostly because of parent interest."[48]

All of this comes at a cost, not only to the children but to other parents. Because some parents have the time to apparently agitate for weekly spelling tests, working parents who are short on time must then sacrifice a bit of the scarce evening hours with their children studying for spelling tests. This ritual takes the place of more useful educational activities, other forms of quality time, or literally anything else that would be less boring and frustrating than memorizing twenty words that will be forgotten within the month. To this complaint, a proponent of the weekly test might reply that all it takes is 'ten minutes an evening' for a student to pass the test (ask me how I know that this is what a teacher would say). But firstly, this isn't true. Studying spelling words might take ten minutes but finding the form, creating a quiet place to practice, and cajoling a second grader into sitting down for ten minutes of spelling practice definitely takes longer. And secondly, even if it did only take ten minutes to study, that's a lot of time for a working parent who only has two hours to spend with their children between daycare pickup and bedtime. Proponents of weekly spelling tests are asking parents to sacrifice at least 10 percent of their nightly family time to each child's *spelling* homework (in addition to other homework) despite the fact that spelling tests are known to be useless!

Pedantic parents have held their grip on elementary education for too long. It's gotten so bad that their love of useless ceremonial spelling is now celebrated outside the classroom as well, in the form of spelling bees. Spelling bees are public competitions where children are required to spell words in ways the correspond to their dictionary spelling. Spelling Bees are primarily held in English-speaking countries, because other languages don't have such nightmarishly inconsistent spelling conventions.[49] The Scripps National Spelling Bee, where American children compete for spelling supremacy, is by far the most famous competition. It has been the subject of a documentary and broadcast on national television. Yet even former Scripps Bee finalists have noticed that the competition isn't especially useful or meaningful. Emily Stagg, who was a three-time finalist in the Scripps National Spelling Bee, argues that the Bee should evolve into a 'Definitions Bee' instead.[50] Stagg asks, "If the bee's format were amended to emphasize excellence in a more valuable skill than spelling, might it not serve the contestants better in the rest of their lives?"[51]

Yet even though it's a patently useless display, the Scripps Bee is unlikely to change its ways for the same reason that spelling tests stick around—grown-ups. Bafflingly, some adults find youth spelling competitions charming and wholesome, so children continue to compete in this useless exhibition. I say it's baffling that adults are so invested in this because the competition, which used to be broadcast on ESPN, is literally just a series of children standing up and spelling words. And I'm not saying that national spelling competitions are as bad as The Hunger Games. As far as I know, no child has been murdered for stumbling on a tricky word. But as an expression of our collective psyche, there is something to this analogy. Both spectacles consist in a televised event where stressed-out adolescents compete in a completely unnecessary high-stakes public ceremony that will determine their future. There can be only one winner, and even then, winning doesn't repay the work that went into it. The entire enterprise serves as a means of social control by promoting compliance not only among the participants but also promoting the authoritarian ideology of the event to all the other children and families that are watching at home.

All that said against the prominence of pedantic parents' preferences for ritualistic spelling competitions, I also acknowledge that are strong reasons for educators to defer to parents' preferences to the extent that those preferences are not seriously detrimental to children's interests. For this reason, spelling and grammar education is a policy area where school choice would be especially useful. Return to the analogy to catechism. If parents are required to send their children to public school, or if there are few feasible alternatives to public school available, then it would be wrong for public school teachers to require that every child learns catechism even if most parents would prefer that they did. So too for spelling and grammar instruction. However, if public officials adopted an educational voucher system that permitted parents to choose which school fit best with their values and family needs, then parents could choose to a Christian school, a school that used evidence-based pedagogies and promoted family harmony, or a school that advanced the ideology of linguistic normativity.

1.5 THE STYLE GUIDE

For all the harmful effects of sticklerism in schools, it wouldn't be *so bad* if people were capable of escaping the ideology of linguistic normativity when they graduated. But at least for people who attend college and those who write for a living, the didacticism of K–12 education follows us into the adult world through the pernicious influence of style guides. Think of the people who post their kids' weekly spelling words on their refrigerators and watch spelling bees on TV. Beyond the school system, they continue their reign of persnicketyness when they criticize writers' grammar in the comment sections of blog posts. At work, they mark up their colleagues' prose with helpful tips and tricks for keeping the less/fewer distinction straight. This is some next-level nit-picking. How did they reach such heights of fussiness? They learned in college when they were assigned a style guide.

Style guides are books that tell people who know how to write that they are not writing in the correct way. The authors of these texts are the worst offenders in perpetuating linguistic normativity because they enable all the other self-appointed sticklers. Here I have in mind, above all else, Strunk and White's *The Elements of Style*.[52] Though Strunk and White do offer some good advice about how to write in a clear, active, and engaging way, they also supply readers with a list of common word-usage errors, pronunciation and grammar rules, and advice about the length of paragraphs and sentence construction. These proclamations about the appropriate mechanics of writing are typical of a style guide. The problem with these guides is that complying with a series of dogmatic prescriptions about split infinitives and the use of 'that' versus 'which' does not make a person's prose more readable or clear. And writers shouldn't get too hung up on these rules as long as they're able to get their point across. Writing is hard enough without the constraints of a style guide to slow down the process even more. And as Strunk and White acknowledge, sometimes it's better to break these rules.

I am not the first person to notice that Strunk and White's prescriptions are counterproductive. In "The Land of the Free and The Elements of Style," Geoffrey K. Pullum argues that not only are Strunk and White's recommendations unnecessary and finicky, but some of their own rules are also inaccurate according to existing conventions![53] Pullum argues that the book's statement about grammar are "actually harmful." More specifically,

> [Strunk and White's rules are] riddled with inaccuracies, uninformed by evidence, and marred by bungled analysis. Elements is a dogmatic bookful of bad usage advice, and the people who rely on it have no idea how badly off-beam its grammatical claims are.[54]

Pullum argues that many of Strunk and White's prescriptions, if followed, would read as ungrammatical to a native American English speaker. For example, Strunk and White claim that the sentence 'none of us are perfect' is incorrect, and people should write 'none of us is perfect' instead. "The arrogance is breathtaking," Pullum writes, before showing that before Strunk and White's pronouncements, both constructions were widely used, and in any case, Strunk and White cite no evidence that their construction is standard. Adding to this example, Pullum cites many more cases which show that Strunk and White's usage pronouncements often depart from typical usage, that celebrated authors routinely violate these rules, and that the rules can make people's writing sound obscure and pompous.

In addition to Strunk and White, there are hundreds of other style guides, and they all have the same problem—they are so concerned with controlling the writing process the risk impeding it instead. Usually, the differences between style guides are mostly just a matter of quibblers quibbling about which of their many quibbles are the most urgent quibbles of all. Most guides are pretty close to Strunk and White's. Of course, there are always a few voicey variations, but they are nearly univocal in their confident yet misguided prescriptivism. Another risk of the style guide is that, if too heavy handed, they might be the enemy of style. If everyone followed the same rules, everyone's prose would sound the same, and readers might miss out on reading their favorite stylists' literary quirks and charming transgressions. One of the worst offenders on this score is the eminent editor Sir Harold Evans, who advises that sentences should, generally, be as concise as possible in his guide "Do I Make Myself Clear?"[55] To illustrate his point, Evans takes it upon himself to edit and improve upon a sentence of Jane Austen's, as if Jane Austen is a paradigmatically deficient communicator? Incredible. Raise your hand if you've heard of Sir Harold Evans. Now hands up for Jane Austen. See my point?

Not all style sages are similarly snooty. In *The Sense of Style* Steven Pinker is admirably laid back about spelling and grammar mistakes.[56] For example, he takes an easygoing approach to the commonplace confusion of 'less' and 'fewer,' and he's not too severe about apostrophe misplacement. Pinker tries to set himself apart from the stodgy prescriptivists who enforce false notions of correctness for other people's speech and writing. He calls himself a card-carrying descriptive linguist. The best case for a style guide is a case for a guide like Pinker's. Sometimes, style guide advice can be useful. It certainly is easier for people to read short, active sentences. Passive voice really can hinder clear communication. These suggestions are especially helpful for a skilled writer whose goal is to hold the attention of a large, potentially inattentive audience. Yet despite its virtues, Pinker concedes that his guide is "avowedly prescriptivist," at points, and he spills considerable ink explaining a new set of rules for writing. In contrast to other style guides that focus primarily on the historical origins of conventions, Pinker bases his advice on data on American usage. This is an improvement in a sense—Pinker trades historical conservatism about language for the conservatism of the status quo. Yet even if the tyranny of the majority is preferable to the tyranny of history, there's still an element of tyranny to it.

Style guides are rarely page-turners. They are reference books that include extensive commentary about common word-usage errors and grammar rules. Yet even though they are so often pompous, partisan, boring and unnecessary, style guides' influence persists—book after book, edition after edition of *The Elements of Style*. Professors correct their adult students' papers by marking them down for 'that/which' misusages instead of actually engaging with the content of their prose. For some authors, few people comment on the content of their work before publication but copyeditors mark their work line by line with suggestions to add commas, delete semicolons, and remove all offending ellipses and em-dashes before publication.

I think the answer to "Why do people buy style guides?" relates to a particular literary identity that some people adopt.

To use a term coined by David Foster Wallace, writers and users of these style guides identify as snoots, they like being snoots, and they want to impose their snooty ideology on everyone around them.[57] Wallace coined the word snoots as an acronym: SNOOTs—the "Syntax Nudnik(s) Of Our Time." To Wallace, snoots were "the last remaining kind of truly elitist nerd." Wallace identifies as a snoot himself. "We are the Few, the Proud, the Appalled at Everyone Else," he writes, using what seems to be a non-standard approach to capitalization. In defense of his fellow snoots, Wallace argues that people who uphold the norms of language usage are similar to those who enforce norms against lying, cheating, or screaming at children. And even though linguistic conventions are arbitrary, unlike morality, presumably, they can nevertheless be instrumentally valuable in structuring a common communicative framework.

Wallace goes further too—he writes that he requires his students to write in Standard Written English (SWE—which he also calls Standard White English) because learning to do this will be useful to them, given that "it is the dialect our country uses to talk to itself." Maybe this snootiness is unfair to people who weren't born and raised to find superfluous commas in the *New York Times* Opinion pages. But it's the way it is! And on Wallace's view snootiness is better than the alternatives.

Snootiness is not better than the alternatives though. It's fine, I guess, for an author to write in a way that sounds affected and pompous. But this style shouldn't be a requirement of 'good writing.' What all this amounts to is academic bullying and what Pullman calls "time-wasting American copy-editor bugaboos."[58] These published usage rules are costly if only because they give authoritarian English teachers and pedantic readers reasons to break out their red pens and write letters to editors. Snooty editorial practices make people who violate the rules doubt their capacities and feel pressure to change prose that is perfectly fine. And they perpetuate the broader ideology of linguistic normativity, which as previously discussed, can be counterproductive and harmful for language learners in lower grades.

1.6 THE GOLDEN AGE

Why are snoots the way they are? Why do people care so much about other peoples' compliance with arbitrary linguistic conventions? Maybe snooty adults are so captivated by spelling tests and children's spelling bees because they view champion spellers as being especially obedient, virtuous, and conscientious. But that doesn't explain why they focus on *spelling and grammar* sites of righteous compliance rather than other forms of compliance-based achievement. In this section I argue that pedants focus on spelling and grammar because these are forms of compliance that they learned as children, when they too were forced to participate in an older generation's pageantry of prescriptivism. As the saying goes, hurt people hurt people. But it's possible, and good, for the current generation of linguistic tastemakers to end the cycle of orthographic tyranny over the young.

The form of sticklerism that holds younger generations to an older generations' linguistic standards is well documented within the sociolinguistic literature. People who speak and write in a language generally maintain that the way that they learned to speak and write is the 'correct way' and that previous and subsequent linguistic norms are incorrect.[59] It is as if each generation views the time that they learned the language as the 'golden age' and the older they get the more it seems like the world of words is going to hell.⁶⁰ Against this backdrop, champion child-spellers give senior sticklers (false) hope that their old standards still matter and that they are not sliding into linguistic irrelevance.

The Golden Age myth explains why a great deal of sticklerism consists in teachers and parents complaining about how children people talk and write. There is a kind of egalitarianism to intergenerational linguistic sanctioning. Each generation starts out as a stigmatized linguistic community. By middle age, each generation has a substantial contingent of members who express righteous indignation about the ways that kids these days talk.⁶¹ Then their numbers dwindle until they become old-timey cranks who complain that people don't write letters like they used to.

Cohorts shift into and out of the role of orthographic oppressors one funeral at a time, and each society's standards of 'good grammar' shift to reflect whatever standards the ruling cohort were taught in grade school.⁶² Even if there is a kind of egalitarianism to this cycle of pedantry, like other kinds of intergenerational injustice these norms can still be oppressive. Even though everyone is at some point young and (if lucky) old, it doesn't follow that a fussy few old people are entitled to hold everyone to the unreasonable linguistic prescriptions of their bygone youth.

The Golden Age myth also highlights how totally arbitrary prescriptive standards for spelling and grammar are.⁶³ What a miracle it would be if the ways of writing and speaking that middle-aged people value *right now* represent the optimal norms for spelling and grammar. Older generations were all wrong about us when we were kiddos and younger generations are defiling their mother tongue. Viewed through the lens of this linguistic reversal test, it's clear sticklers do not have a priori reason to think that the status quo rules for language are functionally better than deviations from the status quo in either direction.[64] This exercise shifts the burden of proof for the enforcers of linguistic normativity to justify their standards, rather than expecting other generations to justify deviations from it.

I suppose middle-aged grammarians could reply that they are entitled to uphold the specific constellation of conventions that they happened to learn in elementary school because it's now their time in the sun. Someone has to maintain some standards around here and at last, they have the power to point out trivial punctuation errors! Where this argument goes wrong is in thinking that someone has to uphold standards around here. As I will argue in the third chapter, speakers and writers don't need the spellocracy and there's good reason to suspect that our language would be richer, more interesting, and more efficient without them. At the same time, as I argue in the next chapter, their standards are not only harmful and inegalitarian in the education system, the perniciousness of pedantry persists throughout society.

If that's not persuasive enough to old sticklers, they might consider going easier on the youth if only because their stuffiness also costs them. Though younger people's speech is stigmatized in many professional contexts, older people can also pay a penalty for failing to understand or talk like younger people, especially in contexts where younger people have a kind of cultural or artistic authority that older generations lack. Consider, for example, the infamous example of a *New York Times* reporter who, in 1992, interviewed a 25-year-old in Seattle for a story about 'grunge slang.' In a move that had very strong 'how do you do fellow kids' vibes, the reporter earnestly echoed the 25-year old's claim that young people called ripped jeans 'wack slacks' and referred to hanging out as 'swingin' on the flippity flop.'[65] The fact that someone credulously printed this in the paper of record is hilarious. But this example also shows that when members of older generations cling to the authority of the linguistic conventions they learned as kids, they risk missing out on new linguistic innovations and beclowning themselves by saying nonsense like "That lamestain was a big bag of bloatation down at the Tom-Tom club." Language is changing all the time. Snoots who can't keep up might just get left behind.

1.7 CONCLUSION

Schooling doesn't have to be the oppressive, snooty, spellocracy that it's become. We can imagine another way. I have described an approach to reading and writing instruction that rejects the status quo's authoritarian approach in favor of a more open, inclusive approach to reading and writing. A one-size-fits all approach to literacy not only fails to promote literacy for many students, it rewards students for compliance, instead of rewarding more valuable verbal skills like critical thinking and reading comprehension.

Real reform in literacy instruction is partly a collective action problem. Education is partly a positional good. By this I mean that the value of a person's education partly depends on the extent that it gives students an advantage over other students in competitions for admissions to selective universities and jobs. Parents and educators are therefore understandably risk averse when it comes to adopting radical reforms. There are few incentives for any parent or school to jump into linguistic anarchism before the other parents and schools do it because to do so would put their children at a disadvantage in a world of sticklers and snoots. Anti-grammarian parents find themselves in a tricky double bind. They are badly off because of the oppressiveness of linguistic prescriptivism, but liberating themselves from this oppressive system involves subjecting themselves to a different kind of mistreatment from their grammarian oppressors.

NOTES

1. Harry Brighouse and Adam Swift, "Equality, Priority, and Positional Goods," Ethics 116, no. 3 (April 2006): 471–97, https://doi.org/10.1086/500524.
2. Gina Schouten, "Fair Educational Opportunity and the Distribution of Natural Ability: Toward a Prioritarian Principle of Educational Justice," Journal of Philosophy of Education 46, no. 3 (August 1, 2012): 472–91, https://doi.org/10.1111/j.1467-9752.2012.00863.x; Debra Satz, "Equality, Adequacy, and Education for Citizenship," Ethics 117, no. 4 (2007): 623–48, https://doi.org/10.1086/518805; Elizabeth Anderson, "Fair Opportunity in Education: A Democratic Equality Perspective," Ethics 117, no. 4 (2007): 595–622, https://doi.org/10.1086/518806.
3. Corey A. DeAngelis and Heidi Holmes Erickson, "What Leads to Successful School Choice Programs: A Review of the Theories and Evidence," Cato Journal 38, no. 1 (2018): 247–64.
4. Amy Gutmann, "Civic Education and Social Diversity," Ethics 105, no. 3 (1995): 557–79.
5. John R. Lott Jr, "Public Schooling, Indoctrination, and Totalitarianism," Journal of Political Economy 107, no. S6 (1999): S127–57, https://doi.org/10.1086/250106.
6. Rashawn Ray and Alexandra Gibbons, "Why Are States Banning Critical Race Theory?" Brookings (blog), July 2, 2021, www.brookings.edu/blog/fixgov/2021/07/02/why-are-states-banning-critical-race-theory/.
7. David Wolman, Righting the Mother Tongue: From Olde English to Email, the Tangled Story of English Spelling, reprint edition (Harper Perennial, 2010), p. 90.
8. E. D. Hirsch Jr, Cultural Literacy: What Every American Needs to Know, updated and expanded edition (New York: Vintage, 1988).
9. Walter Feinberg, "The Influential E.D. Hirsch," Rethinking Schools 13, no. 3 (Spring 1999), https://rethinkingschools.org/articles/the-influential-e-d-hirsch/.

10. For a critical analysis of this view, see Julie Hagemann and Melvin Wininger, "An Ideological Approach to Grammar Pedagogy in English Education Courses," *English Education* 31, no. 4 (1999): 265–94.
11. Private schools and homeschoolers are also required to teach spelling and grammar, at least in some jurisdictions.
12. Bryan Caplan, *The Case against Education: Why the Education System Is a Waste of Time and Money* (Princeton University Press, 2019); Fredrik deBoer, *The Cult of Smart: How Our Broken Education System Perpetuates Social Injustice* (St. Martin's Publishing Group, 2020).
13. See, e.g., the effectiveness of phonics instruction for students who were previously taught to read in other, less effective, ways. Sarah Mervosh, "In Memphis, the Phonics Movement Comes to High School," *The New York Times*, December 25, 2022, sec. U.S., www.nytimes.com/2022/12/25/us/reading-literacy-memphis-tennessee.html.
14. Joy Lin, "The Effects of Code-Based Literacy Interventions on Spelling Achievement: A Meta-Analysis" (The City University of New York, 2013), www.proquest.com/openview/e128610eabbb72a182f466cabc53a7ca/1?pq-origsite=gscholar&cbl=18750; Richard Andrews et al., "The Effect of Grammar Teaching on Writing Development," *British Educational Research Journal* 32, no. 1 (2006): 39–55, https://doi.org/10.1080/01411920500401997; Steve Graham and Dolores Perin, "A Meta-Analysis of Writing Instruction for Adolescent Students," *Journal of Educational Psychology* 99 (2007): 445–76, https://doi.org/10.1037/0022-0663.99.3.445; Steve Graham et al., "A Meta-Analysis of Writing Instruction for Students in the Elementary Grades," *Journal of Educational Psychology* 104 (2012): 879–96, https://doi.org/10.1037/a0029185.
15. "It's Time to Stop Debating How to Teach Kids to Read and Follow the Evidence," April 26, 2020, www.sciencenews.org/article/balanced-literacy-phonics-teaching-reading-evidence; William H. Jeynes, "A Meta-Analysis of the Relationship Between Phonics Instruction and Minority Elementary School Student Academic Achievement," *Education and Urban Society* 40, no. 2 (January 1, 2008): 151–66, https://doi.org/10.1177/0013124507304128.
16. Mark Seidenberg, *Language at the Speed of Sight: How We Read, Why So Many Can't, and What Can Be Done About It* (Basic Books, 2017).
17. Hayley Glatter, "The Ignored Science That Could Help Close the Achievement Gap," *The Atlantic*, November 4, 2016, www.theatlantic.

com/education/archive/2016/11/the-ignored-science-that-could-help-close-the-achievement-gap/506498/.

18. Kathryn Paige Harden, *The Genetic Lottery: Why DNA Matters for Social Equality* (Princeton University Press, 2022); Bryan Caplan, *The Case against Education: Why the Education System Is a Waste of Time and Money* (Princeton University Press, 2019); Fredrik deBoer, *The Cult of Smart: How Our Broken Education System Perpetuates Social Injustice* (St. Martin's Publishing Group, 2020).

19. Kristin Sayeski and David Hurford, "A Framework for Examining Reading-Related Education Research and The Curious Case of Orton-Gillingham," *Learning Disabilities (Weston, Mass.)* 27 (December 21, 2022), https://doi.org/10.18666/LDMJ-2022-V27-I2-11720.

20. In part, these approaches are ineffective because the effects of memorization quickly fade out. See, for example, Vickie Johnston, "Dyslexia: What Reading Teachers Need to Know," *The Reading Teacher* 73, no. 3 (2019): 339–46, https://doi.org/10.1002/trtr.1830.

21. Wolman, *Righting the Mother Tongue*, p. 146–8, Stanislas Dehaene, *Reading in the Brain: The New Science of How We Read*, reprint edition (New York, Toronto, Ontario London Dublin: Penguin Books, 2010), p. 247.

22. James Essinger, *Spellbound: The Surprising Origins and Astonishing Secrets of English Spelling* (Random House Publishing Group, 2007), p. 74.

23. Wolman, *Righting the Mother Tongue*, p. 147.

24. Barbara Riddick, "Dyslexia and Inclusion: Time for a Social Model of Disability Perspective?" *International Studies in Sociology of Education* 11, no. 3 (November 1, 2001): 223–36, https://doi.org/10.1080/09620210100200078.

25. For a clear overview of these arguments (albeit in the service of a different conclusion) see Jacqueline Mae Wallis, "Is It Ever Morally Permissible to Select for Deafness in One's Child?" *Medicine, Health Care and Philosophy* 23, no. 1 (March 1, 2020): 3–15, https://doi.org/10.1007/s11019-019-09922-6.

26. Simon Horobin, *Does Spelling Matter?* (OUP Oxford, 2013), p. 227.

27. Though the good news is that dyslexia alone doesn't seem to undermine kids' overall social wellbeing. Julie-Ann Jordan and Kevin Dyer, "Psychological Well-Being Trajectories of Individuals with Dyslexia Aged 3–11 Years," *Dyslexia* 23, no. 2 (2017): 161–80, https://doi.org/10.1002/dys.1555.

28. Peter Johnston and Donna Scanlon, "An Examination of Dyslexia Research and Instruction with Policy Implications," *Literacy Research: Theory, Method, and Practice* 70, no. 1 (2021): 107–28.
29. Kristin L. Sayeski et al., "Orton Gillingham: Who, What, and How," *Teaching Exceptional Children* 51, no. 3 (2019): 240–9.
30. Elizabeth A. Stevens et al., "Current State of the Evidence: Examining the Effects of Orton-Gillingham Reading Interventions for Students with or at Risk for Word-Level Reading Disabilities," *Exceptional Children* 87, no. 4 (July 2021): 397–417, https://doi.org/10.1177/0014402921993406.
31. In a recent meta-analysis of OG, the authors found no statistically significant effect of OG interventions. One issue is that OG is time-consuming, so it's difficult to implement in large classes. Also, despite certification programs and materials for direct instruction, instructional quality varies a lot. Stevens et al.
32. "Spelling – International Dyslexia Association," October 11, 2014, https://dyslexiaida.org/spelling/.
33. Douglas C. Baynton, *Forbidden Signs: American Culture and the Campaign against Sign Language* (Chicago, IL: University of Chicago Press, 1998), https://press.uchicago.edu/ucp/books/book/chicago/F/bo3683567.html.
34. Susan Burch, "Capturing a Movement: Sign Language Preservation," *Sign Language Studies* 4, no. 3 (2004): 293–304.
35. Burch.
36. Johnston and Scanlon, "An Examination of Dyslexia Research and Instruction with Policy Implications."
37. For this reason, dyslexic students may benefit from additional instructional resources as well, such as the use of spellchecking software for writing assignments. Kara Dawson et al., "Assistive Technologies to Support Students with Dyslexia," *Teaching Exceptional Children* 51, no. 3 (2019): 226–39.
38. Though the good news is that dyslexia alone doesn't seem to undermine kids' overall social wellbeing. Jordan and Dyer, "Psychological Well-Being Trajectories of Individuals with Dyslexia Aged 3–11 Years."
39. Anna Maria Re et al., "Spelling Errors among Children with ADHD Symptoms: The Role of Working Memory," *Research in Developmental Disabilities* 35, no. 9 (2014): 2199–204; Darina Czamara et al., "Children with ADHD Symptoms Have a Higher Risk for Reading, Spelling and Math Difficulties in the GINIplus and LISAplus Cohort Studies," *PloS One* 8, no. 5 (2013): e63859.

40. Flint Simonsen and L. E. E. Gunter, "Best Practices in Spelling Instruction: A Research Summary," *Journal of Direct Instruction* 1, no. 2 (2001): 97–105.
41. Misty Adoniou, *Spelling It Out: How Words Work and How to Teach Them* (Cambridge University Press, 2016), p. 12.
42. Rebecca Putman, "Using Research to Make Informed Decisions about the Spelling Curriculum," *Texas Journal of Literacy Education* 5, no. 1 (2017): 24–32.
43. Linnea C. Ehri et al., "The Roots of Learning to Read and Write: Acquisition of Letters and Phonemic Awareness," *Handbook of Early Literacy Research* 2 (2006): 113–34; Rebecca Treiman and Brett Kessler, "Spelling as Statistical Learning: Using Consonantal Context to Spell Vowels," *Journal of Educational Psychology* 98, no. 3 (2006): 642; Barbara R. Foorman et al., "The Impact of Instructional Practices in Grades 1 and 2 on Reading and Spelling Achievement in High Poverty Schools," *Contemporary Educational Psychology* 31, no. 1 (2006): 1–29; Louisa Moats, "What Teachers Don't Know and Why They Aren't Learning It: Addressing the Need for Content and Pedagogy in Teacher Education," *Australian Journal of Learning Difficulties* 19, no. 2 (2014): 75–91.
44. Belinda Luscombe, "The Massive Effort to Change the Way Kids Are Taught to Read," *Time*, August 11, 2022, https://time.com/6205084/phonics-science-of-reading-teachers/.
45. As scholars note, however, it is difficult to establish a causal link between parental investment and achievement. Frances Van Voorhis et al., "The Impact of Family Involvement on the Education of Children Ages 3 to 8 A Focus on Literacy and Math Achievement Outcomes and Social-Emotional Skills" (MDRC, October 2013), https://files.eric.ed.gov/fulltext/ED545474.pdf.
46. Ericka Mellon, "Some Schools Ditch Traditional Spelling Tests," *Houston Chronicle*, December 25, 2009, sec. Houston & Texas, www.chron.com/news/houston-texas/article/Some-schools-ditch-traditional-spelling-tests-1729815.php.
47. Mellon.
48. Mellon.
49. "Why Is English so Weirdly Different from Other Languages? – John McWhorter | Aeon Essays," Aeon, accessed September 30, 2020, https://aeon.co/essays/why-is-english-so-weirdly-different-from-other-languages.

50. Emily Stagg, "Opinion | Definition, D-E-F-I-N-I-T-I-O-N, Definition," *The New York Times*, May 31, 2006, sec. Opinion, www.nytimes.com/2006/05/31/opinion/31stagg.html.
51. Stagg.
52. William Strunk Jr and E. B. White, *The Elements of Style*, 4th edition (Independently published, 2022).
53. Geoffrey K. Pullum, "The Land of the Free and The Elements of Style," *English Today* 26, no. 2 (June 2010): 34–44, https://doi.org/10.1017/S0266078410000076.
54. Pullum.
55. Ian Jack, "So You Want to Write Better Sentences than Jane Austen? Take Some Lessons," *The Guardian*, May 27, 2017, sec. Opinion, www.theguardian.com/commentisfree/2017/may/27/write-better-sentences-jane-austen-lessons; Jim Holt, "The Value and Virtue of Good Writing (Rule No. 7: Don't Be a Bore)," *The New York Times*, May 17, 2017, sec. Books, www.nytimes.com/2017/05/17/books/review/do-i-make-myself-clear-harold-evans.html.
56. Steven Pinker, *The Sense of Style: The Thinking Person's Guide to Writing in the 21st Century* (Penguin, 2014).
57. David Foster Wallace, "Tense Present: Democracy, English, and the Wars over Usage," *Harper's Magazine* 302, no. 1811 (2001): 39–58.
58. Pullum, "The Land of the Free and The Elements of Style."
59. Kirk Hazen, *An Introduction to Language*, 1st edition (Malden, MA: Wiley-Blackwell, 2014), p. 333. See also James Milroy And Lesley Milroy, *Authority In Language: Investigating Standard English* (Routledge, 2012); Nils Langer and Agnete Nesse, "Linguistic Purism," *The Handbook of Historical Sociolinguistics*, 2012, 607–25.
60. David Marsh, "Why the 'Golden Age' When Everyone Knew Their Grammar Is a Myth," *New Statesman* (blog), October 18, 2013, www.newstatesman.com/uncategorized/2013/10/forget-bad-grammar-and-greengrocers-real-enemies-language-are-politicians-and-businesspeople.
61. Langer and Nesse, "Linguistic Purism," p. 617.
62. James Milroy, "Children Can't Speak or Write Properly Anymore," in *Language Myths*, ed. Laurie Bauer and Peter Trudgill, 0 edition (London; New York: Penguin Books, 1999), pp. 58–67.
63. James Milroy, "Variability, Language Change and the History of English," *International Journal of English Studies* 5, no. 1 (2005): 1–11.

64. Nick Bostrom and Toby Ord, "The Reversal Test: Eliminating Status Quo Bias in Applied Ethics," *Ethics* 116, no. 4 (2006): 656–79.
65. Rick Marin, "Grunge: A Success Story," *The New York Times*, November 15, 1992, sec. Style, https://www.nytimes.com/1992/11/15/style/grunge-a-success-story.html.

Spellocratic Sanctioning

2

No one who has ever started the sentence with the words "I really hate to be a stickler, but ..." has actually hated to be a stickler. Sticklers love to stickle—to correct someone's word usage, to find a spelling error, to gently note that it's generally a bad idea to split infinitives (whatever that means) or to write a run-on sentence. And while the victims of pedantry do not generally respond to these kinds of interventions with unqualified gratitude, sticklers still make it seem like they're doing everyone a favor when they intervene to point out that their fellow speakers and writers are doing it wrong.

In this chapter, I argue that sticklers' so-called gentle corrections and helpful suggestions are anything but gentle and helpful. Rather, people use social sanctions, and sometimes the law, to enforce linguistic rules and to promote ideologies that are tied to language use. I begin by arguing that sticklerism is more politically entrenched than people typically acknowledge. In the most extreme cases, public officials use the legal system to encourage or require people to comply with dominant linguistic norms. Officials enforce national language policies, deter people from using their native languages, and take a stand on how language is taught in public schools. Legal sticklerism is especially egregious because it involves legally disadvantaging or even penalizing people for the way they speak and write. I'll talk about the legal sanctions

DOI: 10.4324/9780429319198-3

related to language first, because thinking through the ethics of legal sanctions for language use can help us understand the ethics of social sanctions for linguistic non-compliance.

In addition to legally mandated grammarianism, anti-grammarians are also disadvantaged by informal sticklerism, which is enforced through social sanctions. This form of sticklersim is far more widespread than the legal enforcement of linguistic normativity. Yet social sanctions can be unfair and harmful in some of the same ways as legal sanctions, and the same kinds of moral reasons that inform whether someone is liable to be legally interfered with can also apply to blaming and shaming.

In the social realm, the ethics of linguistic sanctioning is a bit more complicated in cases where grammarianism isn't straightforwardly about blaming and shaming, but something else. Sometime, snooty sticklers promote their linguistic ideology in the guise of advice. Others equate linguistic compliance with merely having good manners. Norms related to offensive language and speech can also be used to uphold a prescriptive approach to language. In each of these cases, the ethics of social norms related to language is a bit more nuanced than the more straightforward cases of legal sanctions, blame, and shame.

My main point in this chapter is therefore that people who enforce linguistic rules—either through the law or through informal social sanctions—are all doing something that is harmful, even if they do it under the guise of being helpful. Anyone who has been the target of a particularly persistent pedant will already know this to be true, but they may not know just how morally bad the situation is. Along the way, I will argue that the example of using social sanctioning to enforce linguistic norms has broader implications for our understanding of the ethics of manners and advice-giving.

2.1 LANGUAGE AND LAW

Before turning to social sanctions, let's begin by talking about legal sanctions. Sometimes, public officials get into the grammarian game. And when they do, it's not just slang and typos that count as 'bad' speech and writing and they aren't just taking out their red pens to write some rude comments in the margins of an essay. Instead, linguistic authoritarians in the government decide that some whole dialects and languages are better than others, and they use the power of the purse and the police to impose their linguistic preferences on everyone else. In this section, I'll make the case that language policies are usually a mistake to the extent that they go beyond minimal, necessary interference with the linguistic landscape. I argue that it's a mistake for public officials to impose a national language on people in order to promote civic solidarity. And it is also a mistake for public officials to use public resources to preserve minority languages in most cases. My opposition to both kinds of public interventions in the evolution of language stems from a more foundational commitment to liberalism. In both cases, it is wrong for political actors to impose their linguistic preferences on an unwilling population. People should neither be encouraged to abandon their native languages nor to maintain a native language that they no longer find useful.

Some degree of language policy is unavoidable. In every country, public officials enforce laws that influence how people speak and write. As Alan Patten and Will Kymlicka write,

> A state can do without an "official language," if by this is meant a formal declaration that a particular language is to be regarded as official. The United States is an example. But no country can avoid having a language policy in the

broader sense of deciding on the languages of schools, courts, road signs, etc.[1]

So, someone from the government has to get involved in language usage to some extent because officials conduct government business, write official documents, and fund schools. In many political contexts, people are authoritarian about language in ways that go way beyond the pedantry I described in the previous chapter by getting the government involved in suppressing some ways of speaking and writing and building up other ones. These people are the ultimate language police because they enforce their linguistic preferences by calling the actual police.

Political language policing happens in three ways—enforcing the majority language, enforcing bilingualism, and enforcing minority language preservation.

Consider first the kind of language policing that involves legally sanctioning linguistic minorities or using public funds to promote a majority language or two prominent languages. Nowadays, it's unusual for public officials to straight up ban the use of a minority language, but this wasn't always the case. For example, during World War 1, some public officials passed laws that prohibited people from speaking languages other than English in public or even on the telephone.[2] Officials issued fines to people who violated these laws, which were justified as a way to promote national solidarity or to discourage espionage and dissent. Even if a language isn't banned, public officials can still enforce linguistic compliance in favor of the majority language. For example, French people are legally required to pay taxes that fund French language public schools and to send their children to publicly certified schools that teach French. The French government would never incarcerate anyone for speaking Arabic on the street, but they use public funds to strongly encourage French in public life. Contrast France with Canada, where francophones are a majority in Quebec and a minority elsewhere. Canada has two co-official languages, English and French. All federal legislation and documents are bilingual. In Quebec, French is the official language, whereas other provinces either have two official languages or English is the official language. And unlike France or Canada, the United States doesn't have an official language at the federal level, though some states have declared English as their official language.

Hopefully it's clear that banning a minority language is an unnecessary and unfair form of language policing, but beyond that, the ethics of language policy is more complicated. Public officials must make sure that language policies are both efficient and fair. A national language policy like France's might put minority speakers at an unfair disadvantage. A bilingual policy like Canada's could be so inefficient that it makes everyone worse off. Language policy, like other subjects of justice, ultimately come down to debates about how public officials make decisions that determine who gets what. Questions about language policy are ultimately questions about justice.[3]

Should public officials enforce an official national language policy, or should they take a less interventionist approach? Here again, I think people should relax about linguistic variation, which is why I think official language policies are generally misguided. Proponents of an official language might defend the policy for two reasons. First, they may use an official language for reasons of efficiency. After all, it's easier to do business and politics if we're all speaking the same language. This justification for the imposition of a national language may seem credible at first, until we see that many countries do without a national language or accommodate sizeable linguistic minorities and linguistic variation. Linguistic diversity or uniformity seems uncorrelated with governmental efficiency in these cases.

A second justification for having an official language is that it is a way of fostering a nationalist identity.[4] This justification is even worse than the first. At a principled level, nationality is a presumptively immoral social identity because it is a social identity that is defined by allegiance to people who use political violence against outsiders for the benefit of insiders. Contrast nationalism with a cosmopolitan identity, which involves overlooking differences in citizenship and political status when deciding how to treat people. Though there are sometimes compelling instrumental reasons for people to foster a strong national identity (e.g., in order to defend themselves from an unjust aggressor), nationalism is only instrumentally justified in these non-ideal cases. All else equal, it's morally better for people to view themselves as morally equal to people with different political identities.[5]

In any case, even if there was some value in fostering a national identity, public officials have historically done more harm than good when they used their power and authority to foment nationalist sentiment. Subjecting minority linguistic populations to any kind of coercive language policy that encourages them to adopt a national language necessarily makes minority speakers more vulnerable to state interference than majority language speakers. For example, consider the language policies in Tibet, where Chinese nationalist identity-building projects promoted Mandarin language education. These policies discouraged people from speaking which was the language of political resistance. This case is not unusual.

The fact that public officials have historically used national language policies as a way of controlling how indigenous people and immigrants raised their children, or as a way of excluding them from public service further undermines the moral case for an official language. When nationalistic language policies have been effective at cultivating nationwide team spirit, they have achieved this goal by preventing minority speakers from maintaining their own collective identities and networks of political resistance.

Against this historical backdrop of official languages and nationalistic language policy, one might be tempted to think that the problem isn't authoritarian language policy *per se*; the problem is that public officials used their power to enforce the wrong kind of language policy. Here I have in mind proponents of language policies that aim to preserve minority language groups or to provide additional support for minority languages. For example, some scholars argue that it is important to preserve linguistic diversity for its own sake.[6] Many spoken languages are in danger of disappearing. Sue Wright makes the case that language death is bad in its own right.[7] Along these lines, some people think that public officials should try to preserve endangered languages the way they enforce policies that protect endangered species.[8] Will Kymlicka writes that cultural minorities have rights to "tolerance and non-discrimination, but also to explicit accommodation, recognition, and representation."[9] This conception of language rights goes further than toleration for minority speakers; it requires that minority language groups have protected political power.

But just as it's possible to be overly prescriptive in mandating a national language, public officials can also overstep when it comes to promoting a minority-language policy. In both cases, there are costs to trying to control the ways that people choose to speak and write. Policies that actively encourage linguistic preservation for minority languages can have some of the same normative problems as policies that actively discourage minority language use. In both cases, public officials risk taking an overly conservative and authoritarian approach to language which doesn't align with actual speakers' interests.[10] I recognize how the history of language imposition has been a force for oppression for ethnolinguistic minorities worldwide. But even when linguistic preservationists are trying to correct previous linguistic injustices, not all historical injustices can be remedied through policy, and the injustices that can be remedied to some extent needn't be remedied in the coin of the injustice. Members of linguistic minorities have different interests and claims to language preservation, depending on the historical context.

For example, Welsh and Gaelic speakers in the UK have a reasonable claim to support for their nationalist linguistic identities. Historically, Welsh and Gaelic speakers had to learn English if they wanted to read public documents and enjoy taxpayer-funded cultural programming. So, laws like the Welsh Language Act of 1993 or the Irish Official Languages Act 2003, which mandate the provision of bilingual public services and signage, might be understood as a remedy for the harms associated with the previous official English language policy. But if, as some critics have claimed, people persist in preferring to use English in some official contexts—either because they think it is more formal, more familiar, or more efficient—then public officials should not restrict the option to speak English in order to further encourage the use of Welsh.[11] In this case, they may reasonably argue that some documents and programming should be in provided in their minority languages as a way of counteracting policies that encourage them to use the dominant language.

Similarly, in the United States, some members of indigenous communities view the preservation of their linguistic tradition as continuous with the preservation of a set of concepts and ways of understanding the world that cannot be articulated in the dominant language. Sterling Holywhitemountain describes the value of linguistic preservation in these terms, arguing that it's important to preserve the Blackfoot language because the language enables the Blackfeet to understand themselves on their own terms, without being defined in the terms that European colonialists have defined them.[12] The United States government has designated the Blackfeet Nation as a recognized tribe, granting them distinctive territorial authorities which enable them to preserve their culture within the Blackfeet Indian Reservation. Though reservations are not solely justified as a way of preserving indigenous languages, they are a policy that intervenes in a way that makes it more likely that people will continue to speak, and potentially relearn endangered languages.

On the other hand, not all linguistic communities have political claims to linguistic preservation that are as strong as the Welsh or the Blackfeet. When bilingualism or linguistic preservation weighs against other policy priorities, cost-benefit considerations matter. In some cases, linguistic minorities might prefer that public officials offer them other forms of assistance instead of support for linguistic preservation. Linguistic preservation could also be a barrier to prosperity insofar as teaching children an endangered language displaces efforts to teach the dominant language. And in contexts where a language is endangered because members of a linguistic community are assimilating to the dominant culture, efforts at linguistic preservation are unlikely to succeed.[13] It's sad when languages die; language death often occurs because of some other injustice against a minority population, or because it was costly for minority speakers to preserve their language while living in a culture where the majority language was pervasive. The end of a language is not bad in its own right. In the absence of other forms of unjust treatment, it's not unjust if people stop speaking a language.[14]

Proponents of preservationist language policies argue that it's important to actively support endangered minority languages because linguistic diversity is good in its own right, language is an important way for groups to preserve their culture and historical record, language can be important for group member's self-esteem, and linguistic diversity provides researchers with a lot of data about how language works.[15] Most of these arguments are instrumental. They assume that preserving linguistic diversity is necessary for cultural preservation and minority speakers' self-esteem. But if linguistic diversity is so important, minority speakers can voluntarily preserve their languages without getting the law involved, and officials can support members of groups that face language death in other ways.[16] And it would really be overkill to enforce a national language policy just to ensure that researchers have more data about how language works. I think some people who think that public officials should try to preserve languages the way they protect endangered species view linguistic diversity as an aesthetic good—a world with more languages is just more interesting to them. But this shouldn't be a matter of public policy. Some people prefer the simple lines of Japanese watercolors whereas others prefer complex Himalayan mandalas, but neither preference would justify a policy that preserved Japanese watercolors or mandated the inclusion of Himalayan mandalas in public art galleries. So, too, for language policies.

I support a fairly minimal approach to language planning and policy in light of all these considerations. There are moral reasons against having a national language and there are also moral reasons against policies that intervene on behalf of minority languages. The best case for an interventionist approach to language policy is that, in some cases, policies that support minority languages can repair the damage of previous language mandates. But, in the best-case scenario, public officials would stay out language as much as possible.

The political philosopher, Alan Patten, defends an approach to language that nicely balances the moral reasons for and against enforcing language policies. On his view, public officials should not pass laws that disproportionately burdensome linguistic communities more than others. Patten writes,

> People do have a defeasible complaint of injustice when public institutions treat the things they care about non-neutrally—that is, when they impose more burdens on, or extend fewer benefits to, the pursuit of their conception of the good than they do to conceptions that matter to other people.[17]

Since public officials must choose to use some language, this problem is partly unavoidable even in the absence of an official language policy. But minority speakers should be granted exemptions from official language policies to the extent that it is feasible for them to opt out of the dominant linguistic culture, because linguistic rights are a subset of people's broader cultural rights, freedom of speech, and freedom of association. This line of argument weighs in favor of a fairly libertarian approach to language law, and law more generally, since any reason for granting someone an exemption from a policy is also a reason to simply abandon the policy to the extent that it's feasible.[18] Patten then argues that, in some cases, minority speakers can have presumptive rights to bilingual public services. But it doesn't follow from this that public officials must always protect minority speakers' interests in not learning to speak the majority language. For Patten, it depends on the context. If learning the majority language is required for social mobility and full participation in public life, then public schools should teach all students the majority language. Yet officials would not be justified in imposing a language on minority speakers in a place like Spain or Switzerland., where people can socially advance in multiple languages.[19] More generally, Patten is skeptical of any heavy-handed or interventionist approach to language policy. He writes, "we should resist the suggestion that justice ultimately consists in majority and minority each enjoying the opportunity to culturally dominate some part of the state."[20]

Summing up, there are two compelling reasons for public officials to take a stand on how people use language. The first reason is that officials' documents and services must be provided in a language, and it's inefficient for them to choose too many. The second reason is that language policy can sometimes be a way of repairing the harms associated with earlier language policies. Neither argument justifies the official imposition of a national language through. And the second argument for a reparative language policy is tricky to justify, some members of linguistic minorities just stop using their language because the language is no longer useful to them, and policies that aim to counteract the imposition of a dominant linguistic culture could make it more difficult for people to assimilate, even if they want to.[21]

2.2 THE ETHICS OF SOCIAL SANCTIONS

I began this chapter with a discussion of language policy because it is the most extreme case of a more pervasive phenomena. Most people don't have the political power to enforce their authoritarian preferences about language. Though they wish they could, everyday pedants cannot not use violence, fines, and threats of incarceration to tax people who forget the 'i before e' spelling rule. Grammarians cannot lock up offenders who end sentences with prepositions. Though I'm sure there are a few authoritarian sticklers out there who fantasize about bringing down the iron fist of the legal system on people who don't know how to use semicolons appropriately, their legal power mostly ends with the end of compulsory schooling. Yet despite sticklers' (blessedly) limited power over adults, even the informal enforcement of grammarianism, can be harmful to norm-violators in the same way that the official imposition of a national language can harm minority speakers, albeit to a lesser degree.

Political philosophers are obsessed with knowing whether and when coercive public policies are justified—and with good reason. It's really morally risky to impose taxes and fines on people and to use violence to structure the world. But even when congressmen and cops aren't involved in a social practice, everyday public interactions can still affect the distribution of who gets what, whether we're talking about resources, opportunities or esteem. And social norms can also be unfairly punitive, even if they don't involve threats, fines, or jailtime. In this section I argue that social norms that involve sticklerism—enforcing conventions related to speech and writing—can be oppressive because people enforce these norms in ways that sanction rule-breakers and establish a social hierarchy that places people at a social disadvantage for reasons that shouldn't matter for their social status. Obedience to oppressive and inegalitarian social norms is not virtuous. There is no virtue in being well-spoken or in writing clean copy. It's not a flex to tell someone that they mixed up the spelling of 'defiantly' and 'definitely' in an email. If anything, upholding spelling and grammar norms is criticizable because the sanctions that sticklers use to socially enforce these norms inconvenience and stigmatize people who haven't done anything wrong.

Many of the same arguments for getting the government out of language policy are also reasons for ordinary people to chill with the language policing in their own lives. We've all met self-appointed guardians of the grammatical galaxy who blamed and shamed the rebels who violated their precious prescriptive policies. Other social sanctions include things like insults, dishonor, or ostracization. These little social slights can add up to bigger disadvantages. Social sanctions make people feel ashamed, self-conscious, or alone. Because most people want to avoid these penalties, they comply with the sticklers' unreasonable demands for compliance, just to avoid conflict or embarrassment. But why should people who deputize themselves to be the keepers of the speakers set the linguistic agenda for everyone else? People aren't entitled to live in a world where everyone comply with standard communicative norms and non-standard speakers and writers aren't doing anything wrong. The only people who should be blamed and shamed for their linguistic particularities are the self-appointed language police who use the rules of grammar as a tool to assert their dominance over their fellow speakers and writers.

Maybe a stuffy stickler would reply that it's a free country, so if they want to blame and stigmatize people for non-standard languages they're entitled to do it. Of course, just as sticklers don't have a right to live in a world where everyone talks like an NPR reporter, anti-grammarians don't have the right to live in a world where no one criticizes them for their speech.

I grant that blame and stigmatization doesn't violate people's bodily rights or property rights in the way that government coercion does, but not all moral reasons relate to people's rights. Some social norms are better than others when it comes to standards for friendship and inclusion or blame and shame, even if everyone has rights to freely speak and associate with people however they like. As philosophers such as Brookes Brown and Chiara Cordelli have argued, membership in a social community is an especially important part of the good life, and that it is unjust to deny people membership if they do not deserve it. Even if we don't go so far as to say that people who are left out due to their poor spelling and grammar are victims of discrimination, they are at least victims of unkindness and snobbery.

In contrast to norms that relate to inclusion and exclusion and blame and shame, there are other social norms that really are morally neutral. Spelling and grammar norms are like this. This is why the moral landscape favors restraint when it comes to non-standard communication, because the people who violate language norms aren't violating a norm that's as morally charged as the people who are using social sanctions to push their persnickety preferences on everyone else.

Consider an analogy to make this point. People are entitled to make friends with whomever they like. For moral reasons, they should not refuse to make friends with short people, and they shouldn't make fun of people or insult people who are short. Being short is not morally good or bad, but excluding and insulting such people is morally fraught. In most cases, the bare fact that someone is short shouldn't be relevant to whether they would make a good friend, so people shouldn't make height a really salient category that comes up in all their social interactions. Maybe in a few cases (pick-up basketball teams?) it might make sense to exclude short people from a social group. But although excluding and insulting people is always legally allowed, there are moral reasons not to do it. Likewise, snoots have moral reasons to be nice to people who misspell words or who speak and write in a non-standard way, at least in most cases, because non-standard communication isn't immoral whereas there are moral reasons against excluding and insulting people for being different. Unless a social group is united by their love of copy-editing or spelling games, speaking in a non-standard way is extraneous to the things that most people should care about in a friend.

This argument appeals to the intuition that it's just unfair to blame someone when they did not act wrongly. There are approximately one million philosophical theories of blame, and it would be the opposite of helpful to get into this debate just to make a point about grammar. But it's worth noting that on most accounts of blame, people have very strong moral reasons to refrain from blaming people who are not liable to be blamed.[22] Even if blame isn't as serious as legal punishment or fines, it's still pretty morally high stakes because people experience blame as a sanction. To be blamed is to suffer a penalty or a reputational harm, which explains why people are reasonably anxious about undeserved blame.

Because people with bad spelling and grammar aren't doing anything immoral, it is totally reasonable for them to be offended when others blame them for a spelling or grammar mistake. The only exception to this is cases where people knowingly opted into a situation where they agreed to make themselves vulnerable to be blamed for bad spelling. For example, an editor at a newspaper with a specific style guide may reasonably blame her copyeditor for mistakenly misspelling a word because the copyeditor voluntarily took a job where she was being paid to spell things in the standard way. But most people do not voluntarily sign up for obligations to apply particular spelling and grammatical conventions. Why would they? So, most people aren't liable to be subjected to blamey and shamey sticklerism in public life.

For similar reasons, it is also unfair to stigmatize people who have bad spelling and grammar. Like blame, insults and mockery harm a person's self-esteem and it can undermine their reputation. Stigmatization can also limit people's opportunities for professional advancement and social connection because people are less sympathetic to those who engage in stigmatized behaviors, even if the stigma is inappropriate or unfair. And in turn, insults and jokes that are targeted at a group or practice can also foster resentment towards sticklers because people resent being disparaged for things they can't control, which aren't even wrong.

Another downside of policing people's spelling and grammar in social life is that little corrections, slights, corrections, and blame are distracting. When someone is corrected for their speech, listeners discount the content of what they are saying and focus on their mistaken mechanics. This can be dispiriting, and in the worst cases people with bad spelling and grammar might just stop trying to communicate, rather than risking a mistake. Speech act theory can be helpful in understanding how this kind of language policing can be harmful to speakers. Following Rae Langton's description of different kinds of silencing, let's distinguish between three different ways that one person's speech can silence another's.[23] First, a stickler could engage in straightforward locutionary silencing—speakers stop talking entirely because they are afraid of being sanctioned again. Second, a stickler could engage in perlocutionary silencing—speakers with bad grammar lack credibility. And third, a stickler could engage in illocutionary silencing—when some voices are effectively overlooked entirely because they break communicative norms. In these cases, even if the speaker doesn't stay silent in order to avoid further sanctioning by the language police, he might as well because he is not socially recognized as an authoritative speaker.

All three forms of stickleristic silencing impede effective communication under the guise of trying to improve it. People who police others' language act as if they are merely intervening to help people express themselves, but their interruptions make it so that speakers are more reluctant to speak again, listeners are more reluctant to listen, and speakers are less likely to be heard and understood when they do talk. To see what I mean, imagine a person who regularly violates rules about when to say 'fewer' and when to say 'less' and when to say 'me' versus 'I.' She can make these kinds of mistakes but still be perfectly capable of communicating. But if a bunch of word nerds make her feel embarrassed, insecure, or excluded every time she mixes up when to say 'that' or 'which,' she might conclude that it's not even worth it to speak up in those contexts. Or worse, she might continue to speak up, but the sticklers in the room will miss out on what she has to say as they eagerly plan their next little grammarian intervention, perhaps with a patient retelling of whatever rule she broke this time.

The thing is, this cycle of viciousness doesn't even help the snootiest sticklers among us because everyone sometimes makes spelling and grammar mistakes. We're all sinners in the eyes of Strunk and White, so blaming or sanctioning people for so-called grammar mistakes is always a hypocritical enterprise. Most people get that hypocritical blaming is an especially bad look—morally speaking. But there are a few sticklers out there who might nevertheless defend their snooty interjections by casting it as a well-meaning enterprise. It's like free tutoring! Talking about broader ethical questions related to hypocrisy, Daniella Dover defends hypocritical blaming, at least in some cases, because she thinks blame can be a helpful way to educate people about their mistakes.[24] I'm skeptical about this general line. Even if someone is liable to be blamed, I'm not sure they learn from being blamed. When people engage in hypocritical blaming for things that aren't morally blameworthy, like poor spelling, it's even harder to justify because sticklers are sanctioning people for things they do too, which also aren't even wrong! Maybe sticklers think that they're handing out free tutoring, people aren't asking for the lesson.

Maybe this all seems super theoretical, but just as public officials worldwide enforce language policies that privilege some and disadvantage others, there are real sticklers out there who exclude people from their communities on the basis of non-standard communicative practices and poor grammar. Consider, for example, the iFixit CEO Kyle Wiens, who wrote in the Harvard Business Review "I have a 'zero tolerance approach' to grammar mistakes that make people look stupid … they deserve to be passed over for a job—even if they are otherwise qualified for the position."[25] I've heard dozens of people say things like this. Imagine if there were other matters of style where people felt comfortable saying this. Would a CEO say admit to having a zero-tolerance approach to people who fail to match their belt to their shoes during a job interview?

Linguistic social sanctions can be especially high stakes when people make political choices on the basis of a candidate's perceived linguistic competency, rather than on the basis of a candidate's ability to effectively communicate. The most notorious example of this occurred in 1992, when then-Vice President Dan Quayle attended a press event at an elementary school. There, he corrected a 12-year-old student's correct spelling of 'potato' by telling him to add an 'e' to the end and to spell it as 'potatoe.' Members of the public delighted in the error, and today it is perhaps what Quayle is most known for. Even though the error occurred because Quayle was deferring to an incorrect answer key provided by the school, no one cared. After the incident the *New York Times* wrote, "Unscripted, Vice President Quayle often flounders. Even scripted, he suffers frequent embarrassment. With two r's." Quayle wrote in his memoir that the potatoe incident was "a defining moment of the worst imaginable kind."

Similarly, consider President George W. Bush's observation that "Rarely is the question asked—is our children learning?"[26] Or President Joe Biden's inability to spell the number eight in a speech.[27] None of this matters for effective communication. No one should care about this kind of stuff. When it comes to all the things that matter for political leadership, spelling and grammar is the smallest of small potatoes. But in each of these cases, citizens delighted in a rare moment of bipartisanship to mock their political leaders' minor linguistic failures. This is not to say that politicians' language doesn't matter. I grant that that effective communication is an especially important political skill. This is why it's important for public officials in bilingual societies to speak the languages that their constituents use, and why debates and speeches are important components of any political campaign. The point is that poor spelling and grammar doesn't translate to poor communication. In some cases, infelicity with language might plausibly even make someone a more effective communicators, insofar as voters are more open to messages that are delivered in an authentic-sounding, less polished communication style.[28]

Spellocratic sanctioning in cases like these is wrong for two reasons—it punishes people for differences that shouldn't matter, and it distracts people from paying attention to the things that do matter. Here again, an analogy to other forms of discrimination is apt. Just as people are more likely to rate men and tall people as more competent leaders, even though we have reason to think that sex and height are normatively extraneous to a person's capacity to lead, so too with linguistic competency and leadership. And as in these other cases, when people choose and follow leaders on the basis of normatively extraneous traits, they are likely to overlook people who lack these traits but who are more qualified when considering the traits that really do matter. So, when sticklerism influences how people select leaders, it makes leader-selection less reliable. This is yet another way in which grammarianism has negative externalities, beyond the harms it imposes on people who violate prescriptive language rules.

And the harmful effects of sticklerism are not limited to the contexts of employment and political leadership. Throughout a person's life, relentless grammarians not only waste time and insult the people they afflict, they also implicitly reinforce the idea that poor spelling is something to be ashamed of, thereby increasing their own power. Sticklerism begets more sticklerism. The more people correct each other's linguistic errors, the rarer linguistic variation becomes, making linguistic non-compliance even more salient as a social-marker, further isolating grammatical rebels from everyone else and heightening people's incentives to avoid any kind of rule-breaking in their speech or writing.

Am I overstating the problem here? After all, people have a right to associate with whomever they like. We cannot assume that the victims of exclusion or even ostracization have been *wronged* because no one has an entitlement to other people's friendship or to social inclusion more generally. I agree with the claim that no one has a right to association with others. Nevertheless, there are still moral reasons against excluding people on the basis of unfair prejudices. Even if enforcing and upholding social norms does not violate people's enforceable rights, there are still better and worse norms that people can adopt. Prejudices that are based on linguistic competency are unfair.

Consider an analogy to other kinds of social prejudice, which illustrates this point. I think people have moral reasons to be open to dating people of different races. But even if there are moral reasons against restricting one's dating pool based on race, it would also be wrong to legally interfere with people's romantic choices. This point generalizes—moral reasons apply to private and personal choices even if these choices should also be protected from state interference. In some cases, people's private choices can all can add up to unjust patterns of disadvantage. And while these unjust patterns of disadvantage do not merit legal interventions, because a legal response would do more harm than good, it is still important to acknowledge in these cases that people are deciding who to associate with on the basis of considerations that shouldn't matter as much as they do.

This is a longstanding theme in feminist philosophy. When feminist scholars argue that social norms can be a subject of justice, they often focus on things like the distribution of household labor or expectations surrounding caregiving.[29] For example, we might interpret the feminist slogan 'the personal is political' as emphasizing that even if a society had a fully just approach to legislation and law enforcement, it may still be unjust if people's marriages and family obligations were nevertheless unfairly burdensome to women or insufficiently voluntary. In the next chapter, I'll discuss how linguistic sanctioning can contribute to gendered inequalities in the same way that people use informal social sanctions to hold women to higher standards when it comes to their share of domestic labor or appearance.

Similarly, republican political philosophers talk a lot about the ethics of social hierarchy in workplace and the family.[30] For example, workplace republicans argue that people's relationships at work can be objectionable, even though they are private associations, if bosses are empowered to arbitrarily interfere with workers and if workers labor in constant fear of burdensome demands or unexpected job loss. The republican philosopher Philip Pettit also emphasizes the importance of the economy of esteem—which refers to the way that communities can effectively use practices of praise and blame to regulate people's behavior through social pressure, rather than physical force or threats.[31] Linguistic sanctions often function within the realm of the economy of esteem. People are conscious of maintaining their social standing in their family or workplace, so they are sensitive to avoiding social sanctions that would lower their standing and make them more vulnerable to interference or rejection from people who have more status. It's not necessarily the case that people think they will be interfered with or rejected just for misspelling a word or misusing a phrase. Rather, it's that social norms that really play up the importance of talking and writing in a particular way can be used to sort people along a status hierarchy that gives sticklers the social power to arbitrarily interfere and assert their dominance over the people they live and work with. In these contexts, everyone else then lives with a little bit of extra anxiety that they will be the next targets of a grammarian's social sanctioning, which every time imposes a tiny tax on their own social standing.

In recent years, liberal egalitarian philosophers have also turned their attention to the ethics of social norms, and they also find that some social norms can be morally better than others. For example, Aaron James argues that social norms are a subject of justice on the grounds that, just as coercive political institutions are subject to assessment in terms of social justice, other inescapable social practices should be evaluated by the same standards.[32] James discusses social practices concerning how far apart people stand from each other, or how much room they take up in public spaces, such as the norm that men can spread out on the bus whereas women are socially encouraged to sit compactly. He also cites a norm that speakers place more physical distance between themselves and ugly or unfashionable people, compared to attractive and high-status people. These seemingly minor social equilibria can have larger-scale distributive implications—whether someone complies with social norms related to who takes up public space can affect their opportunities and standing going forward. Social norms related to language are like this too. Seemingly small social norms about how people talk and who is included in a conversation can add up to big social disparities, especially if people who violate these norms are themselves subject to further social sanctions or exclusion.

This is not to say that people should abandon all social practices that sort people along a social hierarchy. Sometimes social norms can be useful. Laura Valentini argues that people sometimes have moral obligations to uphold socially constructed norms such as traditions, norms around queuing, and rules of etiquette.[33] Social norms have moral force, Valentini argues, because they arise from people's genuine commitments to upholding them and their autonomous choice to perpetuate their preferred norms. People who violate these norms express disrespect for the people who are trying to uphold them. On the other hand, while Valentini argues that it is disrespectful to interfere with norm-upholders, she also acknowledges that some norms are worth violating, e.g., disrespectful norms. Her point is that unless there are countervailing moral reasons in favor of violating a norm, people have reasons to respect the norms that others construct. When it comes to language policing then, the question is whether social norms around language are more like norms related to queueing or norms related to interracial dating. In the next chapter, I'll argue that the people who uphold norms related to speaking and writing aren't upholding norms of mutual respect, they're upholding inegalitarian norms that maintain an arbitrary status hierarchy. Even if people have moral reasons to comply with and uphold some widespread social practices, sticklerism isn't one of them.

At this point in the dialectic, I can imagine a stickler saying that it's not her fault that some people feel excluded or stigmatized by their snooty sanctions—I'm blaming individual actors for something that's really a structural problem. If people feel oppressed or excluded or judged by the powerful pedants in their lives, then a better solution than asking the pedants to change would be to provide everyone with a universal basic income (UBI) and strong protections for their economic and civil freedom.[34] These policies would liberate everyone from the economic necessity of complying with social norms that they find oppressive without requiring powerful pedants to abandon their love of prose policing in any way.

I don't disagree with this imagined argument from a powerful pedant, but this kind of a remedy could only do so much. Even if everyone in a society were capable of moving where they liked, meeting all their material needs, and pursuing whatever projects they valued, their lives could still go badly if people in their community mocked them, derided their choices, or failed to treat them with respect. For example, a gay person in a very heterosexist society would still be significantly disadvantaged by heterosexism even if she were capable of meeting her basic needs, moving to a different community, and choosing to start her own business or newspaper. People's lives become worse off when they are treated like members of an out-group, and everyone criticizes them for the way they are. If someone thinks that it's not a big deal to ask people to follow a few pretty basic spelling and grammar rules, then they shouldn't think it's a big deal to ask sticklers to chill out a bit and not point out people's linguistic errors. If language policing is a super-important project to some people, then they should recognize that linguistic freedom might be super-important to other people. Either way, debates about social norms surrounding language use are moral debates. Some social practices are better than others and, in this case, the social practices of the sticklers are morally worse than a sanction-free social equilibrium around language use.

All of these reasons support the conclusion that some social norms related to speech and writing are morally better than others. I have argued that social norms surrounding language, like other social norms, should more open and tolerant than they are.

2.3 ADVICE

Are we overthinking this? Almost certainly, yes. Maybe grammarianism isn't the malevolent, stigmatizing force I'm making it out to be. Imagine a friendly, likeable grammarian who thinks of herself as someone who is just trying to help. Maybe people who correct other people's spelling and grammar are genuinely just trying to make the world a more beautiful place, like someone who picks up litter near the river and tidies the public restroom when washing their hands. Maybe grammarians think that giving people unsolicited feedback on their speech and writing makes people feel seen and cared for, the way they felt when their mothers lovingly corrected their essays when they were children. Here I am imagining a stickler who defends themselves by arguing that they are only trying to help people who are seemingly unable to speak and write in the standard way due to their ignorance about conventions. In other cases, people who choose to do acts of charity and volunteering are praised. Even if the beneficiaries asked for help, people do nevertheless sometimes seem grateful for grammarians' free copy-editing services—doesn't that mean that the sticklers were do-gooders, at least in these cases? Think of the friendly neighbor who plows your driveway after a snowstorm. Maybe some sticklers think that cleaning up their neighbors' speech is an act of civic friendship, too.

The first problem with this justification is that, unlike the beneficiary of a neighbor's snowplow, the targets of linguistic sanctioning generally don't experience pedantic corrections in this way. Have you ever heard anyone correct a person's grammar, only for the target of the correction to reply, "Thanks so much!" in a sincere way? Have you ever seen someone follow up when an anonymous poster noted an online typo by saying something like "Fascinating! If it's not too much of hassle, could you also explain to me how apostrophes can be used to distinguish plurals, possessives, and contractions?" These responses read as sarcastic because they almost always are. Whatever the stickler's think they're selling, it doesn't seem to me like there's much of a willing market for it.

Nor can sticklers credibly claim that they're just sharing neutral information that they think might be of interest to their listeners. Though some philosophers claim that advice is merely an attempt to inform people, it rarely functions in this way.[35] Listeners are likely to hear advice about established conventions as prescriptive even when this doesn't take the form of a command. And because advice is prescriptive, it prompts listeners to either comply or to give a justification for non-compliance. This whole book is a justification for non-compliance. It's going to take a while! More often, people don't want to get into it, so they just comply with the advice they're given, even if the conventions themselves are arbitrary and lacking in authority. Sticklers cannot infer that their advice was welcome from the fact that people change their behavior after receiving advice, since compliance is usually just the path of least resistance. Instead, to know whether their advice was warranted sticklers must consider whether they should have offered their advice in the first place.

All advice-givers must consider the moral reasons for and against advice-giving because offering advice puts the advice-receiver in a position where she is then expected to either comply or offer a justification for non-compliance. Consider an analogy to the medical context. When a physician gives medical advice, she is not only informing her patient about the state of the medical literature, she's also encouraging her patient to follow it. Physicians must take care to ensure that they are giving advice that will benefit the patient and that the patient is actually capable of following the advice. Of course, they should also double-check that their advice is never misleading or false. Health workers also know that even truthful information can be harmful to patients, so if they are sharing bad news about a diagnosis or a risk factor, they should ensure that the delivery of the news doesn't compound the emotional burden of the information itself. And health workers should always treat their patients with dignity and avoid insulting them, even when the patient is making a choice that the health worker disapproves of.

Even in the most charitable cases of grammarianism, most people who provide advice about language do not seem to consider the ethics of advice-giving in this way. Grammarians do not take care to ensure that the targets of their interventions will benefit if they follow their advice. If they did, they might consider that most people do not ask for or welcome grammatical advice, which indicates that they don't view it as the kind of thing that would help them. Rarely will people hire speech therapists, language tutors, copyeditors, or writing instructors. (Shout out to the copyeditor for this book! I appreciate your efforts in shielding me from the harmful consequences of my own poor spelling ☺.) Yet only in these contexts can linguistic advice-givers be assured that their insight is welcome, since they are helping someone who asked for it.

Worse, stickler's advice is potentially misleading or false to the extent that they present it as if there is a fixed set of grammatical principles that everyone must follow. Sticklers assume that there is a single 'proper grammar' that everyone has reason to comply with. But language is always changing, so sticklers might be upholding current conventions but they are just as likely deploying their advice to uphold the outdated conventions of their youth. Sticklerism is also risky when the advice-giver lacks context about his advisees' circumstances. For example, a grammarian might advise someone to spell something the American way, not realizing that the British spelling is acceptable in the context that they're writing.

It's also a tell that powerful pedants are giving bad advice because so many sticklers issue public corrections for speech and writing. So many snoots don't bother to ensure that their corrections are delivered in ways that avoid embarrassment or offense. In these cases, language advice isn't just about helping people learn linguistic conventions because sticklers would offer their linguistic suggestions privately after first asking whether their would-be advisees were interested in hearing a few suggestions. Like any good teacher, pedagogical pedants would take care to avoid insinuating that someone is uneducated, rude, or stupid just because they fail to comply with a linguistic rule. Rather, they would frame it merely as a pragmatic suggestion for achieving goals, such as social acceptance or advancement in a context where many other people (unreasonably) care about linguistic compliance.

Maybe a few true pedagogical pedants are out there and we never hear from them because they're only sticklers for the pure love of the grammar game and most people don't sign up for their services. But this cannot be said for all the powerful pedants out there, who are at least in part using advice as a way to punish deviance or raise their own status. In the usual case, a grammarian advice giver would publicly write a comment or say something like "IT'S with an apostrophe means IT IS whereas what you mean to write is ITS which is the possessive of IT." This mode of advice-giving insinuates that the target of the advice never encountered this rule before and that they need to be educated by a volunteer English teacher. This kind of advice also (mistakenly) assumes the legitimacy of these linguistic rules. Alternatively, a more conscientious advice-giver would say something like, "Hey, I don't care either way but I thought I'd let you know that the people who are hiring for these positions are really uptight about typos so you may want to change the spelling of the word 'it's' in the second paragraph of your personal statement to 'its.'" Even in the latter case the advice might be unwelcome and it would be better left unsaid, but at least it is otherwise in keeping with the norms that govern advice-giving in other contexts.

It's striking how unsolicited advice-giving in the linguistic domain is so much more socially acceptable than unsolicited advice giving in other contexts. We can clearly recognize that it is rude and borderline hostile to advise someone who is eating a cheeseburger that they should make lower-calorie choices if they want to avoid developing diabetes or heart disease. But people tell themselves that it's OK to tell people with non-standard spelling and grammar that they should avoid writing things like 'imo ur gr8' if they want to be taken seriously. In both cases, even if this advice were true (which is debatable), the advice-giver shouldn't say it. Likewise for when linguistic advice is couched in aesthetic terms rather than prudential terms. People don't just walk up to each other and recommend that they choose to wear different clothes that are more flattering to one's body type or coloring. Yet so many pendants feel totally comfortable recommending that people choose to speak with different words or that they change the way they write so their speech or prose is more aesthetically pleasing to these sensitive sticklers.

Maybe some pedants are like this because they were hurt by quibblers in the past, so they took up the tools of their oppressors in an effort ensure that their own suffering served some purpose. David Mitchell is a pedant who admits to this, saying that he upholds spelling standards because:

> I did take the trouble to learn them and, having put that effort in, I am abundantly incentivized to make sure that everyone else follows suit. The very last thing I want is for us to return to a society where some other arbitrary code is taken as the measure of a man, like how many press-ups you can do or what's the largest mammal you can kill.[36]

Here Mitchell claims that the grammar game is good for his status, so he upholds it even though he acknowledges that linguistic conventions are arbitrary and burdensome to learn. I suspect that this is what's going on for a lot of advice-givers. If so, then the sticklers of this sort do deserve our sympathy. These quibblers have such low self-esteem that they cannot think of anything to offer the world that would raise their status beyond their knowledge of basic spelling and grammar and a penchant for pedantry. At least when people got status from killing large mammals, the whole neighborhood eat for a week. And it might even be entertaining to watch people compete to do a lot of press-ups. In contrast, stickleristic status seekers reduce their neighbors' wellbeing. Perhaps a less prescriptive linguistic culture would benefit the quibblers as well then, by encouraging them to find a more meaningful and valuable basis of self-respect that doesn't involve knocking other people down a peg just to feel important.

In each of these instances, advice-giving serves as a tool of social control. By prescribing compliance with arbitrary linguistic norms, grammarians are communicating to the world, to their listeners, and to themselves, that they are better than the speakers and writers who fail to comply with these norms. But how are they better? It's not morally better to talk and write in a compliant way rather than a rebellious way. Speakers and writers only have prudential reason to comply with these norms because grammarian advice givers would otherwise sanction or discriminate against them! And as for aesthetic advice, generally people should not give unsolicited advice on matters of taste, especially when they have little reason to assume that their aesthetic judgments are more reliable than others. Grammarians have constructed a maze of burdensome conventions that serve only their own interests. The rest of us remain trapped in their useless little labyrinth because, through seemingly well-meaning advice and subtle social sanctions, sticklers have made linguistic compliance the path of least resistance.

2.4 MANNERS

In virtue of the fact that pedants so reliably contravene the more general, widely-held norms for responsible advice-giving, I'm even not sure that pedants are motivated by the desire to give good advice on matters of morality, prudence, or aesthetics. An alternative explanation is that some pedants think of themselves as the guardians of a dying civilization, as the last defense against social anarchy, as the only true gentlemen left in a society of savages. Here I have in mind a stickler who views social sanctioning as part of a broader project of upholding old-fashioned good manners, or civilized society, or some other high-handed social virtue.

For the sake of argument, let's assume that some modes of communication can violate principles of etiquette, independent of the content of what someone's communicating. For example, let's grant that people may think it's rude for someone to wear casual clothes to a legal hearing because it is disrespectful to the judge. So, too, people might think it's rude to speak in a particularly informal way in professional settings, even if the content of their speech is never inappropriate or rude. In these cases, non-conformist personal styles can violate principles of etiquette. Even granting that people have moral reasons to use good manners in some cases, though, in this section I argue that when it comes to language what passes for etiquette is often morally bad and people should often abandon their fussy commitment to grammar manners. The only exception to this principle arises in contexts where people opt-in to a linguistic community that values a particular linguistic register. But even here, grammarians should proceed with caution because even opt-in, community-based language norms can sometimes become a barrier to effective communication.

Grammarians conflate etiquette and morality when they argue that good grammar or a particular mode of speech and spelling is a way of showing respect for one's interlocutor.[37] A grammarian of this sort might then argue that their grammar policing is just another way of upholding community standards. On this view, grammar policing and legal policing are importantly similar in kind, if not in degree, because both consist merely in upholding a consistent set of norms for a specific community. And the pedants, on this analogy, are like the proponents of broken windows policing. They are enforcing policies that uphold their conception of aesthetic quality, for language, for neighborhoods, in order to uphold more general moral standards within the community.

Some grammarians go further, and specifically link upholding linguistic norms to upholding the more general moral requirement that people respect each other. For example, one pedantic psychiatrist writes,

> I get really annoyed when someone writes up an email for me to review and it's poorly written or edited.... It implies this person doesn't respect me enough because I've pointed out the problem before. Or they don't care about my authority. That might make you actually angry, not just aggravated.[38]

Or here's another person who equates misspelling someone's name with personal disrespect:

> When a client I have corresponded with misspells my name, a little bit of my desire to work with them dies. It shows they do not care about forging a respectful connection with me.[39]

Misspelling someone's name is an especially egregious mistake, it seems, since there are many posts and forums about 'how to deal' when people accidently choose the wrong spelling of 'Kristen' out of the approximately one thousand options available.

Yet even if we grant that etiquette is structurally similar to morality, not all matters of etiquette are matters of morality. Though the line between etiquette and morality can be blurry, it isn't so blurry that we cannot distinguish theft from a broken window from a misspelled name. People who take other people's spelling mistakes super-personally are interpreting what is *at best* a failure of etiquette as a sign of more serious disrespect.

Defenders of etiquette might deny my claim that reasons of etiquette have less authority than moral reasons. Philippa Foot, for example, argues that morality is similar to etiquette. Just as a person who starts eating before the last person is served is rude but not irrational, Foot writes that "the man who rejects morality because he sees no reason to obey its rules can be convicted of villainy but not of inconsistency."[40] On this view, the upshot is that neither morality nor etiquette has any necessary rational force. Say we accept this view (which is controversial!), for the sake of argument. Even if both etiquette and morality were matters of convention, etiquette mistakes are nevertheless conceptually distinct from moral mistakes. And, when the two conflict, morality should take priority when it comes to deciding whether morally charged social sanctions are warranted.

So even if spelling, speech, and grammar rules are matters of etiquette, most people still shouldn't care that much about spelling, speech, and grammar because it's not immoral to have bad language manners and policing people's bad language manners is morally fraught. I say that it's not immoral to have bad language manners because complying with arbitrary linguistic conventions doesn't promote happiness and non-compliance needn't show disrespect for people. And yet the sticklers who uphold grammar manners make people sad and the pedants who are always bringing up violations of the rules of grammar are almost always more disrespectful than the violations themselves. So *even* if it's polite, in some sense, to speak or write in a particular way, it's also polite in those contexts to ignore so-called impolite speech *plus* there are also moral reasons to calm down about people's grammar.

We can go further. Say that I'm wrong and people have moral reasons to have good manners. Those moral reasons are *at best* the kind of moral reasons that are easily outweighed by other moral reasons. To see what I mean by this, say that linguistic etiquette is part of morality because everything that affects people's wellbeing is part of morality, and some people care about language so it affects their wellbeing. But on this view, being free from grammarian etiquette enforcement is also part of morality and our collective liberation from grammarians outweighs the pain a stickler feels when she encounters a misplaced apostrophe.

Or maybe some snoots think poor grammar is a moral transgression because it is a reliable indicator of poor character. After all, people who are rude about little things like language conventions might have more egregiously disrespectful dispositions, and the poor grammar is only a symptom of their broader indifference to others.[41] Is the person who shows up late to a meeting merely rude because he violated a widely held social norm of timeliness, or is a bad person because he lied about when he would arrive? Similarly, is the person who misspelled someone's name inconsiderate of spelling conventions or are they inconsiderate about people's feelings? Maybe both! Someone who values good manners might argue that the kind of person who violates the etiquette norm is likely to be the kind of person who doesn't care about ethics either. This is a better argument for sticklerism. If it's true that people who are chronically late are less trustworthy than people who comply with norms of timeliness, then timeliness manners are a good heuristic for evaluating someone's character. And if it were true that people who misspell people's names are more likely to be inconsiderate of other people's feelings, then spelling manners would also be a good heuristic for evaluating character. I'm not sure whether either of these heuristics are reliable guides to people's character, but if they were then this would be a reason to care about linguistic conventions, albeit only instrumentally.

These examples suggest that people should care about etiquette to the extent that it's a proxy for something they care about morally, like respect or happiness. Grammatical conventions are not the sorts of rules that a person has any necessary reason to follow just for their own sake. There's no objective perspective from which people should care about upholding arbitrary grammar rules. If a person does care about grammar, then they have reason to follow the rules only because other people care about the rules. To borrow Foot's phrasing in her discussion of etiquette, the rules of manners and grammar are like the rules of a club.[42] Club rules have authority only because members of the club give them that authority. They don't have authority for people outside the club and they lack authority in their own right. When it comes to language, there may be different club rules in different contexts, but the rules aren't universal, and people shouldn't be held to a subgroup's club rules when they never agreed to be a part of it.

Consider an analogy to golf. Some fancy golf clubs require everyone to wear a collared shirt on the course. The members of the fancy clubs all know about this rule, they signed up to abide by it, and it generally improves their experience at the club. Private clubs can make their rules however they like, and the people who golf at this kind of club have reason to comply with the club rules simply because the people who own the club want to see golfers in collared shirts. Other golf clubs only enforce rules that enable everyone to play golf safely. The T-shirt clubs are not inferior to the collared shirt clubs; they probably make golf more inviting and accessible. While it's fine for people who choose to golf at a fancy collared shirt club to uphold their club rules those conventions only apply to people who choose to golf at the fancy club. A fancy person at the T-shirt club wouldn't be entitled to encourage his fellow golfers to wear collars, because the T-shirt club doesn't require them.

By analogy, in some contexts people might uphold distinctive linguistic conventions within their subgroup. Linguists call the tone and style that a person uses to communicate their diatype or their linguistic register. People in different contexts talk in different ways. Teenagers communicate differently around their grandparents and their friends. Most people are more polite and honorific at work and more colloquial and even vulgar when they're hanging out with their friends. People change the way they communicate when strangers are listening. A speaker's ability to vary the register of their speech is yet another way in which linguistic variation enables people to communicate more effectively. In these cases, mannered linguistic conventions can be conducive to effective communication.

But as with the two golf clubs, a formal or professional register is not inferior to a casual or intimate register. Rather, norms governing linguistic register should only be determined by norms that are conducive to effective communication in different contexts. And people should only uphold norms related to register if they are fairly certain that everyone in the communicative context is aware of the context-specific linguistic norms and that they are all willing and capable of complying with them. Some families, for example, may have something like 'house rules' for communication where younger people refer to older people as 'sir' or 'ma'am,' but they are not entitled to hold other people's children to these rules outside of their own home.

It's helpful for people to be mindful of contextual communicative norms because when people violate others' expectations about register, it can be a barrier to effective communication in the way that wearing a T shirt at the fancy club undermines the other golfers' experience in that context. For example, when a job candidates' speech is excessively informal, she might lead potential employers to infer that she's not interested in the position. But in these cases, the authority of the contextual norms derives from people's decision to opt in to a particular communicative context. Members of a linguistic subculture aren't entitled to impose their contextual communicative preferences on people who did not choose to join that context.

In other cases, speakers can subvert expectations related to register in a way that enhances their ability to communicate. Consider a public intellectual who hopes to make her work more inviting and accessible to everyone, so she delivers a complicated talk at a prestigious university in an easygoing casual tone. In each case, contextual linguistic conventions don't have any special authority in their own right, but the context can be relevant for speakers' ability to effectively communicate.

2.5 GRAMMARIAN GASLIGHTING

There is a kind of gaslighting that can occur when people pedantically correct other people's speech. Gaslighting occurs when a person (typically from a place of higher status) causes someone to doubt her capacity, such as her capacity to use language or to competently perceive her circumstances. In the context of language policing, the corrector makes it seem as if there is broad consensus about their preferred linguistic norms, and that it should have been obvious that it was a mistake to transgress them. In so doing, correctors gain power over those who they interfere with. They establish a position of social or intellectual dominance by making their targets doubt their own capacities. But there are not clear facts about proper usage, at least not in English, so correctors make people think that they are violating a norm when previously they, correctly, thought that their pattern of speech was acceptable.

Several philosophers have sought to explain why gaslighting is wrong. On one account, it's wrong as a general matter to make someone believe falsehoods and that's why it's wrong to gaslight someone about their own perceptual capacities or capabilities. Call this the deception account. On another account, gaslighting is wrong because it is manipulative. Call this the manipulation account. Another view is the egalitarian account, wherein gaslighting is wrong because it introduces or widens an objectionable asymmetry in power between the gaslighter and the gaslit. On another view of gaslighting, it's wrong because it is politically bad.

On each of these accounts of gaslighting, grammarianism can be a form of it. Consider first the deception account of gaslighting.[43] Grammarianism is deceptive simply because it's not true that people have anything other than instrumental reasons to comply with the dominant grammatical standards. Pointing out that someone is not compliant with a linguistic convention should only communicate that she's not compliant with the convention, but that's not how people say or hear corrections in everyday life. When a person corrects someone's speech or writing they aren't pointing out mere non-compliance (why would they?!). Rather, they insinuate that a grammatical error is a sign of sloppiness, low status, or stupidity. When this happens, a stickler makes a speaker unnecessarily doubt her own capacities by causing her to believe that her linguistic errors mean more than they actually do.

Turning to the manipulation account, grammarianism can also be manipulative insofar as sticklers interject their corrective advice as a way of establishing dominance over speakers.[44] When a stickler makes someone doubt her own communicative capacities by issuing a grammatical correction, he may cause the target of the correction to feel inferior or indebted to the stickler. This dynamic can make a speaker or writer more vulnerable to the stickler's influence on other matters going forward. When this happens, grammarianism is empowering for grammarians and disempowering to the targets of correction. I think this is part of the appeal of grammarianism—it makes pedants feel powerful. People feel pressured to signal their gratitude towards pedantic interjectors even when the only reason linguistic compliance matters is because it matters to pedantic interjectors.

On the egalitarian account of gaslighting, it is wrong to make a person doubt their linguistic capacities because sticklerism is not deployed against the powerful with the same force and frequency as it is deployed against those with less power. Nora Berenstain describes the broader phenomenon of structural gaslighting, which "arises when conceptual work functions to obscure the non-accidental connections between structures of oppression and the patterns of harm they produce and license."[45] The concept of a single normative linguistic standard functions to obscure the connection between social differences and social inequalities, since social groups differ in their compliance with that single standard and their differential compliance with the standard correlates with different levels of credibility and social status. The single linguistic standard is historically contingent and arbitrary, but people treat these communicative norms as if they are a reliable guide to the amount of social status and credibility a person should have.

Alternatively, say we adopt a political view of gaslighting, which states that it is wrong for public officials to disempower a person or group by undermining their confidence in their own capacities.[46] Public schools and official government language policies can disempower people in these ways. When a group's communicative norm does not conform to dominant linguistic standards, schools and official language policies can make people from that group doubt whether they are educated or smart enough to participate as equals in public life.

According to any of these views of why gaslighting is wrong, the upshot is the same. As friends and as citizens, we all have moral reason to build each other up and promote a kind of egalitarian spirit in our conversations. In virtue of these reasons, we should just assume that everyone talking is a competent speaker of her language. People should try to avoid social practices that make people doubt their capacities unless they have very strong reason to believe that they really are incompetent. Rarely will this be the case when it comes to policing language. The people who claim the status of 'dictionary boss' and make the rest of us doubt our linguistic capacities introduce an inegalitarian dynamic into the conversation even when we're all perfectly capable of communicating and understanding each other.

2.6 OFFENSE

Imagine starting from scratch to create social norms for communicators. The main priority would be to adopt norms that help people communicate clearly. People would have good reason to adopt linguistic norms that treated everyone with the respect, that helped people flourish, made people happy or advanced whatever other values are morally important. Linguistic norms that made the world more beautiful, interesting, or entertaining could be justified as well. But what purpose would it serve to add a bunch of sanctioning, punitive, exclusionary norms around language? One answer to this question is that it might be important to have mechanisms for policing language in place because some speech isn't just a matter of bad manners, it's unethical in its own right.

In this section I address a very limited case for language policing, focused on offensive language and slurs. This kind of an argument doesn't really land against people who misspell proper names or forego capitalization. But grammarian-types do advocate for sanctions against people who use taboo words. I myself have encountered a puritanical pedant of this sort when I said the word 'bullshit' on a Zoom call and someone wrote 'language!' in the chat.[47] Everyone probably had their language policed in this way when they were children, but to pull this with a grown-up is insulting because it treats an adult like she's a misbehaving child. Parents can make the language rules in their own houses, but puritanical pedants shouldn't feel empowered to make language rules for everyone around them!

Though not all sticklers are puritanical pedants, the puritanical pedants are among the most powerful of the sticklers because they have the law on their side. George Carlin didn't make up his famous list of "seven words you can never say on television," they were words that broadcasters censored at the time.[48] Lenny Bruce had previously been arrested for using these words in a routine, and Carlin was also arrested for saying these words on the grounds that he was disturbing the peace. Subsequently, federal officials enforced decency standards that enabled them to fine broadcasters for content that included taboo words. In the UK, public officials also censor profanity in public advertisements and fine people who swear in public.[49] At least in the United States the first amendment protects people's rights to use profanity in advertising and political protests but, even in the States, taboo words remain one of the most policed forms of everyday language.

A drawback of imposing legal limits on obscene speech is any limits on obscenity and offensive speech could potentially deprive people of the benefits of using taboo words. For one thing, swear words can be cool and fun, in the way that it's often cool and fun for people to present themselves in ways that are shocking or unexpected.[50] And, in my experience, profanity can also promote group-cohesion and bonding in contexts where some people might find the dominant social norms to be oppressive or confining. For example, if a speaker at a talk says the word 'fuck' it may be liberating for people in the audience to hear it, because it serves as a signal that the social dynamics in the room are less likely to be punitive and censorious. And when (as happened on my Zoom call) someone in the room then openly criticizes a profane speaker, the critic re-asserts a social dynamic that is less open and welcoming. These puritanical pedants already have too much social power when they punish profanity in the ordinary way, through stigmatization and social sanctions. Giving them the power of the police would only exacerbate fusspots' misplaced sense of entitlement to chide people for saying the forbidden words.

To this, one might object that some taboo words and patterns of speech are rightly stigmatized because they are discriminatory. For example, people should refrain from using derogatory slurs to describe people with different identities. Some philosophers argue that slurs, like threats, are speech-acts that can violate people's rights through the expression of the speech alone.[51] Others have argued that it's wrong for speakers to use racist slurs because it makes listeners complicit in the speaker's racism.[52] A simpler view of slurs holds that slurs are prohibited just because people view them as prohibited, often because the words have a distinctive social function.[53] In any case, insofar as a speaker who uses a slur is liable to be sanctioned it is not because they used the slur, but because they used the slur in a way that was insulting or degrading someone or because they expressed an opinion about a group of people that reflects an immoral ideology. In these cases, the language itself isn't the problem, it's what the slur expresses.

Are people who use slurs liable to be sanctioned for expressing insulting or degrading views or for expressing immoral opinions? Legally, the foregoing arguments support speech policies that permit people to use slurs, and weigh in favor of communicative norms that are fairly tolerant towards the use of slurs as well.[54] At the same time, other speakers and listeners should sometimes feel empowered to criticize and discourage people from using slurs in ways that are insulting, degrading, or immoral, just as they people should criticize insulting and degrading speech more generally and argue against other expressions of immoral viewpoints too.

That said, it's not straightforward that social sanctions for slurs are a good idea in most cases. One problem with imposing legal or social sanctions for offense speech is that restrictions on taboo expressions are not likely to be fairly enforced. People from different cultural and class backgrounds have different views of obscenity and different preferences for communicative norms. Sanctioning profanity and offensive words is likely to exacerbate inequalities of social power insofar as the people who control standards of obscenity are those that have the social power to do so. At the same time, people with less social power may have a legitimate interest in engaging in profane or offensive speech, either because their preferred cultural norms are more permissive with respect to taboo speech or as way of subverting the dominant culture. Consider, for example, musical artists who use profanity in punk, rap, and metal songs specifically as a way of subverting the dominant culture. The puritanical pedants who have the social or legal power to influence the ways that people communicate should not spend their time trying to silence these subversive kinds of speech. Instead, they should use their power to adopt communicative norms that permit rude and offensive speech, even speech that is seemingly inegalitarian or stigmatizing. When high status people instead feign dismay at everyone else's alleged linguistic transgressions, they performatively denounce people as a way of reinforcing their own high status.

A puritanical pedant may defend their position by pointing to the most egregious forms of inegalitarian, profane, and offensive speech. For example, in the United States burning crosses are a form of legally protected speech as long as they are not deployed to convey a targeted violent threat. Holding up large photos of dismembered fetuses outside of abortion clinics is a form of protected speech too, as is displaying pictures of dead bodies at an antiwar protest, or protesting military funerals with signs that say, "Thank God for Dead Soldiers." Panhandlers are entitled to shout obscenities at people who drive by. Catcallers are legally permitted to shout insults or comments about women in public. Even if all this is legal, a proponent of some puritanical language policing might argue that this kind of behavior should be publicly criticized.

I'm not keen to defend these kinds of speech against social sanctions and criticism. But in each of these cases, speakers should be sanctioned for the content of their message and not for the profanity of it. For example, antiwar protesters should not be socially sanctioned or criticized for displaying images that depict war crimes that were committed by their own government. In this case, the offensive speech is a public service because it alerts their fellow citizens to the atrocities that are being committed by their elected officials.

Obscene and offensive speakers also provide a public service, albeit unintentionally, when they subvert puritanical pedants' inappropriate sense of entitlement to dictate how everyone else behaves in public spaces. I grant that some forms of public speech can be genuinely disgusting, insulting, and disturbing. But permitting even the worst speech in public spaces is a way of holding the line against the most mannered and hypersensitive people in society who type 'language!' in the chat of a Zoom call. People should tolerate a wide range of communicative practices that they'd rather avoid in part because we all disagree about which speech needs more limits. If all the puritanical pedants got their way, then speech standards would be excessively burdensome for all speakers. That's why it's better if the puritanical pedants never get their way, because almost everyone values their own ability to say minor profanities so we should, in solidarity, resist puritanical language policing when it's targeted at linguistic transgressions we would never say.

In *Offense to Others*, Joel Feinberg provides a philosophical argument that broadly justifies the legal status quo in the United States.[55] In general, Feinberg argues, it is very difficult for public officials to justify legal limits on offensive speech. However, Feinberg agrees that some obscene forms of speech can amount to 'fighting words' where speech is not merely an utterance or a form of communication, but an injurious action as well. In these cases, Feinberg writes, legal limits on obscene speech are not justified in virtue of the obscenity of the speech but rather in virtue of the fact that public officials are entitled to restrict actions that incite violence or other rights violations. Implicit in this analysis, Feinberg seems to assume that fighting words, while distinct from direct threats of violence, are close enough to threats that they ought to be governed in the same way.

Even this fairly permissive approach to offensive language cedes too much to puritanism and sanctioning though. This standard sanctions and limits some speech on the grounds that listeners could potentially commit violence after hearing certain words—but speakers shouldn't be held responsible for people's unreasonable violent reactions to their words.[56] For example, if a listener is excessively sensitive and they take a mild insult to their country (e.g., flag burning) to be a justification to engage in violence, it seems like the speaker is not responsible for the listener's response to her speech.[57] Even when speech could plausibly "produce a clear and present danger of a serious intolerable evil that rises above mere inconvenience or annoyance" the thing that should be prohibited is the evil, not the speech that inspired it.[58] And so, too, for social sanctioning—an excessive focus on calling out and discouraging offensive and profane speech diverts attention from more pressing social problems. Puritanical pedants should focus far less on the language of injustice and far more on actual injustices.

2.7 CONCLUSION

In this chapter I've argued that people should refrain from language policing because it's OK to have bad spelling and grammar, or any communicative style really. For many people, spelling and grammar just isn't their thing. They are not making any moral or social mistakes when they communicate in a nonconforming way. This is why sticklers should not enforce punitive social or legal sanctions against linguistic deviants because the rebels, innovators, and dgafs haven't done anything wrong. And since even sticklers have moral reason to be inclusive and egalitarian, they shouldn't try to flex on linguistic deviants by offering unsolicited advice, enforcing fussy etiquette standards, or gaslighting gaslit people into doubting their own capacities. In a few cases, language can be pretty bad, but even in these cases, puritanical pedants should be very wary of stepping in to make people feel bad or ashamed about the manner of their speech. It is, of course, fair game to criticize the content of people's speech.

NOTES

1. Will Kymlicka and Alan Patten, "1. Language Rights and Political Theory," *Annual Review of Applied Linguistics* 23 (2003): 3–21.
2. *Meyer v. Nebraska* ruled in 1923 that these laws were unconstitutional, as were mandates for English-only education. For more on this see, e.g., John C. Maher, *Multilingualism: A Very Short Introduction* (Oxford University Press, 2017).
3. Alan Patten, *Equal Recognition: The Moral Foundations of Minority Rights* (Princeton University Press, 2014). 186
4. And this process can reinforce itself as nationalist identities grow more salient. See, e.g., Eugen Weber, *Peasants into Frenchmen: The Modernization of Rural France, 1870-1914* (Stanford University Press, 1976), p. 89.
5. Paul Gomberg, "Patriotism Is Like Racism," *Ethics* 101, no. 1 (1990): 144–50.
6. Ken Hale, "Endangered Languages: On Endangered Languages and the Safeguarding of Diversity," *Language* 68, no. 1 (1992): 1–42; Anthony Woodbury, "Documenting Rhetorical Aesthetic and Expressive Loss in Language Shift," in *Endangered Languages: Language Loss and Community Response*, ed. Lenore A. Grenoble and Lindsay J. Whaley (Cambridge University Press, 1998).
7. Sue Wright, *Language Policy and Language Planning: From Nationalism to Globalisation* (Springer, 2016).
8. Daniel Nettle and Suzanne Romaine, *Vanishing Voices: The Extinction of the World's Languages* (Oxford: Oxford University Press, 2000).
9. Will Kymlicka, *Politics in the Vernacular: Nationalism, Multiculturalism, and Citizenship* (Oxford University Press, 2001), p. 41.

10. Suzanne Romaine, "Preserving Endangered Languages," *Language and Linguistics Compass* 1, no. 1–2 (2007): 115–32, https://doi.org/10.1111/j.1749-818X.2007.00004.x.
11. Catrin Fflur Huws, "The Welsh Language Act 1993: A Measure of Success?" *Language Policy* 5, no. 2 (June 1, 2006): 141–60, https://doi.org/10.1007/s10993-006-9000-0.
12. Heather Horn, "Assessing the Value of Dying Languages," *The Atlantic* (blog), December 19, 2009, www.theatlantic.com/national/archive/2009/12/assessing-the-value-of-dying-languages/347198/.
13. John Edwards, "Language Revitalization and Its Discontents: An Essay and Review of Saving Languages: An Introduction to Language Revitalization," 2007, https://journals.lib.unb.ca/index.php/CJAL/article/download/19736/21414.
14. Heather Horn, "Assessing the Value of Dying Languages."
15. These four arguments appear in Sue Wright's defense of language preservation Wright, *Language Policy and Language Planning*.
16. David Crystal, *Language Death*, Canto (Cambridge: Cambridge University Press, 2002), https://doi.org/10.1017/CBO9781139871549.
17. Patten, *Equal Recognition*, p. 203.
18. For a further argument to this effect see, Brian Barry, *Culture and Equality: An Egalitarian Critique of Multiculturalism* (John Wiley & Sons, 2013).
19. Patten, *Equal Recognition*, p. 208.
20. Patten, p. 6.
21. Wright, *Language Policy and Language Planning*, p. 272.
22. Consequentialists who claim that standards of blaming should simply promote overall wellbeing are a notable exception here.
23. For a helpful overview of how these categories matter for applied ethics, see Rae Langton, "Speech Acts and Unspeakable Acts," *Philosophy & Public Affairs* 22, no. 4 (1993): 293–330.
24. Daniela Dover, "The Walk and the Talk," *Philosophical Review* 128, no. 4 (2019): 387–422.
25. Kyle Wiens, "I Won't Hire People Who Use Poor Grammar. Here's Why," *Harvard Business Review*, July 20, 2012, https://hbr.org/2012/07/i-wont-hire-people-who-use-poo.
26. Simon Jeffery, "Rarely Is the Question Asked, Is Our Children Learning?" *The Guardian*, April 13, 2010, sec. Politics, www.theguardian.com/politics/blog/2010/apr/13/labour-spelling-mistake.

27. Steven Nelson, "Biden Misspells Number 8 as 'E-I-G-H' in Maryland Speech," NY Post, April 19, 2023, https://nypost.com/2023/04/19/biden-misspells-number-8-as-e-i-g-h-in-maryland-speech/.
28. Farhad Manjoo, "So Trump Makes Spelling Errors. In the Twitter Age, Whoo Doesn't?" The New York Times, August 27, 2017, sec. Technology, www.nytimes.com/2017/08/27/technology/donald-trump-twitter-spelling.html.
29. Susan Moller Okin, Justice, Gender, and the Family, 50843rd edition (New York: Basic Books, 1991).
30. Elizabeth Anderson, "Equality and Freedom in the Workplace: Recovering Republican Insights," Social Philosophy & Policy 31, no. 2 (2015): 48. Anca Gheaus, "Child-Rearing with Minimal Domination: A Republican Account," Political Studies 69, no. 3 (August 1, 2021): 748–66, https://doi.org/10.1177/0032321720906768.
31. Philip Pettit, Republicanism: A Theory of Freedom and Government (Clarendon Press, 1997).
32. Aaron James, "Power in Social Organization as the Subject of Justice," Pacific Philosophical Quarterly 86, no. 1 (2005): 25–49, https://doi.org/10.1111/j.1468-0114.2005.00213.x.
33. Laura Valentini, "Respect for Persons and the Moral Force of Socially Constructed Norms," Noûs 55, no. 2 (2021): 385–408, https://doi.org/10.1111/nous.12319.
34. Justin Tosi, "Relational Sufficientarianism and Basic Income," in The Future of Work, Technology, and Basic Income (Routledge, 2019). One might make a similar case in favor of free migration, free speech, free association, or economic freedom—protections which would blunt the harmful effects of violating norms in communities that would otherwise demand compliance.
35. Darwall, e.g., argues that advice is merely informative and that it is not disrespectful per se to either give nor to ignore advice. Rather, advice giving and receiving can convey appraisal of someone's epistemic authority while not taking a stand on their authority to decide for themselves. Stephen Darwall, "Respect and the Second-Person Standpoint," Proceedings and Addresses of the American Philosophical Association 78, no. 2 (2004): 43–59, https://doi.org/10.2307/3219724.
36. Horobin, Does Spelling Matter? p. 229.
37. In making this point in a more general way, Sarah Buss argues that "all else being equal, people have a basic moral obligation to make

themselves agreeable to others." Sarah Buss, "Appearing Respectful: The Moral Significance of Manners," Ethics 109, no. 4 (1999): 795–826.
38. Max Plenke, "This Is What Bad Grammar Does to You're Brain," Mic (blog), October 21, 2015, www.mic.com/articles/127144/this-is-what-bad-grammar-does-to-youre-brain.
39. Bri Williams, "Why Misspelling a Name Is More of a Problem than You Realise," SmartCompany, July 30, 2018, www.smartcompany.com.au/marketing/networking/why-misspelling-name-more-problem-than-you-realise/.
40. Philippa Foot, "Morality as a System of Hypothetical Imperatives," The Philosophical Review 81, no. 3 (1972): 305–16.
41. Karen Stohr, for example, argues that impoliteness can be a sign that someone lacks a moral imagination, that they are insensitive to others, or that they have a deficient grasp of moral concepts. Karen Stohr, "Manners, Morals, and Practical Wisdom," in Values and Virtues: Aristotelianism in Contemporary Ethics, ed. Timothy Chappell (Clarendon Press, 2006).
42. Foot, "Morality as a System of Hypothetical Imperatives."
43. On this view, gaslighting is wrong because it causes someone to have a false view of their capacities. See, e.g., Cameron Domenico Kirk-Giannini, "Dilemmatic Gaslighting," Philosophical Studies 180, no. 3 (2022): 745–72, https://doi.org/10.1007/s11098-022-01872-9.
44. Abramson advances an account of the wrongfulness of gaslighting that emphasizes manipulation. Kate Abramson, "Turning up the Lights on Gaslighting," Philosophical Perspectives 28, no. 1 (2014): 1–30, https://doi.org/10.1111/phpe.12046.
45. Nora Berenstain, "White Feminist Gaslighting," Hypatia 35, no. 4 (2020): 733–58, https://doi.org/10.1017/hyp.2020.31.
46. Eric Beerbohm and Ryan W. Davis, "Gaslighting Citizens," American Journal of Political Science n/a, no. n/a, accessed May 5, 2023, https://doi.org/10.1111/ajps.12678.
47. Tell Harry Frankfurt that the word bullshit is unprofessional! Harry G. Frankfurt, On Bullshit (Princeton University Press, 2009), https://doi.org/10.1515/9781400826537.
48. Though, as an aside, people seem to swear nowadays more than ever! See Jean M. Twenge, Hannah VanLandingham, and W. Keith Campbell, "The Seven Words You Can Never Say on Television: Increases in the Use of Swear Words in American Books, 1950–2008," SAGE Open 7,

no. 3 (July 1, 2017): 2158244017723689, https://doi.org/10.1177/2158244017723689.
49. Rebecca Roache, "Where Does Swearing Get Its Power – and How Should We Use It?" *Aeon*, n.d., https://aeon.co/essays/where-does-swearing-get-its-power-and-how-should-we-use-it.
50. Roache, "Where Does Swearing Get Its Power – and How Should We Use It?"
51. See, e.g., Chang Liu, "Slurs as Illocutionary Force Indicators," *Philosophia* 49, no. 3 (2020): 1051–65, https://doi.org/10.1007/s11406-020-00289-0; Cameron Domenico Kirk-Giannini, "Slurs Are Directives," *Philosophers' Imprint* 19 (2019): 1–28.
52. Roache, "Where Does Swearing Get Its Power – and How Should We Use It?"
53. Luvell Anderson and Ernie Lepore, "Slurring Words," *Noûs* 47, no. 1 (2013): 25–48.
54. Alec Greven and I expand on this point elsewhere. Jessica Flanigan and Alec Greven, "Speech and Campus Inclusivity," *Public Affairs Quarterly* 35, no. 3 (July 1, 2021): 178–203, https://doi.org/10.2307/48628247.
55. Joel Feinberg, *Offense to Others* (Oxford University Press, 1984).
56. Robert M. O'Neil, "Hate Speech, Fighting Words, and Beyond – Why American Law Is Unique Symposium: What Are We Saying – Violence, Vulgarity, Lies and the Importance of 21st Century Free Speech," *Albany Law Review* 76, no. 1 (2013 2012): 467–98.
57. Street v. New York, 394 US 576 (Supreme Court 1969).
58. Terminiello v. Chicago, 337 US 1 (Supreme Court 1949).

Sticklers and Stigma

3

In the previous chapter I made the general case that social norms, including linguistic norms, can be a subject of justice. There, I focused mainly on the claim that justice requires that people refrain from sanctioning, shaming, stigmatizing, or ostracizing people who aren't doing anything wrong. I focused a lot on the ways that people should avoid inappropriately sanctioning others. I didn't say much about an alternative vision for how people *should* relate to each other when it comes to language. In this chapter, I discuss the ethics of grammarians from a social egalitarian perspective. Social egalitarianism is the view that people should relate to each other as social equals.[1] This is an intuitive ideal for social norms; it just means that people shouldn't relate to each other in ways that sort people along a hierarchy of esteem and status based primarily on their social identities.

When it comes to communication, people should communicate in ways that establish a level playing field between different kinds of communication styles. Language policing is incompatible with a social egalitarian ideal because when sticklers police other people's language they aim to raise their own social status by lowering the status of people who communicate in a different way. Because people's social identities often influence the ways that people communicate, sticklers therefore uphold a practice that sorts people into a hierarchy based

DOI: 10.4324/9780429319198-4

on their social identities. This practice can also widen existing social divides, because sticklers uphold the communication styles of more advantaged subgroups, whereas members of socially disadvantaged groups are more likely to be sanctioned and further disadvantaged based on the way they communicate.

In the first section I make the general case that language policing worsens existing social disparities. I then turn to a few examples of how linguistic sanctioning maintains social hierarchies and stigmatizes people who speak in non-standard ways. Specifically, I address language policing as it affects lower class speakers, women, gay people, racial and ethnic minorities, and immigrants. Whenever someone's identity is stigmatized or disadvantaged, so too are the patterns of speech that are associated with those identities. Pedants and snoots uphold these patterns of stigma and disadvantage when they take it upon themselves to hold everyone to their normative speech standards.

Next, I turn to a subgroup of grammarians who attempt to make language policing a force for egalitarian justice. Here I have in mind egalitarians who police people's language to ensure that they use other people's pronouns, and people who argue against cultural appropriation, including the appropriation of different cultures' patterns of speech. A proponent of 'egalitarian language policing' may argue that the problem isn't grammarianism *per se*, the problem is that most pedants correct disadvantage speakers too often and they don't sanction privileged people's speech enough.

I disagree with even these egalitarian cases for language policing. For one thing, just as sticklerism often doesn't stick as a way to get disadvantaged speakers to change the way they speak and write, it is also unlikely to inspire meaningful reform for privileged speakers. For another, even if egalitarian language police could use social sanctioning and correction to get privileged groups to change their speech, they shouldn't. Some pronoun refusers have legitimate reasons for refusing to comply with egalitarian pronoun norms. Some people from socially advantaged groups have legitimate reasons for adopting marginalized peoples' patterns of speech. Egalitarian language policing is too blunt an instrument to capture the moral nuance of these cases. Instead, egalitarians should criticize people who fail to treat others with dignity and respect, rather than looking for opportunities to callout and criticize people who talk in ways that they don't like.

3.1 SOCIAL EGALITARIANISM

Social egalitarians, aka relational egalitarians, argue that in a just society, everyone would relate to each other as equals. This doesn't mean that in a just society everyone would be the same or that they would control the same level of resources. Rather, social egalitarians argue that no one should have higher or lower status than other people simply by virtue of features of their social identity.[2] This is not to say that all social hierarchy is bad. Social egalitarians do not argue that people who are unkind, people who break just laws, and people who are responsible for their own disadvantages should have the same social status as everyone else. And in a socially egalitarian society, some people would still have more or less money, political power, cultural influence, or social support than others, due to differences in people's preferences, talents, and values. Social egalitarianism only requires that people do not have more or less primarily because of their sex, gender, race, sexuality, class, ethnicity, or any other social identity category. On their own, these identity categories should be irrelevant to how much money, power, influence, or support someone has.

There are lots of reasons to value social equality, but the most compelling reason is the idea that everyone has equal moral status, and social practices should reflect that fact.[3] Another reason to care about social equality relates to the value of freedom. If one group treats another group as if they are inferior, the subordinated group is less free or more vulnerable to domination.[4] Social hierarchies also constrain people's options for reasons that are beyond any individual's control, so social inequality undermines autonomy too.[5] Or, if you care about wellbeing, social hierarchy is bad for people's wellbeing in the long run because when members of lower-status groups are shut out of economic and social life, everyone misses out on the opportunity to trade with and learn from them. Social egalitarians also sometimes argue that it's important for everyone to have roughly equal social status in order for democratic institutions to function well.[6]

Each of these moral reasons to value social equality are reasons that weigh against language policing. People's social standing shouldn't be determined by irrelevant demographic differences. When sticklers promote their stuffy views about linguistic competency, they often socially disadvantage people on the basis of demographic differences that should be irrelevant to whether someone merits esteem or disapproval. Additionally, as I argued in the previous chapter, sticklers interfere with people who speak in counter normative ways, both through formal legal sanctions and informal social sanctions. Sticklers also stigmatize, dominate, exclude, and subordinate linguistic transgressors. Grammarians use the social sting of a correction to preserve existing social hierarchies in the same way that other people use makers caste, scarlet letters or punitive head shaving to raise their own status by knocking other people down a rung on the social ladder.

Some social egalitarians are more sympathetic to interference and sanctioning than I am. They argue that public officials should uphold institutions and enforce policies that encourage everyone to relate as equals. For example, a lot of social egalitarians defend democratic institutions, speech restrictions, mandatory public schooling, laws that prohibit discrimination, or even laws that mandate that everyone speak a common language in order to promote civic friendship and national solidarity. In the previous two chapters, I argued that even when laws and social practices are enforced for the sake of equality, they are likely to backfire because enforcement so often ends up entrenching the advantages of the people who already have a lot of social power, because they are the ones who are doing the enforcing. In this chapter, I'll also show that when it comes to the legal or social enforcement of language rules, these practices can widen existing identity-based social divides. Here again, language policing exacerbates the disadvantages of people who are already disadvantaged, even when it's done in the name of social equality.

3.2 CLASS

Social egalitarians reject social practices that sort people into high-status and low-status social categories on the basis of traits that shouldn't matter for social status. To illustrate what this means for language policing, let's begin with the example of class hierarchy. People from different economic classes often speak in different dialects and they construct sentences in different ways. Consider, for example, a speaker who says, "I seen da tree fall" versus "I saw the tree fall." The first speaker's sentence construction marks him out as having a working-class background whereas the second speaker sounds like he is from a more advantaged class. Both speakers can effectively communicate that they witnessed the falling of a tree, so one way of constructing the sentence isn't better than the other. In this instance, the fact that the first sentence is coded as working-class should not lower the status of the speaker, because the speaker's class background doesn't affect his ability to communicate. But if a pedantic person heard the first sentence and said "You mean to say you *saw the* tree fall" they would mark out the first speaker's sentence as deviant and wrong. This kind of sticklerism is inconsistent with social egalitarianism.

Paul Fussell, a notoriously perceptive commentator on the American class system, writes that language is the most clearly visible marker of an American person's social class.[7] According to Fussell, lower- and middle-class people are differentiated by their different grammatical constructions (as in the seen/see distinction) whereas distinctions in pronunciation and annunciation differentiate the middle and upper classes. He also argues that different classes have different vocabularies (e.g., consider the class valance of the words crapper, can, John, commode, toilet, little girls' room, bathroom, rest room, facilities, lavatory, and 'WC' pronounced 'vay-say'). Other linguistic differences also correspond to class. Slang, for example, is primarily a working-class and urban phenomenon. Even when wealthier people eventually adopt slang terms, the terms typically originate in poorer and younger communities.[8] In America, people can face labor-market disadvantages if they use terms that are associated with working-class urban dialects or southern accents. For example, when listeners hear speakers use the southern 'y'all' they perceive the speaker to be less competent than a non-southern speaker.[9] In contrast, people with more posh accents are viewed as more competent, so they are advantaged by their speech and vocabularies.

One might think that sticklerism is not inegalitarian as long as everyone has an equal opportunity to comment on other people's spelling and grammar. But grammarianism often backfires when people from lower classes try to play the grammarian game. As Fussell writes, many lower-class people self-consciously try to adopt the normative rules of grammar that upper-class people use, but they don't quite succeed. It's difficult for people to adopt the linguistic norms of other social groups because so many grammar rules are arbitrary, so lower-class people frequently misapply grammar rules by mimicking other groups' patterns of usage, resulting in 'pseudo-correct' constructions like 'between he and I.'[10]

This dynamic further illustrates why grammarianism undermines social equality. The conventions that sticklers uphold are the linguistic conventions that educated and wealthier people use, and it's really hard for someone who isn't from this kind of class background to out-pedant someone who's been born into the stickler class. Sometimes, people from lower socioeconomic classes try their hands at pedantry, perhaps in an attempt to use bourgeoise word weapons as tools of resistance or self-defense against class-based sanctions. But in these cases, sticklerism still makes class divides stick, rather than narrowing gaps in socials status. For example, lower middle-class women are more likely than other speakers to engage in 'hypercorrection,' which involves erroneously correcting sentences that are in fact grammatically correct to begin with.[11] Think of a woman who corrects a friend who says, "She gave the photos to my brother and me" and instructs them to say, "She gave the photos to my brother and I." In this case, the friend's initial construction would be considered grammatically correct according to the style-book rules of grammar. But using 'me' instead of 'I' is generally socially coded as lower class. A class-anxious stickler suggests saying "My brother and I" and thus outs herself as someone who has not mastered high-status linguistic conventions.

It gets worse. People from privileged economic classes are already advantaged, but sticklerism compounds their advantages because compliance with linguistic normativity is rewarded in the labor market. Perhaps because so many people attend public schools, which unnecessarily promote spelling and grammar, many adults value linguistic competency when they are selecting employees. This means that people who are prone to make spelling and grammar mistakes are routinely excluded from more lucrative positions, even if they are otherwise qualified and even if perceived linguistic competency is not especially important for the job, so the cycle of high-class grammarianism perpetuates itself through the labor market because employers mistakenly think that linguistic compliance matters.

At this point, one might push back on the class-based case against grammarianism by questioning whether linguistic compliance really is irrelevant to most jobs. In a 2013 commentary by Brad Hoover, the then-CEO of a grammar-checking software company called Grammarly, makes an argument like this in the *Harvard Business Review*.[12] Hoover's commentary is called "Good Grammar Should be Everyone's Business." There, he describes an analysis of LinkedIn profiles that used Grammarly software. The analysis found that people who had lower rates of grammar errors received more promotions, achievement of higher positions, and more frequent job changes. Hoover's analysis was confined to a small sample of profiles, but he speculated that it made sense that grammar was correlated with professional success because people who paid attention to detail, thought critically, or had high intellectual aptitude were both more likely to avoid grammar errors when writing a profile and more likely to be successful.

Other employers also equate professional conscientiousness and intelligence with linguistic competency. The CEO of a popular online recruiting website claimed that spelling and grammar errors were one of the main reasons that employers overlooked applicants' resumes.[13] Some companies use pre-employment spelling tests to screen candidates, even for positions that do not involve copyediting or clerical work.[14] For example, Google uses a resume screening software that removes applications with spelling errors from consideration.[15] As one workplace consultant writes, "Employers and customers are quick to jump on people who make bad spelling mistakes, even when they frequently use poor spelling and grammar themselves."[16] Another study finds that spelling errors were as harmful to an applicant's chances as a lack of professional experience—only the recruiters who are poor spellers themselves seem to go easier on applicants with poor spelling.[17]

Are employers correct in saying that poor spellers and applicants with non-standard grammar really are more likely to have other deficits that are relevant to the job? Maybe! The question is whether screening on the basis of grammar is the best way to identify these deficits. If employers are interested in conscientiousness or cognitive ability or whatever they think spelling is a proxy for, they should just craft a screening instrument that can measure these skills directly. Screening on the basis of linguistic non-compliance is a poor procedure, because linguistic differences can sometimes irrelevant demographic differences even if it also sometimes uncovers relevant skill deficits. Because spelling and grammar screening is so unreliable, business professor and HR consultant John Sullivan argues, excluding applicants on these grounds is inefficient, counterproductive, and potentially discriminatory.[18] Sullivan notes that many leaders in the technology, entertainment, and finance industries struggled with spelling and grammar, and may therefore have been overlooked by employers who used spelling and grammar tests and software to screen applicants.

The issue isn't that screening for linguistic errors is never useful, it's that language-based screening is an unreliable way to find qualified applicants and it can set off a cycle of class inequality insofar as the screening perpetuates the economic disadvantages of people from already disadvantaged groups. Screening for spelling and grammar mistakes can also severely limit an applicant pool, given that on some estimates more than half of all resumes contain errors.[19] Employees might miss out on a great applicant just because he starts his cover letter by saying 'I seen' instead of 'I saw.' In these cases, sticklerism in HR departments doesn't just harm potential applicants, it harms the bottom line.

Moving beyond the economic realm, grammarianism also widens class divides in political contexts. Spelling and grammar policing enables lawmakers to signal their class-affiliation without directly saying that it's bad to be working class, which would alienate their own constituents. Consider an example from 2021, which illustrates this point.[20] At the time, the Republican representative Marjorie Taylor Greene (MTG) was aligned with a more populist faction of the Republican party, which supported Donald Trump and primarily appealed to white working-class voters. MTG publicly criticized a fellow Republican representative, Nancy Mace, writing, among other mean things, "Your out of your league." Mace, an anti-populist Republican who was critical of the Trump administration, simply replied "*you're." Another anti-Trump republican,

Adam Kinzinger, also made fun of MTG for the error, as did several Democratic lawmakers.

Everyone knew what MTG was saying. Mace and Kinzinger sought to embarrass MTG by pointing out that she was writing in a way that made her look uneducated and low-class. At the same time, MTG's faction of the Republican party embraces misspelling because they also view politics through the lens of class hierarchy, and mimicking the grammar of the poorly educated serves their populist interests. Trump's aides allegedly introduced grammatical errors into his tweets on purpose, to signal his affinity with the working class.[21] In this way, public officials on both sides can advance their political interests by ignoring or agonizing about apostrophes, but the stigmatization of non-standard spelling also widens class divides and further stigmatizes people who communicate in a low-class way.

This dynamic plays out on the left too. So many educated progressives in the United States are incredibly pedantic about their working-class political enemies' spelling, grammar, and speech. Consider, for example, Taylor Swift's "You Need to Calm Down" video, where anti-LGBT protesters are portrayed holding signs that misspell words. Swift's intention in the video is to insinuate that people who are against LGBT rights are immoral or mistaken. But by linking poor spellers to anti-LGBT protesters, Swift also is implying that poor spelling is correlated with ignorance or immorality, or that the fact that people with anti-LGBT views have poor spelling would be further evidence of their lack of credibility.[22] Swift purports to support broadly progressive values (the lyrics of her capitalist girl boss anthem "The Man" notwithstanding), but the classism on display in her depiction of the protesters is inconsistent with the values she is championing in the rest of the video.

Or, consider Democratic representative Alexandria Ocasio-Cortez (AOC)'s reply to a different MTG insult tweet, where MTG implied that AOC was stupid. In response, AOC wrote, "You seem to have some trouble spelling your own insults correctly. Next time try 'single-handedly,' it'll work better. Good luck writing legislation!" Elsewhere, democratic lawmakers and too-online progressive pundits have long reveled in making fun of Donald Trump's unorthodox orthography, which only strengthens his brand as a populist class warrior. In each of these cases, sticklerism enables people with ostensibly progressive politics to indulge in perpetuating class-based stigma against their working-class political enemies without having to explicitly criticize them for being lower class, which would be inconsistent with their progressive values.

In each of these contexts—social, economic, and political—sticklerism perpetuates existing class divides by punishing people whose language deviates from the linguistic conventions of high-status speakers. These pedantic social practices might serve politicians, who promote their own electoral prospects by encouraging people to think in terms of their class-based interests, but it doesn't serve the rest of us.

3.3 GENDER

Grammandos don't just maintain existing class hierarchies, they also perpetuate a bunch of other social hierarchies that confer advantages on the basis of people's identities. Specifically, language policing disadvantages women, gay people, ethnic and racial minorities, or immigrants.

Begin with the claim that linguistic normativity disadvantages women. Stickleristic sanctioning sets back women's status in part because existing linguistic standards have developed in a context where women's patterns of speech were stigmatized or corrected. For example, back in 1922 the linguist Otto Jepperson published a comprehensive study of language which included a chapter called "The Women," where he argues that female patterns of speech are inferior to the way that men talk because women were less likely to complete sentences and because women had less extensive vocabularies than men.[23] These linguistic values persist today, as people continue to prize the ability to communicate in complete sentences or an extensive vocabularies for its own sake, even when complying with these conventions isn't important for clear communication.

Gendered differences in communicative styles are culturally specific.[24] While American women may communicate in a more stereotypically friendly and submissive way, women in Madagascar stereotypically communicate in a way that is more aggressive and direct than male speakers, a norm that they likely developed while haggling in markets.[25] Yet in both contexts, people look down on the more female-coded ways of communicating, because social norms in both contexts are shaped in part by a patriarchal ideology that assumes that the male way of doing things is the standard or ideal.

In the United States, for example, people often hear women's voices and patterns of speech as distractingly deviant from the standard male way of speaking. Within the community of amateur language police, public-radio-listeners probably issue the most citations for feminine-coded patterns of speech like up-speak and vocal fry, with some listeners claiming that these patterns make female reporters sound "unlistenable!"[26] Adding to the chorus of NPR complainers, a few scholars who study vocal fry have even gone so far as to suggest that it could be harmful to women's vocal health to speak in this way.[27]

But up-speak and vocal fry never impede a women's ability to make themselves understood, but for the fact that some people don't like the sound of women's voices and turn off the radio whenever they hear a young woman. Moreover, it's not like other groups don't have their own verbal quirks and idiosyncrasies that are grating to some listeners. I, for one, cannot stand it when people talk in an affected academic tone, but I would never write a letter to NPR to complain about it! As the linguist Penny Ekert writes, "People are busy policing women's language and nobody is policing older or younger men's language."[28] This is ESPECIALLY egregious because, as Ekert notes, "the biggest users of vocal fry traditionally have been men, and it still is [for] men in the U.K, for instance. And it's considered kind of a sign of hyper-masculinity."[29] Yet when women speak in that way it is coded as unprofessional?!?

Beyond the example of vocal fry, my claim that grammarianism is bad for women's social equality might seem surprising to some readers, given that the ideology of grammarianism begins in elementary school, where most of the teachers are women. Also, women generally have stronger verbal abilities.[30] And there are certainly many notorious examples of female grammaristas. But we shouldn't forget the classic feminist observation that women are often complicit in social practices that merely compound their own disadvantages. In this case, grammarianism often entrenches a kind of male-normativity for language, even when women are the grammarians.

To illustrate this point about how some women sanction female-coded language, consider the practice of criticizing women for frequently saying 'like' as a filler word. I *love* to use 'like' as a filler word, but many women in my life have advised me to knock it off because it sounds unprofessional and annoying. Sometimes, they've couched their 'advice' in the language of sisterhood, as if they just want me to be taken seriously when I talk in public. But the only reason my use of 'like' would undermine my credibility is that people like them have made this speech pattern a target of social sanctioning and correction! Like the women who have told me to drop the 'likes,' the linguist Robin Lakoff once criticized the use of filler words like 'like' on the grounds that women use these words as hedges in order to appear more likeable. Lakoff was critical of the practice, because she thought that the practice caused women to preemptively undermine their own authority and convey a lack of confidence.[31] And somehow Lakoff thought that publicly calling out all the girls who talked this way would help the situation.

What critics of girl-coded filler words miss is that the use of 'like' in speech can serve several important purposes. It can signal a person's membership in a community of like-minded women (see what I did there?) Or the use of like can give women time to collect their thoughts while guarding against interruption. Or, as the linguist Jennifer Coates writes, words like 'like' and 'you know' can function as conversational hedges that enable women to more effectively communicate uncertainty or manage the emotional needs of all conversational participants.[32] So like, if I say "Fixing the car will cost like $600" I can convey that I'm not exactly sure how much it will cost to repair the car. By saying, "It was like, a really good birthday cake" I can diminish the braggy tone of a sentence. Or I can avoid hyperbole by using filler words in a statement such as, "You're like, really good at this game. It's like so impressive to see you make like so many points," because the word 'like' diminishes the rhetorical force of each evaluative claim. In these cases, I'm not undermining my own authority, I'm using language to communicate in a way that establishes the precise authority relations that I intend to establish.

In written communication, people also perceive feminine-coded ways of writing, such as the use of multiple exclamation marks, as unprofessional.[33] And here again, language policing serves to not only disadvantage women for linguistic practices that are coded as girl-talk, norms against enthusiastic punctuation also limit everyone's communicative possibilities. People lose a lot of context when they communicate through text. It's hard to convey tone through the written word alone, and it's especially hard to write a short text that sounds both friendly and engaging. Exclamation marks solve this problem. !!!s can make emails more emotionally expressive and reassuring, unlike the flat direct email style that some people use. When I receive an email without any !!!s, it often sounds like an email accusing me of hitting someone's trash cans as I backed out of my driveway. When I receive an email with a bunch of !!!s it puts me at ease and makes me more receptive to the message.

People's aversion to excessive exclamation points cannot be grounded in any functional considerations about effective professional communication. Instead, their fussy views about !!!s is a reflection of their more general anxieties about sex differences in communication styles. Because male ways of communicating are widely perceived to be the professional standard, when sticklers uphold professional standards of communication, they put women who want to use a ton of !!!s in a difficult position. On the one hand, people also encourage women to be warm and friendly and they punish women who are perceived as cold or unfriendly. On the other hand, the most reliable way to seem friendly in written communication is counter normative. Facing this dilemma, women must ask "How many exclamation marks are too many?" for every email they write. Refrain from using any exclamation marks and recipients may worry that they're mad. Use too many, and some stickler might think they're unserious.

This isn't just a problem for women. It's an issue for anyone who occupies a social role where they are expected to communicate in ways that are both professional and friendly. And there's no winning this game, because it's rigged from the start. However many !!!s appear in an email, there's a chance that a reader will think it sounds standoffish and a chance it will come off as hyper and weird. There's no magical number of !!!s per paragraph that will avoid the punctuation police in our heads because the conventions that govern professional text are both arbitrary and inconsistent. The only way out of the dilemma is to banish the punctuation police in our own heads, as we read and write emails, and use however many !!!s we think are useful to convey the appropriate emotional tone.

3.4 SEXUALITY AND SEXUAL IDENTITY

Just as enforcing normative linguistic standards can maintain sex-based status inequalities, linguistic norms can also be used as a way of stigmatizing people for their sexuality. At the same time, just as a female-coded way of talking enables women to communicate more effectively, gay-coded communicative styles can also enable more effective communication.

In English, some men speak in a way that people associate with homosexuality. The gay voice is a cultural trope that identifies the extended s-sound (known as the gay lisp), certain variations in tone and pitch, some vowel sounds, and upspeak as signifiers that the speaker is a gay man.[34] Like all research on stereotype accuracy, it's controversial whether what researchers call 'auditory gaydar' is accurate.[35] But people in the gay community widely acknowledge the accuracy of the stereotype, with some gay men reporting that "My voice knew who I was before I did."[36] One of the touchstone discussions of this topic is David Thrope's 2014 documentary "Do I Sound Gay?" which proceeds from the assumption that the gay voice stereotype is accurate, while also featuring a straight man who has a gay voice and a gay man who does not.[37]

Because the gay voice is overrepresented among gay men, all men who speak with a gay voice face stigmatization and sanctions for the way they talk in any contexts where gay men are stigmatized.[38] The stigmatization of the gay voice is another example of how language policing can widen and reinforce social divides. People discriminate against men who speak with a gay voice, in the same way people might discriminate against people who use non-standard grammatical conventions, or people who speak with a southern accent.[39] People who sanction or stigmatize gay-coded patterns of speech are also engaged in the same kind of misogynistic language-policing I discussed in the previous section, because many aspects of the gay voice are also feminine-coded ways of talking.[40] One theory for the development of 'gay voice' speculates that men who are raised in a more female-dominated environment are more likely to have gay sounding voices because they adopt female-coded speech patterns early in life.[41] Gay-sounding patterns of speech might also be more prominent among gay men if, as children, they engage more with female speakers and come to emulate their speech.[42] Gay kids might do this if, for example, they encounter more homophobia from male speakers and therefore choose to spend time with girls and women instead. As for the gay lisp, gay children are not more likely to speak with a lisp.[43]

Because the gay voice is stigmatized in heterosexist cultures, some people try to avoid it in order to avoid stigmatization. The writer David Sedaris recounts his own experience going to speech therapy as a child to address a lisp. Sedaris was embarrassed by the experience at the time. He writes, "no one seemed to make any significant improvement. The only difference was that we were all a little quieter."[44] Guy Branum tells a similar story of growing up with a gay voice. He writes,

> By the fourth grade, I learned that there was something about me that made me audibly different from the other boys my age. I could not mask it, I could not change it, I could not fight so well that I could earn the respect of my classmates. My voice evoked rage and disgust from my peers and teachers. I kept it hidden and tried to fit into a role that did not fit me. I played football, I tried to date girls. None of it worked, so I became quiet, very quiet, for a long time.[45]

On Branum's account, the stigmatization of his gay voice was inexorably linked to the broader culture of heterosexism he encountered as a child. Like Sedaris, the social sanctions he faced for his speech effectively silenced him throughout his childhood. As Dan Savage comments, "for many gay men, that's the last vestige, that's the last chunk of internalized homophobia, is this hatred of how they sound."[46] Even though Sedaris and Branum are comfortable with their identities as gay men today, they both continue to feel ambivalently about their voices because they partly internalized the heterosexist culture of their childhoods.[47]

Straight men with gay voices are also disadvantaged by social sanctions that stigmatize this way of talking. For one thing, women may not think they're romantically interested in them because they might assume that these men are gay. And, more generally, straight men with gay voices are disadvantaged by homophobia too, insofar as people assume that they're gay based on their voices. Bob Corff is a vocal coach who trains actors to speak with different accents, including training to sound straight. According to Corff, both gay and straight actors have asked him to speak in a way that sounds more straight in order to improve their chances of being cast in leading roles.[48]

But for the very same reasons that young people may try to diminish the gayness of their voices, older gay men might deliberately adopt deliberately adopt a gay voice or a campy gay accent as a way of signaling that they are gay.[49] Throughout the nineteenth century, gay men in England even spoke a distinctive dialect, Polari, which enabled them to communicate in public without revealing their sexuality.[50] Polari fell out of favor in the twentieth century as homosexuality was decriminalized and some gay rights activists thought the dialect perpetuated derogatory stereotypes. But more recently, gay men have reappropriated gay voice in the same way that they have reappropriated the word 'queer.' There is even some recent renewed interest in Polari among some gay rights activists.

More generally, gay men now adopt gay-coded patterns of speech as a way of cultivating in-group pride and solidarity and enabling them to identify other gay men more easily. Like anyone else who is a member of a minority social group, older gay men may also just come to adopt the patterns of speech that people in their community view as more stylish or aesthetic. In these cases, the gay voice becomes a self-reinforcing phenomenon that fosters camaraderie among gay men while widening the social distance between gay men and the dominant culture. In these cases, the policing of the gay voice still widens social divides between gay men and the broader heterosexist culture, but the gay voice also fosters social equality among gay people.

Language policing doesn't only affect men who speak with a gay voice. Lesbians' speech may differ from heterosexual women's speech, too, but this claim is controversial among researchers.[51] There are also mixed results regarding whether bisexual men or women speak in ways that are systematically distinctive.[52]

Trans people can also face social sanctions when their speech departs from normative standards for speech and language. Unlike gay children, there is some evidence that children who later identify as transgender are more likely to speak with a lisp during childhood.[53] As adults, trans people may struggle to gain social recognition as men or women because their voice is socially coded as being inconsistent with their gender identity. For this reason, some trans people invest in transgender vocal training so that they can learn to speak in a way that affirms their gender identities.[54] In some cases, trans people get surgery to change the pitch of their vocal folds. Vocal training often involves imitating and adopting gendered patterns of speech as well. On the one hand, this process can be liberating and validating for trans speakers. But the fact vocal training is so important to trans speakers also highlights how authoritative and restrictive gendered linguistic standards are for all speakers. Given people's attitudes about speech and gender, trans people have a legitimate interest in modifying their voices, but it would be better for all involved if the self-appointed speech supervisors in our lives abandoned the practice of subtly encouraging everyone to comply with their gendered expectations for speech and voice.

These examples aren't about spelling and grammar specifically, but they demonstrate how spelling and grammar pedantry is part of a broader phenomenon of monitoring people's communications and punishing social deviance by sanctioning linguistic deviance. When gay men embrace and aim to reappropriate gay voice, they are working to change the perceptions of homosexuality more generally, but advocating for more inclusive norms surrounding linguistic variations is part of this broader project of working for social equality.

3.5 RACE, ETHNICITY, AND REGIONALISM

So far, I've made the case that people shouldn't sanction the way others speak or write in cases where speakers and writers aren't doing anything wrong, and that grammarians are especially out of line when they sanction people's speech in ways that exacerbate existing social inequalities. This is especially clear in cases where sticklers target racial minorities or people from socioeconomically disadvantaged regions.[55]

One of the clearest examples of how language policing can widen social inequalities is the policing of African American Vernacular English (AAVE). Researchers find, for example, that people who speak in a dialect associated with being black are plausibly more likely to experience race-based employment or housing discrimination.[56] There are two ways to remedy these patterns of discrimination. On the one hand, educators could encourage people who use AAVE to communicate in Standard American English (SAE) instead. Or educators could reject linguistic normativity and embrace AAVE as an equally legitimate way of communicating.

Unsurprisingly, I favor the second strategy of embracing regional dialects in education. Yet this approach has been controversial in educational policy debates. In the 1970s, a division of the National Council of Teachers of English adopted the position that "affirm[s] the students' right to their own patterns and varieties of language—the dialects of their nurture or whatever dialects in which they find their own identity and style."⁵⁷ Yet, in 1979, a federal judge in Michigan found schools were required to identify that students who spoke AAVE only in order to "use that knowledge in teaching such student how to read standard English."⁵⁸

By the 1990s, the debates over AAVE and education became an even greater source of public controversy when a school district in Oakland, California passed a resolution instructing educators not to disparage the use of AAVE (also known as Ebonics). The resolution instructed the superintendent of the district to "devise and implement the best possible academic program for imparting instruction to African American students in their primary language" and stated that this requirement was important for "maintaining the legitimacy and richness of such language."⁵⁹

Though many public figures were harshly critical of the Oakland Ebonics resolution, sociolinguists were uncharacteristically united in their agreement with the Oakland school district.⁶⁰ Looking back on the controversy, the linguistic anthropologist Laura Ahearn writes "Opinions that would have been unacceptable had they been expressed about African Americans themselves became acceptable when they described the way some African Americans talked." For some, the public debate about linguistic standards served as a proxy for an unspoken debate about racial hierarchy.

Though it might be more instrumentally useful for people to be fluent in SAE, it is not as if AAVE is in any sense less functional or communicative than SAE. As John McWhorter writes, AAVE is even "more ingrown and intricate than Standard English in some ways" because it includes grammatical constructions that can convey context in a more streamlined way.⁶¹ For example, Black English speakers can use the construction 'up at your house' to convey that the speaker had an intimate relationship with the location, in contrast to 'at your house.' This is why McWhorter claims, "Black English is not 'bad grammar' under any logical conception—unless we can seriously condemn our own mainstream English as crummy Anglo-Saxon."[62] People can be as articulate and well-spoken in speaking AAVE as in any other dialect, meaning that they can communicate as accurately and efficiently as anyone else. It's disingenuous for people to claim that people who speak in dialect should change their speech to be more comprehensible. With few exceptions, all speakers of American dialects can understand people who speak in other American dialects.

Part of the reason that people who speak in AAVE, or other 'non-standard' American dialects might face discrimination is that their speech is different from the way that English is typically written. Verbal communication changes more quickly and has more variation than written communication, and people who value written communication may hold other people's speech to the more conservative standards that they apply to writing. That's changing though, according to McWhorter, because people now communicate in writing so much more than they did before the internet. As a consequence, written language is evolving and becoming less formal in the same way that people have historically developed less formal dialects in their oral communication.[63]

Alongside this recent, large-scale shift in formality and standardization of written communication, some writing instructors have moved to embrace dialect, or at least to refrain from penalizing people who speak and write in dialect. In 2020, the Rutgers English department announced that they would deemphasize grammar in their Graduate Writing Program (a program for all graduate students at Rutgers) as a way of resisting racism and standing with the

Black Lives Matter movement. The open letter announcing the change stated that the department would incorporate "critical grammar" into their writing pedagogy "so as to not put students from multilingual, non-standard 'academic' English backgrounds at a disadvantage." It also clarified that writing instructors would instead aim to equip students to "push against biases based on 'written' accents." In other words, instead of teaching people to comply with the demands of linguistic prescriptivism, the English professors at Rutgers would teach people to resist these demands.

These proposed changes to instruction at Rutgers are very similar to the pedagogical reforms that I advocated for in the first chapter. The department is to be commended for their anti-grammarianism. When the department announced these laudable changes, though, some conservative commentators mocked the Rutgers reforms for insinuating that proper grammar is racist. In response, a variety of non-conservative news outlets published 'fact checks' which denied that the department had declared grammar to be racist and which included a statement from the department chair saying that her view had been misrepresented. Which was a shame because popular conceptions of 'proper' grammar actually are upheld in ways that can be racist and bad in all sorts of other ways too!

In addition to the policing of AAVE, people who speak in regional dialects are similarly disadvantaged by widespread linguistic normativity. For example, in the United States people are more likely to perceive those who speak with a southern accent as less intelligent but nice, whereas they are more likely to people with northern accents as being smarter yet unfriendly.[64] In England, people with lower-class dialects or with accents from lower-class regions also face significant discrimination throughout their lives.[65] For example, Fiona Hill was a national security advisor in the United States, but she was born in England. While testifying before the U.S. Congress during former President Trump's impeachment hearing, Hill explained her American patriotism by referencing the fact that her accent didn't hold her back in the States. Hill said,

> I grew up poor with a very distinctive working-class accent. In England in the 1980s and 1990s, this would have impeded my professional advancement. This background has never set me back in America.[66]

Hill's story is only one illustration of the ways that accent biases arise when people in power unfairly hold other speakers to standards of linguistic normativity in educational contexts, housing, and employment.

In response, one might question why people don't just abandon or change their accents in order to avoid being subject to discrimination. This practice is a form of code-switching. In some instances, code-switching is used to establish intimacy within groups and to differentiate in-group members from out-group ones. But when a group is likely to be treated unfairly due to their dialect or accent, or due to the identity traits that are associated with their dialect or accent, code-switching can also be a form of self-defense against mistreatment.[67]

Though many speakers can use code-switching, it would be unfair to expect people who are subject to accent biases to change the way they talk. Speakers with accents and dialects aren't doing anything wrong by failing to use the standard grammar and pronunciation. And the expectation that people engage in codeswitching can be especially burdensome for people perceive their communities as under threat due to biases or forced assimilation. Writing about the films *Sorry to Bother You* and *BlacKkKlansman*, Doreen St. Felix writes "For the black social actor, the use of white voice can trigger the treacherous assimilation of the black bourgeoisie to the white status quo." At the same time, sometimes people's opposition to codeswitching or the adoption of a more widely used dialect can also be a way of unfairly policing people's language. For example, it would be similarly unfair for people to disparage a black person who used Standard American English instead of AAVE on the grounds that she was "talking white."[68] In both instances, it's wrong to punish or exclude people for their failure to comply with arbitrary linguistic standards.

People also have compelling social reasons to preserve their regional dialects rather than assimilating. For one thing, a dialect may enable members of a group to express familiarity or friendliness between group members. Consider, for example, the linguist Jennifer Smith's work with people who spoke a regional Scottish dialect called Buckie.[69] Smith finds that adults use the dialect with varying frequency depending on the social context. Adults used the dialect more with their children in contexts where they were being playful and intimate, and they used a more widely used standard grammar when they were correcting or scolding their children. In this context, the dialect could communicate social meanings that would have been lost if everyone in the community adopted the standard grammar.

Linguistic gatekeeping is also especially detrimental to people who are non-native speakers of a language, whose linguistic innovations are liable to be interpreted as linguistic errors.[70] Linguistic natives police the boundaries of their mother tongues just as geographic natives police their borders. And often the causes and effects of this policing align.

For example, it can be more difficult for immigrants who are less fluent than native speakers to find employment, even for jobs that do not require fluency in the dominant language.[71]

Just as some gay men felt that their linguistic preferences to avoid the gay voice reflected their own internalized homophobia and the heterosexism of the broader culture, people's preferences against racialized or regional patterns of speech are also hard to distinguish from broader discriminatory attitudes and practices of stigmatization. People who cling to their prescriptivist linguistic commitments uphold norms for communication that enable them and others to disparage people from different ethnic and cultural backgrounds under the guise of grammarianism.

3.6 CULTURE, LANGUAGE, AND APPROPRIATION

In the previous sections, I argued that it's not wrong for people to communicate in ways that seem working class, female, gay, Black, or southern. Language policing is especially unfair when it targets people in these groups, because monitoring and correcting the way that people speak and write can widen existing social inequalities. But some egalitarians might reply that while pedants should not police the speech patterns of women, gay, Black, and southern people who speak in ways that reflect their identities, it's fair to police the speech patterns of people who speak in identity-coded ways that don't match their social identities.

Here I have in mind a kind of egalitarian language policing, which sanctions modes of communication that mirror marginalized people's speech. Proponents of this argument claim that it is disrespectful when people from a more socially dominant group appropriate the accents or patterns of speech that are more commonly used by a socially disadvantaged group. In this section I will first lay out the egalitarian case against linguistic appropriation, and then I'll argue that linguistic appropriation is not intrinsically objectionable, and that there are many compelling reasons to tolerate linguistic appropriation.

Linguistic appropriation consists in using language that is associated with people who have marginalized identities. Arguments against linguistic appropriation parallel arguments against cultural appropriation. Philosophers who write about cultural appropriation cite various reasons that cultural appropriation could be wrong. On one account, it's wrong to appropriate a culture when appropriation is a form of dominating speech that contributes to the oppression of a marginalized group.[72] Others argue that it's wrong to appropriate cultural practices when there is an intimate relationship between group members that non-group members have duties to respect by refraining from doing things that group members do as part of their shared identity.[73] On another view, cultural appropriation is wrong because it consists in "the appropriation of elements of a subordinated culture by a dominant culture without substantive reciprocity, permission, and/or compensation" to members of the subordinated culture.[74]

These broader arguments against cultural appropriation all apply to the narrow case of linguistic appropriation. Non-Black people's use of a 'Blaccent' is one of the most commonly cited examples of objectionable cultural appropriation. To say that someone has adopted a Blaccent is to say that they are using AAVE when they are not Black. Yet this objection to Blaccents overlooks the ways that many groups borrow from different vernaculars to express their own, distinctive cultural identity. For example, linguistic anthropologists find that some Asian American teenagers, who generally do not use a distinctive ethnic dialect, use either SAE or AAVE or a mix of the two as a way of asserting a distinctive social and ethnic identity.[75] Others find that white, middle-class American teenagers incorporate elements of AAVE into their dialect if they are fans of hip-hop, only to revert to SAE in adulthood.[76]

These examples of linguistic cultural appropriation may not be objectionable, even to critics of cultural appropriation. In these cases, people adopt elements from different dialects to assert their own identities in contexts where the boundaries between cultures are diffuse. In contrast, objections to linguistic cultural appropriation are especially salient in the entertainment industry where people profit from their deliberately crafted identities and modes of self-presentation. Specifically, people have long criticized hip hop artists and actors for using Blaccents, likening the practice to a kind of sonic blackface.[77] Consider, for example, the actor Nora Lum, who is also known professionally as Awkwafina. Early in her career as a comedian and rapper, Awkwafina adopted a Blaccent in her work. As Awkwafina's career advanced, activists criticized her patterns of speech on the grounds that she used AAVE for comedic purposes, which "upholds white supremacy by turning the voices of a community into a joke."[78] Others worried that Awkwafina's linguistic appropriation of AAVE could make it more difficult for Black actors who used AAVE to get non-comedic roles because she encouraged people to perceive AAVE as unserious.[79] In response to public criticism, Awkwafina apologized for her use of AAVE and clarified that she did not intend for people to interpret her patterns of speech as mocking or degrading Black Americans and she did not intend to harm anyone.

These arguments against linguistic appropriation often conflate two things that might be objectionable in practice.

On my view, adopting another culture's speech pattern or an accent is not intrinsically bad, but mocking a marginalized group is bad. In seemingly objectionable cases of linguistic appropriation, it's not the language *per se*, it's the mockery of an ethnic group. Granted, it can be difficult to tell if linguistic appropriation is used for mockery. For example, Hank Azaria adopted an Indian accent to portray the character of Apu on the Simpsons. In this case, some people argued that Azaria was mocking Indian people through his portrayal of Apu, which they compared to blackface. In contrast, others argued that Azaria was not mocking Indian people by portraying Apu, but rather that he was simply interpreting an Indian character.

Whether Azaria's portrayal of Apu was objectionable would depend not on whether Azaria was engaged in linguistic appropriation (he clearly was) but on whether he was degrading or mocking Indian people. Similarly, whether people should criticize fiction authors for using a variety of dialects doesn't depend on whether they grew up using those dialects, it depends on whether the dialects are used in a way that makes the whole novel degrading to a particular group. Linguistic appropriation on its own is not immoral, but we do have moral reasons to refrain from insulting people on the basis of their social identities.

There are three problems with the argument that linguistic appropriation is wrong in itself. First, it erroneously assumes an essentialist view of groups and suggests that that groups can collectively own their cultural products in ways that give them an entitlement to exclude other people from using it.[80] But groups do not own their cultural products. It's wrong to claim that particular groups are entitled to act as the guardians or the gatekeepers of their language whether the snoots or anyone else does it.[81] And to acknowledge that group members are entitled to act as self-appointed communication cops as long as they are policing the language of the privileged, is to implicitly endorse a reductive view of groups, assuming that everyone in the group agrees about the ethics of linguistic communication. This might hold for small groups, but for large identity-based groups such an approach is misguided because it cedes the norms for communication to the most protectionist individuals within a group who claim to speak for anyone who shares their identity.

The second problem with the egalitarian argument for language policing is that discouraging linguistic appropriation deters innovation and learning that could be for all speakers. Returning to the example of Black patterns of speech, Black English speakers are more likely than non-Black speakers to use African American Vernacular, which has the 'habitual be'. For example, linguistic researchers conducted an experiment where they showed Black and white children two pictures, one of the Cookie Monster sick in bed and one of Elmo eating cookies. The researchers then asked the children "Who be eating cookies?" or "Who is eating cookies?"[82] For Black children, they identified the Cookie Monster as the answer to the first question but Elmo as the answer to the second question. For White children, they identified Elmo for both questions. The 'habitual be' is a useful linguistic innovation. Other languages have a habitual aspect as well, and non-Black speakers may have an interest in adopting this linguistic convention to communicate more precisely.

As another example, consider British English speakers' recent incorporation of Topics into their grammar. Topics are grammatical phrases that emphasize which noun is or will be the most important in the subsequent conversation. Japanese, Lakhota, Central American Ayaucuho Quechua, and American

Sign Language grammars include Topics, but English generally does not.[83] Yet English speaking children who were raised in multilinguistic communities in England seem to use the words 'who' and 'that' as a marker for Topics in English. For example, they may say something like 'people that were on the bus' to emphasize that the subsequent speech will be about the people on the bus, and not about other people that the speaker will reference next.[84] This innovation creates a new way of communicating more precisely, which had previously been unavailable to English speakers.

Another example—verbal habits of active listening, interjecting small affirmation and responses to reassure a speaker that the listener is engaged in the conversation, are more common among women and, especially, Black women. Yet it would quite plausibly be beneficial to speakers and listeners if they were more widely adopted. As Sonja Lanehart finds, these patterns of crosstalk and reinforcement can promote consensus and community-building among speakers.[85] Each of these linguistic variations can, if more widely adopted, make communication more precise, effective, or more welcoming. If people were reluctant to adopt these modes of communication out of fear about inappropriate linguistic appropriation, all speakers would miss out on communicative practices that might improve how their language functions.

And third, to claim that borrowing is only permissible when it consists in adopting dominant linguistic norms is to entrench the aforementioned egalitarian problems with linguistic normativity. The problem with snoots is that they adopt privileged linguistic norms and sanction or punish people who fail to comply with these norms. Critics of linguistic appropriation argue that people who natively speak a privileged dialect or who comply with the dominant prescriptive standards when writing cannot adopt less privileged people's modes of communication. Yet critics of linguistic appropriation do not criticize code-switching to privileged linguistic norms. So, effectively, critics of linguistic appropriation are in partial agreement with the snoots in that they argue that only a few people should speak in non-standard ways whereas it is not problematic to adopt the dominant linguistic conventions. For this reason, critics of linguistic appropriation are advancing the inegalitarian stickler agenda under the guise of social equality.

This argument for the general permissibility of linguistic appropriation sheds light on broader debates about cultural appropriation. More generally, it's not wrong to appropriate a cultural practice but people shouldn't adopt other cultures' practices in order to insult or degrade them. Yet in these cases, the wrong of cultural appropriation isn't the appropriation *per se*, it's just that it's wrong to insult people.[86]

3.7 PRONOUNS AND POLITICS

Another form of egalitarian language policing concerns recent debates about pronouns.[87] Egalitarian language police argue it is disrespectful to refer to someone by a pronoun that they do not identify with. Pronoun refusers sometimes argue that it's ungrammatical to refer to people with non-binary pronouns, or that it's inaccurate to use pronouns that correspond to gender identity rather than someone's sex assigned at birth. Against both egalitarian and pedantic language policing related to pronouns, I argue that the directive to comply with egalitarian pronoun norms is a good one, but that doesn't mean that people who refuse to comply with this directive should have their own speech sanctioned or criticized in all cases. In some cases, pronoun refusal can be disrespectful. But not all instances of pronoun refusal are disrespectful, so pronoun refusal on its own is not grounds for social sanctioning by egalitarian language police.

Egalitarian language police argue that it's important for people to refer to people by pronouns that correspond to their gender identity. This is usually only an issue for trans and nonbinary people, because some people, pronoun refusers, do not want to refer to them with pronouns that correspond to their gender identities. Egalitarian language police therefore stigmatize and criticize speakers who do not use people's preferred pronouns, and they also advocate for legislation that would compel speakers to refer to people by their pronouns. In these cases, egalitarian language police get the actual police on their side, and pronoun refusers can face fines and criminal charges.[88] Pronoun refusers sometimes try to police people's language too, either in the name of promoting 'good' grammar or out of a commitment to using words in ways that correspond only to their preferred definitions. As it is with other examples of language policing, people on both sides often aim to advance a broader political agenda that goes beyond their specific commitments to how language is used, and they use language policing as a way of promoting their ideology.

I am against linguistic sanctioning in both cases. I do not think pronoun refusers should oppose the singular use of they/them pronouns or pronoun norms that use pronouns to refer to people's gender identities rather than their sex assigned at birth. But egalitarian language police should not sanction pronoun refusers either, not only because a punitive and sanctioning approach to language is likely to be ineffective but also because this approach to language is counterproductive to the broader egalitarian goal of making communicative norms more inclusive.

Let's start by discussing where pronoun refusers go wrong in terms of language policing. There are four kinds of pronoun refusers who oppose using people's pronouns in at least some cases—pedantic refusers who oppose the use of a singular they/them as a grammatical construction, punitive refusers who aim to deny trans and non-binary people's claims about their own genders, principled refusers who refuse to use people's preferred pronouns because they are committed to an ideology that does not recognize the legitimacy of gender self-identification, and political refusers who are making a statement about free speech.

The first kind of pronoun refuser is just like all the other pedants we've encountered so far. Pedantic pronoun refusers resist using they/them pronouns on the grounds that it is clunky or ungrammatical.[89] They are so committed to upholding the linguistic conventions they learned as children that they are prepared to shame, stigmatize, and sanction anyone fails to speak or write in ways that match the pedants arbitrary and idiosyncratic communicative preferences. When these pronoun refusers notice that some pronouns no longer comport with the standards of grammaticality that they, as middle-aged native speakers, learned in elementary school, it's the grammatical non-compliance that drives them crazy about new pronoun conventions.

Savvy egalitarian sticklers might respond to this group of pronoun refusers by questioning their authority as the arbiters of 'good grammar.' While middle-aged pronoun refusers are right to point out that they learned in school that 'they/them/their' refers only to groups of two or more people, and individual people must be referred to with 'she/her' and 'he/his' pronouns, they're wrong to think that these rules of grammar still apply today. As people increasingly acknowledged that some people are non-binary, linguistic conventions have shifted to recognize these new identities and they/them is now a widely accepted linguistic convention—making pedantic pronoun refusers the ones who are non-compliant with existing standards.[90]

I wouldn't respond to pronoun refusers in this way though, because it doesn't matter who's right about existing grammatical conventions. But if I had to take a side, I prefer the newer convention because it is more effective for communication. Some languages don't have gender-specific pronouns, so people are clearly capable of communicating without them, but these pronoun conventions are less efficient insofar as pronouns can quickly convey information about gender.[91] On the other hand, a language without a singular non-binary pronoun is less efficient too, because it cannot communicate gender for non-binary people. They/them is a useful singular non-binary pronoun because it a widely known gender-neutral word that English speakers already know how to use as a pronoun.

None of these considerations of this should matter to pedantic pronoun refusers because they should just relax about linguistic conventions for pronouns. To the extent that a pedantic pronoun refuser's commitment to 'correct' pronoun conventions makes her incapable of using non-binary people's pronouns, due solely to her fidelity to linguistic prescriptivism, she is essentially saying that she thinks it is more important to uphold the rules of pronoun usage that she learned in the 1980s than to make people feel recognized and respected. Grammarianism has about zero authority in my book (this book!), so this group of pronoun refusers clearly has the wrong priorities here.

A second group of pronoun refusers do not use people's pronouns because they want to communicate that trans and non-binary people are wrong about their gender and they refuse to use pronouns as a way of delegitimizing trans and non-binary people.[92] There are also some of these pronoun refusers who either only use non-binary pronouns, or presumptively always use them, in order to avoid reenforcing essentialist or inegalitarian gender ideologies.[93] Some of these pronoun refusers think that using someone's pronouns amounts to mollifying mentally ill people instead of encouraging them to seek treatment.[94] In the most extreme of these cases, people may refuse to use someone's preferred pronouns as a way of insulting them, hurting their feelings, or insinuating that their self-presentation is somehow deceptive or immoral.

Punitive pronoun refusals aren't committed to linguistic conventions, they are committed to delegitimizing and stigmatizing trans and non-binary people. In these cases, pronoun refusal *per se* isn't objectionable, the moral objection to punitive pronoun refusal is that it functions as an insult or a sanction against gender non-conforming people. Trans and non-binary are not liable to be stigmatized or sanctioned for their gender identities. This group of pronoun refusers seems to think that refusing to use pronouns in an effort to insult and stigmatize gender non-conforming people is likely to deter gender non-conformity. But making gender non-conformity more socially costly doesn't seem to deter it, it just seems to make trans and non-binary people worse off. The moral case against punitive pronoun refusal is similar to the case against grammarians—it's as if they are trying to 'correct' people who fail to conform with their stickleristic gender ideology by imposing a social penalty or insult. In both cases, non-conformity isn't wrong and non-conforming people aren't liable to be stigmatized for social deviance. So punitive pronoun refusers are a fair target from the egalitarian language police. They aim to stigmatize people that they disapprove of, so they cannot complain that egalitarians likewise stigmatize pronoun refusal because they disapprove of it.

The third group of refusers is similar to punitive pronoun refusers in that they are also sticklers about their gender ideology. But this group doesn't refuse to use people's pronouns in an effort to insult them, rather, they refuse to use people's pronouns because to do so would be to make them feel complicit in a practice that they find immoral. [95] Principled pronoun refusers oppose using people's pronouns for religious reasons. For example, in 2018, Nicholas Meriwether, a philosophy professor at Shawnee State, refused to use a transgender student's pronouns because he felt that using her pronouns would imply that God made mistakes when creating people as male or female.[96] Meriwether was disciplined by his university, but he ultimately won his case on the grounds that he refused to use people's pronouns out of religious conviction.

Other principled refusers decline to state their pronouns or to ask others about their pronouns because they think that participating in pronoun practices heighten the social salience of their gender.[97] Others worry that the practice might make them complicit in the perpetuation of gendered stereotypes. For example, Colin Wright draws the following analogy:

> Consider the Human Rights Campaign urging people to begin conversations with "Hi, my pronouns are _____. What are yours?" Now imagine a similar request from the American Federation of Astrologers encouraging everyone to begin conversations with, "Hi, I'm a Sagittarius. What's your sign?" To respond with your own star sign would be to operate within and signal your tacit agreement with the belief system of astrology. If you reject

astrology and respond to the question with "I don't have a sign," the reply might be "Of course you do! When were you born?" But that's a completely different question.[98]

On Wright's view, "Pronoun rituals are extremely effective at normalizing and institutionalizing the abolition of biological sex in favor of gender identity."[99] He claims that encouraging people to state their pronouns and use other's preferred pronouns is a mistake because this practice tacitly equates a person's gendered identity with their adherence to gendered roles and stereotypes.

As with punitive pronoun refusers, Meriwether's and Wright's arguments for principled pronoun refusal derive from their sticklerism about gender compliance. They are not like the grammarian pronoun refusers who are insisting on fidelity to the language they learned in grade school. Unlike the punitive pronoun refusers though, they do not refuse to use people's pronouns out of a desire to stigmatize and degrade trans and non-binary people. Rather, principled refusers are engaged in a kind of revisionist interpretation of the meaning of words, just as proponents of they/them pronouns are. Principled pronoun refusers choose to use language in a way that associates gendered pronouns with a person's sex as assigned at birth, whereas historically pronouns attached to people's gendered social identities. To the extent that principled refusers like Meriwether aren't engaged in language policing, but are merely refusing to comply with pronoun requests, their conduct avoids moral objections to linguistic prescriptivism and objections to the unfair stigmatization of trans and non-binary people. Principled pronoun refusers may incidentally insult, stigmatize, or disrespect trans and non-binary people, but they should not be subject to social sanctions from egalitarian language police because they are also not liable to social sanctioning on the grounds that they use language in a way that egalitarians view as socially undesirable.

The fourth group of pronoun refusers includes people who oppose using people's pronouns solely because they view pronoun proponents as trying to control their speech. For political pronoun refusers, their primary reason for refusal stems from their opposition to egalitarian language policing. For example, the psychologist Jordan Peterson once notoriously vowed never to use non-binary pronouns because he viewed egalitarian directives that required pronoun compliance as a threat to freedom of speech. Peterson claimed that he should not feel compelled to use trans and nonbinary people's pronouns out of fear of sanctioning, rather than his own motivations. He feared that complying with a request to use someone's pronouns would make him a tool of "radical left political motivations."[100] In this case, Peterson's pronoun refusal was a form of political speech.

Critics of Peterson are correct in arguing that Peterson has moral reasons to use people's pronouns, just as people have moral reasons to pronounce other people's names correctly and to try to make others feel as welcome and comfortable. But pronoun refusers like Peterson are similar to religious pronoun refusers in that they refuse to use pronouns for ideological reasons. In Peterson's case, his pronoun refusal was a strategic act of linguistic non-compliance that aimed to counteract pronoun proponents' linguistic prescriptivism. Pronoun proponents are correct in saying that the existing standards of linguistic normativity are not politically neutral.[101] People are using language rules that advance a political conception of gender when they only use she/her pronouns, or when they only use these pronouns in ways that correspond with people's sex assigned at birth. People use language rules that advance a different political conception of gender when they use they/them pronouns, or trans people's pronouns.

It can be hard to know whether someone is a pronoun refuser because they are sticklers about grammar or gender, or whether their pronoun refusal reflects their interest in avoiding complicity with an ideology they reject. I've argued that pedantic and punitive pronoun refuses have bad reasons for refusal, whereas principled and political refusers have a point. To lay my cards on the table, I support pronoun norms; I think speakers should generally use people's pronouns. But as a liberal, I also support speech norms that permit people with different pronoun preferences to avoid social sanctions.

Egalitarian language police would sanction all four pronoun refusers. I don't think any of them are liable to be scolded merely for their pronoun refusal, and only the punitive refusers are liable to be socially sanctioned at all. Linguistic dispositions are rarely morally wrong in a way that would make people who fail to comply with the dominant conventions liable to be shamed or criticized. And *even* if a person is using language in a way that is morally criticizable, sanctions may still be inappropriate or misguided if they are unlikely to effectively deter those morally criticizable uses of language. And sanctioning language is especially difficult to justify when it risks backlash, as in the case of the pronoun debate where sanctioning principled pronoun refusers inspired people like Peterson to engage in political pronoun refusal.

Egalitarian language policing is even harder to justify when it involves enforcing punitive workplace rules and governmental regulations.[102] People who refuse to comply with linguistic norms that don't align pronoun proponents' communicative preferences and ideology do not make themselves liable to be sanctioned on these grounds. A person who refuses to use someone's preferred pronouns may be rude or insulting or inconsiderate, but that alone is insufficient grounds for workplace sanctions and legal penalties. It matters whether their rudeness is grounded in their principled interests in non-compliance or matters of conscience. And though I agree that pedantic pronoun refusers who maintain their position out of mere snootiness, rather than moral reasons, are especially misguided, even in these cases, a person's failure to adhere to prescriptive pronoun pronouncements is not a human right's violation, or any kind of rights violation at all. Peterson is right to say that other people don't have an entitlement to determine which pronouns he uses to address them, even if it would be impolite or hurtful for Peterson to deliberately use pronouns that a person did not choose.[103]

Summing up, the only pronoun refusers who are liable to egalitarian language policing are the punitive pronoun refusers, not because they fail to comply with pronoun proponents' directives but because they are using language in a way that intends to stigmatize or sanction trans and non-binary people. Since punitive pronoun refusers are using language to lower the social standing of trans and nonbinary people because they disapprove of gender non-conformity, they have little standing to complain about egalitarian language police who try to lower the social standing of punitive pronoun refusers because they disapprove of them. Even in this case, though, I don't think that the cycle of shaming is productive for either side of this debate. Egalitarian language police might think that they are benefiting trans and non-binary people by lowering the social standing of their political enemies, but this punitive impulse is at odds with their broader egalitarian commitments. And it's risky to stigmatize punitive pronoun refusal because the practice is likely to misfire insofar as it also affects principled and political pronoun refusers. Instead of trying to cajole pronoun refusers into compliance with social sanctions, workplace policies, and law, egalitarian language police should just make the positive case for using people's pronouns and engage with pronoun refusers' reasons on their own terms. When punitive pronoun refusers are disrespectful towards trans and non-binary people, egalitarian language police may be entitled to defensively disrespect them in return, but it still doesn't follow that they should.

This discussion of pronoun refusal and egalitarian language policing illustrates a broader point about how language policing functions as a means of social control. Pronoun refusers and proponents are both right when they say that their opponents in the pronoun debate are trying to sanction people for using language in ways that reflect a controversial ideology. I'm a pronoun proponent, but I don't think my fellow proponents should use social sanctions or institutional penalties to shame pronoun refusers into compliance. There is a tension within the case for egalitarian language policing between the commitment to egalitarianism and the impulse to use social sanctions to lower the status of disfavored groups. Egalitarians are correct in saying that people have moral reasons to use people's pronouns, or more generally, to speak in an inclusive and respectful way. But the same reasons for encouraging respectful and inclusive language are also reasons against using social sanctions and penalties to stigmatize people who disagree.

3.8 GENDER, GRAMMAR, AND POLITICS

We can apply the lessons from the pronoun debate to other debates about gendered language too. Some languages are genderless. In English, for example, the only gendered nouns are those which correspond to objects with gendered attributes. This means that the English language has gendered nouns such as 'goose' and 'gander' and gendered pronouns, which linguists call 'natural gender,' but it does not have gendered nouns for objects that do not have clear gendered attributes. Mandarin Chinese does not ascribe gender to nouns or pronouns when they are spoken, but the written characters are gendered.[104]

Many other languages ascribe grammatical genders to nouns that do not have gendered attributes. Grammatical genders are linguistic categories that determine which articles precede a noun, which adjectives describe a noun, and which pronouns describe a noun. In some cases, spelling conventions for nouns align with the nouns' grammatical genders. Widely used languages—including French, Italian, Spanish and Hindi—have noun classes that assign nouns as either feminine or masculine. Other languages—such as German, Latin, and Greek—also have a third, neutral noun class. Over time, some languages—like Danish and Swedish—have dropped the feminine/masculine distinction such that they now differentiate nouns along a common/neutral distinction, where common refers to nouns that were once feminine or masculine.

Other languages have grammatical genders that do not correspond to differences between nouns that describe different genders (as a masculine/feminine distinction would). Somewhat confusingly, linguists refer to these kinds of distinctions between noun classes as grammatical genders as well. For example, Algonquin languages divide nouns into animate/inanimate grammatical classes.[105] Other languages, such as Polish and Russian, differentiate some nouns based on a human/non-human classes. Sometimes, grammatical genders for nouns align with the properties of whatever the noun describes. Many African languages have grammatical conventions for nouns that generally correspond to the perceived properties of the things that the nouns describe.[106] For example, Supyire is an African language that has five gender classes for nouns, which align with whether a noun descries a human, small thing, big thing, a mass noun/abstract concept, or a liquid. Interestingly, while the Swahili language has many noun-classes that operate like grammatical gender, and which correspond to different kinds of things that the nouns describe, it does not have a distinction in its noun classes that corresponds to sex or gender.[107]

For our purposes in this section, I will first focus on the subset of languages that have grammatical gender along masculine/feminine lines. In these languages the masculine/feminine grammatical gender that attaches to a noun is not necessarily linked to the qualities of whatever the noun describes. For example, in the German language, the word for 'girl' (*das Mädchen*) has the neutral (neuter) gender and the word for person (*die Person*) has the feminine gender class. Sometimes the grammatical gendering of nouns can encode gender-based stereotypes. For example, written Chinese characters are constructed out of radicals, pictographic signifiers of a word's meaning. Some characters that describe seemingly gender-neutral nouns include gendered radicals. And, in some cases, the inclusion of gendered radicals in these written characters can reflect gender-based stereotypes. For example, the characters for rape, jealousy, monster, and reckless include female radicals.[108] Or, in the French language prestigious jobs are grammatically masculine, whereas jobs for caretakers and servant are grammatically feminine.[109] Researchers have suggested that grammatical gender can cause people to describe objects that are assigned gendered nouns in ways that reflect gendered stereotypes.[110] For example, when researchers asked Spanish and German speakers to describe the same objects, speakers would describe the objects in different terms depending on the grammatical gender that their language assigned to the object.[111]

In these contexts, speaking in the 'traditional' way amounts to speaking in a sexist way that entrenches patriarchal values. These gendered linguistic conventions can also entrench stereotypes about men and women, making it harder for men and women who speak these languages to behave counter to the stereotypes. Partly out of concerns that grammatical gender in languages can perpetuate stereotypes, some people who speak these languages with masculine/feminine grammatical genders deploy gaps, stars, and colons to avoid using gender-specific words. For example, the word for 'student' is '*Schüler*' for a male student or for a group of students and '*Schülerin*' for a female student. To avoid gendering subjects through one's word choice, some German speakers prefer to use conventions like '*Schüler_in*' or '*Schüler*in*' instead.[112] Yet like egalitarian efforts to encourage people to use trans and nonbinary people's pronouns, efforts to promote gender-inclusive linguistic reforms can be controversial because speakers view these proposed reforms either as an ideological imposition or as a barrier to effective communication.[113]

Seemingly egalitarian proposals for linguistic reform can also be culturally insensitive, especially when they originate from people who whose native languages are genderless. For example, consider the conversation surrounding the word Latinx. Some activists have advocated for using the word 'Latinx' instead of the words Latina/Latino to describe Hispanics. Yet many Spanish-speaking Americans viewed these proposed reforms as non-native speakers attempting to control how recent immigrants used their native language. In this case, Spanish speakers viewed an egalitarian call for linguistic reform as a condescending and unwelcome linguistic intervention.[114] Even if speakers should be open to changes in their language, it's also important for linguistic reformers to be mindful of the broader social context when they advocate for gender-neutral reforms.

Similar issues arise for English speakers, too. Even though English has only natural gender, not grammatical gender, the English language still includes a range of subtle gendered stereotypes and phrases that reinforce the male perspective or sideline women's perspectives. For example, the term 'penetrative sex' characterizes sex as something that a man does to a woman (in contrast to a word like *envelopment*, which would make women the protagonists of sexual experience).[115] English speakers also tend to use masculine generics, meaning that they use the 'he' pronoun to refer to people whose gender is unknown and say things like 'hey guys,' or 'mankind' or 'the dawn of man' to refer to groups of people.

And as in other linguistic communities, some egalitarian linguistic reformers have advocated for the minimization of gendered language in English.[116] And here again, egalitarian language policing that aims to minimize the use of masculine generics and gendered language in English communication can do more harm than good, from an egalitarian perspective. For example, the podcaster Clementine Morrigan described an experience where she used the term 'hey guys' in a social community that was dedicated to inclusivity and subsequently experienced significant distress related to her fear of social sanctioning for using a masculine generic.[117] This experience is not unusual, even for people who are broadly committed to using inclusive language.[118]

These accounts of the social dynamics of changing gendered language reaffirm my earlier point that egalitarianism is generally inconsistent with language policing, even when social sanctions aim to reduce social inequalities. When people use language policing as a tool for egalitarian social change, they attempt to lower the status of people who use language in an inegalitarian way, rather than addressing people's underlying inegalitarian attitudes or attempting to convince them to change the way they communicate for egalitarian reasons.

Egalitarian language police might claim that there is no reason to accept an inegalitarian linguistic status-quo as given. But there are egalitarian reasons against using social sanctions to promote linguistic reforms that native language speakers find offensive or difficult to adopt. As with the pronoun debate, I am calling for linguistic liberalism. Though a linguistic status quo may merit reform, reformers should take care to make the case for language change in ways that don't stigmatize or sanction members of linguistic communities that already lack social power relative to egalitarian linguistic reformers.

3.9 EGALITARIAN LANGUAGE POLICING

Taking stock, I have suggested that egalitarian language policing, like all language policing, is misguided. This kind of language policing is misguided in part because it is likely to be ineffective, in part because it risks widening unfair social hierarchies, and in part because egalitarian language policing shifts conversations about social equality from substantive debates to semantic squabbles. Even if egalitarian language policing does get some speakers to change the way they communicate, if speakers only reform the way they talk in an effort to avoid sanctions stigma and punishment then egalitarian language policing can still backfire because people resent being threatened into submission.

The more general egalitarian reason to reject egalitarian language policing is that this practice is often more burdensome to people who are already socially disadvantaged. For example, consider the "euphemism treadmill."[119] Egalitarians discourage people from using words or phrases that they perceive as derogatory, only to replace those words and phrases with new terms that describe the same things. The new terms are eventually also perceived as derogatory, and a new euphemism must enter the inclusive lexicon. But this process has an egalitarian cost. As Pinker writes,

> Using the latest term for a minority often shows not sensitivity but subscribing to the right magazines or going to the right cocktail parties. Shifts in terms have an unfortunate side effect. Many people who don't have a drop of malice or prejudice but happen to be older or distant from university, media and government spheres find themselves tainted as bigots for innocently using passe terms like "Oriental" or "crippled."[120]

Even worse, just as taxes are more harmful to poor people, social sanctions are more harmful to low-status people. The people who lose out the most from this language game are the people who have the least status to lose. And when political language policing reflects the political attitudes of an elite class, and I've suggested it does, non-elite low status people are additionally burdened by this practice because linguistic norms change to reflect high-status political values which makes it harder for members of lower-status groups to articulate their positions.

Egalitarian language policing has other political costs too. Language can be used as a tool of social and political control. In some instances, egalitarian language policing directly materially disadvantages the people who are subject to it. As discussed in Chapter 2, officials in the UK censor racist and offensive speech in public spaces, and people who violate these speech restrictions face fines or even jail time. In the U.S., people have been fired just for mentioning (not using!) taboo words. The egalitarian reasons against subjecting socially and politically disadvantaged people to disproportionately burdensome laws and punishments also weigh against egalitarian language policing, because the people who violate these policies are often socially and politically disadvantaged.

Say an egalitarian language cop is confident that her egalitarian social and political values are correct, and she is also sure that she is on the side of justice when she threatens her fellow citizens with social, legal, and economic sanctions. She should still be wary of using language to promote her political ideology because policing other people's language in this way might make people comply with her linguistic demands without actually getting them to internalize her egalitarian values. People who encounter a lot of language cops in their lives might get into the habit of unthinking compliance, not because they agree with their censors but because they are afraid of sanctions and conflict. Committed egalitarians should want people to think about the moral reasons against using taboo and politically charged terms, but language policing prompts people to bypass this process of moral reasoning in favor of just watching their language around egalitarians, because self-censorship is the path of least resistance.

Another cost of egalitarian language policing is that when people self-censor in order to avoid violating the prevailing social and moral norms their language can become less precise, less evocative, and less expressive. Consider, for example, the euphemism slide from 'slum' to 'ghetto' to 'inner city' to 'urban neighborhood' to 'low-income/low-SES community' to 'underserved populations.' The word 'slum' is derogatory, but it expresses the concept in a way that clearly communicates the idea that some geographic areas are crowded and poor and the people who live there face distinct challenges. In contrast, inclusive revisions of the term lose some of this conceptual content. Lots of people who live in affluent communities are underserved. Lots of people who live in cities are affluent. Lots of people who are low-income/low-SES do not live in slums.

The overarching theme here is that social egalitarians should not support egalitarian language policing because sanctioning people in the name of equality is still not a very egalitarian thing to do. So why do so many social egalitarians seem so eager to socially sanction people for their egalitarian sins? The answer might lie in the social egalitarian origin story that Elizabeth Anderson tells in her work on social egalitarianism. Anderson argues that all people have an 'egalitarian impulse.' In support of this claim, she writes that even the earliest humans established social orders that granted all adult males' equal status despite the fact that some were older or stronger or smarter than others, and they all had different capacities to contribute to their communities.[121] Anderson thinks that this shows that humans naturally desire to live under conditions where there isn't a social hierarchy.

On the other hand, there's also evidence to suggest that even the earliest human communities adopted conventions that sorted people into higher and lower status groups, just like other primates.[122] Human children catch onto these status-based distinctions very early on, and when they do, younger children distinguish people primarily based on their language, rather than, e.g., their race.[123] People have an interest in social equality, but they also have an interest in maintaining social status distinctions. Egalitarians who raise their own status and foster in-group solidarity by sanctioning outgroup members for the sake of equality can serve both interests at once.

The history of linguistic development reflects people's dueling interests in social equality and status for themselves. On the one hand, language evolved in a way that enabled people to coordinate in large groups, working together to advance collective projects that would benefit the whole group more than any individual. On the other hand, even the earliest forms of language developed as a way of keeping track of who had what, who was in debt, and who had power.[124] Language developed to promote social equality and to undermine social equality because people have interests in both solidarity and status. Today, social egalitarians language police should not overlook how these two forces shaped today's linguistic norms. Any attempt to reform a linguistic practice for the sake of equality risks backfiring because even egalitarians have an interest in using social sanctions and egalitarian ideologies to raise their own status by lowering the status of their political rivals.

3.10 CONCLUSION

A just society is one where people don't feel stigmatized, excluded, or ostracized on the basis of their social identity or their economic class. Language policing is counterproductive to egalitarian justice, because it does just this. Often, people experience language policing because they communicate in a way that also identifies them as someone who is a member of a group that already lacks social power. Women, gay people, racial and ethnic minorities, and immigrants are all exposed to identity-based language policing, which sanctions and stigmatizes them for the way they communicate. This kind of language policing exacerbates existing social inequalities.

Someone might think that if language policing is bad because it's inegalitarian, then egalitarian language policing can be a force for good. Grammarian language cops might be tempted to stick with their practice of condemning nonstandard communication but aim their condemnation away from socially disadvantaged speakers towards inegalitarian speakers instead. This might involve sanctioning non-Black speakers who use AAVE, pronoun refusers, or people who use gendered nouns. The problem with this strategy is that even egalitarian language policing is often inegalitarian and unfair, and it can also be ineffective and counterproductive. Better for proponents of egalitarian justice to just walk away from old habits of stigmatization and sanction all together—instead of telling people how to speak, we should just listen to what they're trying to say.

NOTES

1. Or at least that people should be disposed to relate as equals. For an overview of this view, see Carina Fourie, Fabian Schuppert, and Ivo Wallimann-Helmer, *Social Equality: On What It Means to Be Equals* (Oxford University Press, 2015).
2. Sophia Moreau, "What Is Discrimination?" *Philosophy & Public Affairs* 38, no. 2 (2010): 143–79, https://doi.org/10.1111/j.1088-4963.2010.01181.x.
3. Niko Kolodny, "Rule Over None II: Social Equality and the Justification of Democracy," *Philosophy & Public Affairs* 42, no. 4 (September 1, 2014): 287–336, https://doi.org/10.1111/papa.12037.
4. Anderson, "Equality and Freedom in the Workplace."

5. Charles R. Beitz, *Political Equality: An Essay in Democratic Theory* (Princeton University Press, 1989), p. 190.
6. James Wilson, for example, develops an instrumentalist argument for reforming existing institutions with an eye to establishing social equality in the service of creating a well-functioning democracy, which is then instrumental to further promoting social equality. *Democratic Equality*, 2019, https://press.princeton.edu/books/hardcover/9780691190914/democratic-equality.
7. Paul Fussell, *Class: A Guide through the American Status System* (Simon and Schuster, 1992), p. 151.
8. Jonathon Green, *Slang: A Very Short Introduction* (Oxford University Press, 2016), p. 71.
9. Cheryl J. Boucher et al., "Perceptions of Competency as a Function of Accent," *Psi Chi Journal of Psychological Research* 18, no. 1 (2013).
10. Fussell, *Class*. Fussell, *Class*, p. 168.
11. Amanda Montell, *Wordslut: A Feminist Guide to Taking Back the English Language* (HarperCollins, 2019), p. 137.
12. Brad Hoover, "Good Grammar Should Be Everyone's Business," *Harvard Business Review*, March 4, 2013, https://hbr.org/2013/03/good-grammar-should-be-everyon.
13. Kathleen Doheny, "When a Worker's Grammar and Spelling Are Embarrassing," SHRM, September 15, 2020, www.shrm.org/resourcesandtools/hr-topics/people-managers/pages/poor-grammar-and-spelling-.aspx.
14. Doheny, "When a Worker's Grammar and Spelling Are Embarrassing"; Catherine Rampell, "With Positions to Fill, Employers Wait for Perfection," *The New York Times*, March 6, 2013, sec. Business, www.nytimes.com/2013/03/07/business/economy/despite-job-vacancies-employers-shy-away-from-hiring.html; "Spelling Skill Test | Online Skills Test for Employment," *Skillsarena* (blog), accessed January 4, 2021, https://skillsarena.com/skills-tests/english/spelling/.
15. John Sullivan, "Rejecting Resumes with Spelling Errors: A Silly and Costly Hiring Mistake," ERE, February 10, 2020, www.ere.net/rejecting-resumes-with-spelling-errors-a-silly-and-costly-hiring-mistake/.
16. Quentin Fottrell, "3 Ways Bad Spelling Could Alter the Course of Your Life," *MarketWatch*, April 9, 2016, www.marketwatch.com/story/3-ways-bad-spelling-could-alter-the-course-of-your-life-2015-08-20.

17. Christelle Martin-Lacroux and Alain Lacroux, "Do Employers Forgive Applicants' Bad Spelling in Résumés?" *Business and Professional Communication Quarterly* 80, no. 3 (2017): 321–35.
18. Sullivan, "Rejecting Resumes with Spelling Errors."
19. Sullivan.
20. Jim Saksa, "What 'Your' vs. 'You're' Says about Congress Right Now," *Roll Call*, December 2, 2021, https://rollcall.com/2021/12/02/what-your-vs-youre-says-about-congress-right-now/.
21. Annie Linskey- Reporter, "Does Donald Trump Write His Own Tweets? Sometimes – The Boston Globe," *BostonGlobe.Com*, May 22, 2018, www.bostonglobe.com/news/nation/2018/05/21/trump-tweets-include-grammatical-errors-and-some-them-are-purpose/JeL7AtKLPevJDIIOMG7TrN/story.html.
22. Swift reaffirms her commitment to linguistic prescriptivism in the song "Me" where she exclaims "Hey kids, spelling is fun!" This line operates on two levels. On one hand she recognizes the absurdity of it and means it to read somewhat ironically. On the other hand, she then engages in a recitation of how to spell words, in an (unsuccessful) attempt to cast spelling as genuinely fun.
23. Montell, *Wordslut*, p. 80.
24. Jennifer Coates, *Women, Men and Language: A Sociolinguistic Account of Gender Differences in Language*, 3rd edition (Harlow; New York: Routledge, 2004).
25. Laura M. Ahearn, *Living Language: An Introduction to Linguistic Anthropology* (John Wiley & Sons, 2021), p. 223.
26. Liana Van Nostrand, "Sounding Like a Reporter—And a Real Person, Too," NPR, August 7, 2019, sec. Language, www.npr.org/sections/publiceditor/2019/08/07/749060986/sounding-like-a-reporter-and-a-real-person-too.
27. Lesley Wolk, Nassima B. Abdelli-Beruh, and Dianne Slavin, "Habitual Use of Vocal Fry in Young Adult Female Speakers," *Journal of Voice* 26, no. 3 (May 1, 2012): e111–16, https://doi.org/10.1016/j.jvoice.2011.04.007.
28. "From Upspeak to Vocal Fry: Are We 'Policing' Young Women's Voices?" *Fresh Air* (NPR, July 23, 2015), www.npr.org/2015/07/23/425608745/from-upspeak-to-vocal-fry-are-we-policing-young-womens-voices.
29. "From Upspeak to Vocal Fry."
30. Andrea Scheuringer, Ramona Wittig, and Belinda Pletzer, "Sex Differences in Verbal Fluency: The Role of Strategies and Instructions,"

Cognitive Processing 18, no. 4 (2017): 407–17, https://doi.org/10.1007/s10339-017-0801-1.

31. For a critical overview see Kristina Sommerlund, "Critical Overview: Gender and Tentative Language," *Leviathan: Interdisciplinary Journal in English*, no. 1 (2017).
32. Jennifer Coates, *Women, Men and Language: A Sociolinguistic Account of Gender Differences in Language* (Routledge, 2015), pp. 89–91.
33. John McWhorter, "The Linguistic Evolution of 'Like,'" *The Atlantic*, November 25, 2016, www.theatlantic.com/entertainment/archive/2016/11/the-evolution-of-like/507614/.
34. Rudolf P. Gaudio, "Sounding Gay: Pitch Properties in the Speech of Gay and Straight Men," *American Speech* 69, no. 1 (1994): 30–57, https://doi.org/10.2307/455948.
35. Arianne E. Miller, "Searching for Gaydar: Blind Spots in the Study of Sexual Orientation Perception," *Psychology & Sexuality* 9, no. 3 (July 3, 2018): 188–203, https://doi.org/10.1080/19419899.2018.1468353.
36. "What Does It Mean to Sound Gay?" *The New Republic*, accessed August 19, 2024, https://newrepublic.com/article/122287/what-does-it-mean-sound-gay.
37. *Do I Sound Gay?* (IFC/Sundance, 2014), www.doisoundgay.com.
38. "Stigmatization of 'Gay-sounding' Voices: The Role of Heterosexual, Lesbian, and Gay Individuals' Essentialist Beliefs - Fasoli - 2021 - British Journal of Social Psychology - Wiley Online Library," accessed July 7, 2022, https://bpspsychub.onlinelibrary.wiley.com/doi/full/10.1111/bjso.12442.
39. See, e.g., Ana Beatriz Gomes Fontenele, Luana Elayne Cunha de Souza, and Fabio Fasoli, "Who Does Discriminate Against Gay-Sounding Speakers? The Role of Prejudice on Voice-Based Hiring Decisions in Brazil," *Journal of Language and Social Psychology*, June 30, 2022, 0261927X221077243, https://doi.org/10.1177/0261927X221077243.
40. Ana Swanson, "What It Means to 'Sound Gay,'" *Washington Post*, November 25, 2021, www.washingtonpost.com/news/wonk/wp/2015/07/28/what-it-means-to-sound-gay/.
41. David Thorpe, "Video: Opinion | Who Sounds Gay?" *The New York Times*, June 23, 2015, sec. Opinion, www.nytimes.com/video/opinion/100000003757238/who-sounds-gay.html.
42. *Do I Sound Gay?*

43. Kelly Servick, "Where Did the 'gay Lisp' Stereotype Come From?" November 9, 2015, www.science.org/content/article/where-did-gay-lisp-stereotype-come.
44. David Sedaris, "Go Carolina," *Me Talk Pretty One Day* (New York: Little, Brown and Company, 2000).
45. Guy Branum, "Opinion | My Gay Voice," *The New York Times*, July 28, 2018, sec. Opinion, www.nytimes.com/2018/07/28/opinion/sunday/my-gay-voice.html.
46. *Do I Sound Gay?*
47. *Do I Sound Gay?*; Branum, "Opinion | My Gay Voice."
48. Jeff Gordinier, "Hollywood's Secret Weapon for Losing the Gay Accent," *Details*, May 19, 2019, www.corffvoice.com/wp-content/uploads/Details-Bob-Corff-Article-5-2010.pdf.
49. David Adger, *Language Unlimited: The Science Behind Our Most Creative Power* (Oxford: Oxford University Press, 2019), pp. 234-6.
50. Paul Baker, "A Brief History of Polari: The Curious after-Life of the Dead Language for Gay Men," *The Conversation*, February 8, 2017, http://theconversation.com/a-brief-history-of-polari-the-curious-after-life-of-the-dead-language-for-gay-men-72599.
51. Salina Cuddy, "Can Women 'Sound Gay'?: A Sociophonetic Study of /s/ and Pitch of Gay and Straight British-English Speaking Women" (PhD Thesis, University of York, 2019), https://etheses.whiterose.ac.uk/27430/; Simone Sulpizio et al., "Auditory Gaydar: Perception of Sexual Orientation Based on Female Voice," *Language and Speech* 63, no. 1 (March 2020): 184–206, https://doi.org/10.1177/0023830919828201; John Van Borsel, Jana Vandaele, and Paul Corthals, "Pitch and Pitch Variation in Lesbian Women," *Journal of Voice: Official Journal of the Voice Foundation* 27, no. 5 (September 2013): 656.e13–16, https://doi.org/10.1016/j.jvoice.2013.04.008.
52. Chloe Willis, "Bisexuality and /s/ Production," *Proceedings of the Linguistic Society of America* 6, no. 1 (2021): 69–81; Mariya Yoshovska, "Understanding the Speech Cues to Bisexuals," *The Journal of the Acoustical Society of America* 143, no. 3_Supplement (March 1, 2018): 1970, https://doi.org/10.1121/1.5036491; James S. Morandini et al., "BIDAR: Can Listeners Detect If a Man Is Bisexual from His Voice Alone?," *The Journal of Sex Research* 60, no. 5 (June 13, 2023): 611–23, https://doi.org/10.1080/00224499.2023.2182267.

53. Servick, "Where Did the 'Gay Lisp' Stereotype Come From?"
54. Hyung-Tae Kim, "Vocal Feminization for Transgender Women: Current Strategies and Patient Perspectives," *International Journal of General Medicine* 13 (February 12, 2020): 43–52, https://doi.org/10.2147/IJGM.S205102.
55. "English with an Accent: Language, Ideology and Discrimination in the United States," Routledge & CRC Press, accessed July 15, 2022, www.routledge.com/English-with-an-Accent-Language-Ideology-and-Discrimination-in-the-United/Lippi-Green/p/book/9780415559119.
56. Faye K. Cocchiara, Myrtle P. Bell, and Wendy J. Casper, "Sounding 'Different': The Role of Sociolinguistic Cues in Evaluating Job Candidates," *Human Resource Management* 55, no. 3 (2016): 463–77, https://doi.org/10.1002/hrm.21675.
57. https://cdn.ncte.org/nctefiles/groups/cccc/newsrtol.pdf
58. *Martin Luther King Jr., etc. v. Ann Arbor Sch. Dist.*, 473 F. Supp. 1371 (Dist. Court, Ed Michigan 1979).
59. "Full Text of 'Ebonics' Resolution Adopted by Oakland Board," *Education Week*, January 15, 1997, sec. Equity & Diversity, www.edweek.org/leadership/full-text-of-ebonics-resolution-adopted-by-oakland-board/1997/01.
60. Walt Wolfram, "Language Ideology and Dialect: Understanding the Oakland Ebonics Controversy," *Journal of English Linguistics* 26, no. 2 (June 1, 1998): 108–21, https://doi.org/10.1177/007542429802600203.
61. John McWhorter, *What Language Is* (New York: Gotham, 2011), p. 128.
62. McWhorter, p. 131.
63. McWhorter, pp. 163–6.
64. Katherine D. Kinzler and Jasmine M. DeJesus, "Northern = Smart and Southern = Nice: The Development of Accent Attitudes in the United States," *Quarterly Journal of Experimental Psychology* 66, no. 6 (June 1, 2013): 1146–58, https://doi.org/10.1080/17470218.2012.731695.
65. Devyani Sharma, "British People Still Think Some Accents Are Smarter than Others – What That Means in the Workplace," *The Conversation*, accessed July 14, 2022, http://theconversation.com/british-people-still-think-some-accents-are-smarter-than-others-what-that-means-in-the-workplace-126964.
66. Kate Cooper, "The English Obsession with Accents is Bad for Business," *Forbes*, accessed May 5, 2023, www.forbes.com/sites/katecooper/2020/02/04/the-english-obsession-with-accents-is-bad-for-business/.

67. Jennifer M. Morton, "Cultural Code-Switching: Straddling the Achievement Gap," *Journal of Political Philosophy* 22, no. 3 (2014): 259–81, https://doi.org/10.1111/jopp.12019.
68. For a further discussion of this issue see Jamelle Bouie, "Talking White," *Slate*, October 1, 2014, https://slate.com/news-and-politics/2014/10/talking-white-black-peoples-disdain-for-proper-english-and-academic-achievement-is-a-myth.html.
69. Adger, *Language Unlimited*, p. 238; Jennifer Smith, "'You Ø Na Hear o' That Kind o' Things': Negative Do in Buckie Scots," *English World-Wide* 21, no. 2 (January 1, 2000): 231–59, https://doi.org/10.1075/eww.21.2.04smi.
70. Jennifer Jenkins, "Global Intelligibility and Local Diversity: Possibility or Poroolox," in *English in the World: Global Rules, Global Roles*, ed. Rani Rubdy and Mario Saraceni (Bloomsbury Publishing, 2006).
71. Gerrit B. Smith, "I Want to Speak Like a Native Speaker: The Case for Lowering the Plaintiff's Burden of Proof in Title VII Accent Discrimination Cases Note," *Ohio State Law Journal* 66, no. 1 (2005): 231–68.
72. Erich Hatala Matthes, "Cultural Appropriation and Oppression," *Philosophical Studies* 176 (2019): 1003–13.
73. C. Thi Nguyen and Matthew Strohl, "Cultural Appropriation and the Intimacy of Groups," *Philosophical Studies* 176, no. 4 (April 1, 2019): 981–1002, https://doi.org/10.1007/s11098-018-1223-3.
74. Richard A. Rogers, "From Cultural Exchange to Transculturation: A Review and Reconceptualization of Cultural Appropriation," *Communication Theory* 16, no. 4 (2006): 474–503.
75. Laura M. Ahearn, *Living Language: An Introduction to Linguistic Anthropology*, 3rd edition (Hoboken, NJ: Wiley-Blackwell, 2021), pp. 252–3.
76. C.A. Cutler, "Crossing over: White Youth, Hip-Hop and African American English," 2003, 1, p. 213.
77. Jeff Guo, "How Iggy Azalea Mastered Her 'Blaccent,'" *Washington Post*, November 25, 2021, www.washingtonpost.com/news/wonk/wp/2016/01/04/how-a-white-australian-rapper-mastered-her-blaccent/.
78. CNN Staff, "What a 'blaccent' Is, and Why It's Wrong," *CNN*, February 8, 2022, www.cnn.com/2022/02/08/entertainment/blaccent-explainer-cec/index.html.
79. Steffi Cao, "Awkwafina's Statement Finally Addressing Her 'Blaccent' Controversy Is Drawing More Backlash," *BuzzFeed News* (blog), February 6,

2022, www.buzzfeed.com/stefficao/awkwafina-blaccent-appropriation-backlash.

80. For a further argument about the complexities involving making claims of collective ownership over culture, see James O. Young, *Cultural Appropriation and the Arts*, 1st edition (Chichester: Wiley-Blackwell, 2010).

81. For a compelling counterpoint to this claim, see C. Thi Nguyen and Matthew Strohl, "Cultural Appropriation and the Intimacy of Groups," *Philosophical Studies* 176, no. 4 (April 1, 2019): 981–1002, https://doi.org/10.1007/s11098-018-1223-3.

82. Lisa Green and Thomas Roeper, "The Acquisition Path for Tense-Aspect: Remote Past and Habitual in Child African American English," *Language Acquisition* 14, no. 3 (2007): 269–313; Janice E. Jackson and Lisa Green, "Tense and Aspectual Be in Child African American English," *Perspectives on Aspect*, 2005, 233–50.

83. Adger, *Language Unlimited*, p. 246.

84. Adger, p. 246.

85. Montell, *Wordslut*, p. 85.

86. James O. Young, "Profound Offense and Cultural Appropriation," *The Journal of Aesthetics and Art Criticism* 63, no. 2 (2005): 135–46.

87. For an example of pronoun debates in another language (Swedish) see Nathalie Rothschild, "Sweden's New Gender-Neutral Pronoun: Hen," *Slate*, April 11, 2012, https://slate.com/human-interest/2012/04/hen-swedens-new-gender-neutral-pronoun-causes-controversy.html.

88. See, e.g., David McConnell who was initially fined for publicly misgendering someone in the UK before his sentence was overturned. "Leeds Preacher's Sentence for Trans Woman's Harassment Quashed," March 9, 2023, www.bbc.com/news/uk-england-leeds-64905216.

89. "Opinion | Gender-Neutral Pronouns: The Singular 'They' and Alternatives," *The New York Times*, October 9, 2021, sec. Opinion, www.nytimes.com/2021/10/09/opinion/letters/gender-neutral-pronouns.html.

90. Jessica A. Clarke, "They, Them, and Theirs," *Harvard Law Review* 132, no. 3 (2019 2018): 894–991.

91. For a further discussion of this aspect of the ethics of pronouns see Cameron Domenico Kirk-Giannini and Michael Glanzberg, "Pronouns and Gender," in *The Oxford Handbook of Applied Philosophy of Language*, ed. Luvell Anderson and Ernie LePore (Oxford University Press, n.d.).

92. Paul Sacca, "Matt Walsh Joins Gender Pronoun Debate on Dr Phil," *TheBlaze* (blog), January 20, 2022, www.theblaze.com/news/matt-walsh-dr-phil-gender-pronoun-debate.
93. Robin Dembroff and Daniel Wodak, "He/She/They/Ze," *Ergo: An Open Access Journal of Philosophy* 5 (2018), https://doi.org/10.3998/ergo.12405314.0005.014.
94. "Why I'm Done with 'Preferred Pronouns,'" *National Review* (blog), June 5, 2023, www.nationalreview.com/2023/06/why-im-done-with-preferred-pronouns/.
95. In this way, the argument against pronoun requirements is similar to the complicity-based arguments against using slurs that I discussed in the previous section on offense.
96. Jonathan Franklin, "A University Pays $400K to Professor Who Refused to Use a Student's Pronouns," NPR, April 20, 2022, sec. Education, www.npr.org/2022/04/20/1093601721/shawnee-state-university-lawsuit-pronouns.
97. "Why I Don't Have Pronouns In My Bio. | Practical Ethics," October 2, 2023, https://blog.practicalethics.ox.ac.uk/2023/10/why-i-dont-have-pronouns-in-my-bio/.
98. Colin Wright, "When Asked 'What Are Your Pronouns,' Don't Answer," *Reality's Last Stand* (blog), February 1, 2021, www.realityslaststand.com/p/when-asked-what-are-your-pronouns.
99. Wright.
100. Jason McBride, "A Professor's Refusal to Use Gender-Neutral Pronouns, and the Vicious Campus War That Followed," *Toronto Life* (blog), January 25, 2017, https://torontolife.com/city/u-t-professor-sparked-vicious-battle-gender-neutral-pronouns/.
101. Dembroff and Wodak, "He/She/They/Ze."
102. Nina Dragicevic, "Canada's Gender Identity Rights Bill C-16 Explained," CBC, 2018, www.cbc.ca/cbcdocspov/features/canadas-gender-identity-rights-bill-c-16-explained; Matt Gonzales, "LGBTQ Inclusion: Using Pronouns at Work," *Society for Human Resource Management* (blog), September 9, 2022, www.shrm.org/resourcesandtools/hr-topics/behavioral-competencies/global-and-cultural-effectiveness/pages/lgbtq-inclusion-using-pronouns-at-work.aspx.
103. McBride, "A Professor's Refusal to Use Gender-Neutral Pronouns, and the Vicious Campus War That Followed."

104. "How Gender Stereotypes Are Built into Mandarin," *The Economist*, accessed May 2, 2023, www.economist.com/the-economist-explains/2018/09/06/how-gender-stereotypes-are-built-into-mandarin.
105. Ives Goddard, "Grammatical Gender in Algonquian," *Algonquian Papers-Archive* 33 (2002).
106. Francesca Di Garbo and Yvonne Agbetsoamedo, "Non-Canonical Gender in African Languages: A Typological Survey of Interactions between Gender and Number, and between Gender and Evaluative Morphology," in *Non-Canonical Gender Systems*, ed. Sebastian Fedden, Jenny Audring, and Greville G. Corbett (Oxford University Press, 2018), 0, https://doi.org/10.1093/oso/9780198795438.003.0008.
107. P. J.L. Frankl, "The Indifference to Gender in Swahili and Other Bantu Languages: Part 2 in Consultation with Yahya Ali Omar," *South African Journal of African Languages* 13, no. 3 (January 1993): 85–9, https://doi.org/10.1080/02572117.1993.10586970.
108. Victor Mair, "Misogyny as Reflected in Chinese Characters," *Language Log* (blog), December 25, 2015, https://languagelog.ldc.upenn.edu/nll/?p=23043.
109. Montel, *Wordslut*, p. 145.
110. Webb Phillips, "Can Quirks of Grammar Affect the Way You Think? Grammatical Gender and Object Concepts," January 1, 2003.
111. Lera Boroditsky, Lauren Schmidt, and Phillips Webb, "Sex, Syntax, and Semantics," in *Language in Mind: Advances in the Study of Language and Thought*, ed. Dedre Gentner and Susan Goldin-Meadow, vol. 22 (MIT Press, 2003), pp. 61–79.
112. Grigorios Petsos, "(Gender) Stars in Their Eyes," kontextor, August 31, 2021, www.kontextor.org/en/blog/gender-stars/.
113. Christopher F. Schuetze, "'Gender Star' Stirs Linguistic Conservatives to Battle in Germany," *The New York Times*, March 7, 2019, sec. World, www.nytimes.com/2019/03/07/world/europe/germany-language-gender.html.
114. Marc Caputo and Sabrina Rodriguez, "Democrats Fall Flat with 'Latinx' Language," *Politico*, December 6, 2021, www.politico.com/news/2021/12/06/hispanic-voters-latinx-term-523776.
115. Montell, *Wordslut*. 17
116. Brian D. Earp, "The Extinction of Masculine Generics," *Journal for Communication and Culture* 2, no. 1 (2012): 4–19.

117. Blocked and Reported, "Episode 136: How The Left Can Fight Cancel Culture (With Clementine Morrigan)," October 22, 2022, www.blockedandreported.org/p/episode-136-how-the-left-can-fight.
118. Joe Pinsker, "The Problem With 'Hey Guys,'" The Atlantic, August 23, 2018, www.theatlantic.com/family/archive/2018/08/guys-gender-neutral/568231/.
119. Steven Pinker, "Opinion | The Game of the Name," The New York Times, April 5, 1994, sec. Opinion, www.nytimes.com/1994/04/05/opinion/the-game-of-the-name.html.
120. Pinker.
121. Elizabeth Anderson, "The Problem of Equality from a Political Economy Perspective: The Long View of History," in Oxford Studies in Political Philosophy, Volume 3, ed. David Sobel, Peter Vallentyne, and Steven Wall (Oxford University Press, 2017), 0, https://doi.org/10.1093/oso/9780198801221.003.0003.
122. R. I. M. Dunbar, "Structure and Function in Human and Primate Social Networks: Implications for Diffusion, Network Stability and Health," Proceedings of the Royal Society A: Mathematical, Physical and Engineering Sciences 476, no. 2240 (August 26, 2020): 20200446, https://doi.org/10.1098/rspa.2020.0446.
123. Katherine D. Kinzler and Jocelyn B. Dautel, "Children's Essentialist Reasoning about Language and Race," Developmental Science 15, no. 1 (2012): 131–38, https://doi.org/10.1111/j.1467-7687.2011.01101.x.
124. Daniel L. Everett, How Language Began: The Story of Humanity's Greatest Invention (Liveright Publishing, 2017), p. 102–3.

Pedants and Progress

4

Though I've mostly focused on examples of grammarianism in the English-speaking world, the problem is universal. In most non-English speaking linguistic communities, people with the impulse to police people's grammar can appeal to the actual grammar police. The French language, for example, is governed by the Académie Française, a 389-year-old council, consisting of 40 linguistic authorities who publish official advisory rules for French usage and (no joke) call themselves 'the immortals.'

In contrast to French and many other languages, the English language is open source, disordered, and democratic. Maybe too democratic, the grammarians would allege. After all, someone needs to keep the semicolons sorted from the em-dashes. Someone needs to keep track of all the their, they're, and there's out … there. Someone needs to switch the misplaced 'ei's with 'ie's. Right?!?

The thing is—that's not true. Language has evolved and functioned for millennia without the immortals. Languages can continue to function and evolve without a cadre of self-appointed guardians of the grammar galaxy dragging everyone down. Nowadayz, when people see or hear linguistic errrors or anomalies, they are very capable of interpreting a text or utterance by uzing context clues to discern the meaning of a seemingly misspeled or ungrammarrly linguistic construction.[1] See what I did there?

DOI: 10.4324/9780429319198-5

In this chapter, I'll make the case that anti-grammarianism isn't *just* a more humane, compassionate, and egalitarian way to approach language. Anti-grammarianism is just flat-out better as a way of communicating. A more anarchic, less prescriptive approach to language allows for more flexibility, diversity, interest, innovation, and efficiency. It's more fun! It's exciting to see where language will take us next. And when speakers and writers throw out the rule books and style guides, their languages function better *as languages* because they enable people to communicate more effectively and precisely.

There are many reasons to doubt the necessity of linguistic prescriptivism. People's use of a language today very often departs substantially from the norms of proper usage, but still functions. In some cases, we do struggle to understand each other, but grammarianism doesn't really help matters in these cases. There was once much more variation in the English language. The chaotic history of English serves as a proof of the conceptual point that fixed linguistic rules are not required for a language to function, persist, and evolve. I argue, then, that language police are not only unnecessary for a language to function, they are counterproductive if the main purpose of a language is effective communication. Linguistic innovation happens when people break the rules of language in ways that make it more efficient, beautiful, interesting, or accurate. Examples of these kinds of innovations include the recent use of emojis, jargon, non-standard trade names and internet slang. To these arguments, grammarians may reply that the anarchic approach to language I'm defending is unsustainable as communication becomes ever-more globalized and universal. In lower-context environments, they argue, standardization is even more valuable than it has been as language developed to date. In the fourth section, I address this concern. There, I argue that people should prefer technological solutions to communicative divides over snoots' and sticklers' social sanctions. Not only can these solutions avoid the moral problems with language policing, assistive technology is also more accurate and effective.

4.1 THE ANARCHIC ORIGINS OF LANGUAGE

Grammarian rule followers might grant the moral arguments against excessive peevishness but worry about letting go of all standards. After all, language *just is* a system of social rules. Without a few pedantic police keeping everyone in line, wouldn't society just descend into disorder and madness. Might all communication break down? Families split apart? Left could mean right. Right could mean wrong. Lawless language would lead to lawless society. Maybe this is an exaggeration, but I imagine grammandos do think that they are providing a public good of some sort—holding the line against orthographic anarchy.

But orthographic anarchy would be ok! People don't need to uphold prescriptive linguistic rules for the sake of preserving the communicative benefits of their language. When a person says, "I seen you there" rather than "I saw you there" or "I have seen you there," even snoots know what he means. They just nevertheless find this construction so grating that they feel the need to correct people who say it.[2]

To further illustrate this point, let's consider a seemingly basic rule for English, which is that every sentence should have a verb. It seems like a good idea, right? But now imagine that your toddler points to her doll and says, "Her sick." Or imagine someone in the break room complaining, "Candy there no more." These sentences are perfectly intelligible, even though they don't include a verb. Sticklers don't hear people say, "Game Over!" and wonder what's being implied by that locution. Arabic language speakers use this convention for present-tense sentences all the time. In Arabic, the verb 'is' is implied in the same way that the verb is implied in an English sentence like "Sarah helpful." Verbless sentences are common in other languages too, and people still manage to understand each other.³

Sticklers act like it's a tough job informing the checkout clerk that the sign should say "Ten items or fewer" (rather than 'or less') but someone's gotta do it. No one's gotta do it though. We don't need any self-appointed immortals to understand how many items we can purchase at the express check out. Social enforcement is not required for maintaining a language that enables people to communicate. The same goes for any other benefits associated with having a language. People need language to coordinate in large complex groups, but they don't need language cops for this. People write beautiful prose in order to express themselves, but they don't need spelling sanctions to make this happen. Language is what sets us apart from non-human animals, not our systems for mapping sentences. Maybe language is a precondition for all moral reasoning, but moralistic grammarians certainly are not.

If you were looking for proof that the English language (and any other language) can carry on just fine without widespread standardization and enforcement of spelling and grammar conventions, look no further than the history of language. The cognitive scientist Daniel Everett estimates that human language first developed about a million years ago among the *Homo erectus*, who are our evolutionary predecessors.⁴ These communities used a primitive language with features that every existing human language now shares—nouns, some kind of grammar. Human language is not instinctive or innate. People invented language long ago and they've passed this technology on for tens of thousands of generations, along with knowledge about how to use tools, social norms, and the rest of their culture. They used language, like other cultural conventions, to track people's status, transactions, relationships, and feelings, just as we do today.

Human language evolved as humans evolved. Though all humans may have once spoken a single language, as soon as people started migrating across the world and developing their own cultures, they developed their own languages as well.[5] The linguistic distance between languages typically mirrors the cultural and geographic distance between the groups that speak them. Like cultural practices, languages sometimes split apart alongside new political divides, and languages spread alongside patterns of political dominance and colonization.[6] Or, languages can fade away as groups become more culturally similar and people become more mobile. Language is always in flux because culture is always in flux.

This is why the history of English is a hodgepodge mess of borrowing and innovating, and why the language continues to change over time. For most of the history of the English language, spelling was not standardized, to the extent that people would spell their own names differently from one week to the next. Few people were literate, and those who could read and write weren't too fussy about the form as long as it served its functional purpose.

If we travel back to the earliest forms of English, we find examples of how English spelling could function without the rulebound sticklerism we see today. When the Germanic tribes of the Saxons, Angles, and Jutes moved to what is now Britain in the fifth century a new language developed (named after the Angles' tribe). So began the spoken English language, which like other languages, was not centrally planned but which emerged spontaneously from a mix of different cultures and dialects. Written English did develop with a bit more authoritarian intervention. When the Anglo-Saxons in Britain converted to Christianity at the end of the sixth century, they adopted the Roman alphabet and discarded the pagan Runic writing system that was used to that point.[7] Likely, the adoption of this alphabet was due to religious and political leadership, but also due to considerations of efficiency, given the widespread use of the Roman alphabet in the rest of Europe.

From there, the first written English documents were mostly legal codes. People who wrote things down were just trying to make themselves understood in a way that couldn't be misremembered or misconstrued. If someone wrote something down, he could later appeal to the written document to press a claim about property or criminality. Maybe it's no surprise then that people still love harping on about the rules of written English, since the written language got its start as a tool of enforcement.

Substantial linguistic variation persisted between regions until the tenth century when England became fairly united under the West Saxon royal house, King Alfred the Great. Alfred and his scribes established a unified set of Anglo-Saxon spelling and usage conventions, which is sometimes called Old English. As James Essinger writes, "such a convention had never existed before, and there must have been many people who found that during their lives they were spelling English one way at the age of twenty and spelling it another way twenty or thirty years later."[8] These scribes were the first English sticklers. Today's professional copyeditors and grammar schoolteachers can only dream of reaching this boss level of pedantic power. The rest of us English speakers and writers still haven't recovered from the scribes' pernicious influence.

Though the Anglo-Saxon language was more unified than the linguistic tapestry that preceded it, Old English was still largely phonetic and remarkably inconsistent compared to today's English. David Wolman observes that, "Back then, most spellings represented—not perfectly, but closely—the way a word sounded when read aloud."[9] Can you imagine!? Literally it sounds wonderful. There is no evidence that most Old English speakers and writers had a consistent concept of incorrect spelling, and at the time, as "a notion of more formal Standard English was still centuries away."[10]

Two things happened in the centuries that followed that set the stage for spelling standardization. First, in the eleventh century William the Conqueror invaded England and established French as the language of the government. The introduction of French brought about greater variation in the spelling of English words as the two languages mixed. Even back in the day, the French also had a particular penchant for linguistic standardization. Since English people still didn't care that much about spelling, the French had an especially strong influence on the spelling of English words.

Around this time, the first English spelling reformer entered the scene. In the twelfth century, a monk named Orrm got real fired up when he heard people mispronounce words. His friend Walter, who was also a monk, agreed with Orrm's complaint, and asked Orrm to develop a novel phonetic spelling system for religious texts. Orrm's goal was seemingly to write homilies that were accessible to less educated clergy, in a way that made it super-clear to them how everything should be pronounced.[11] Ironically, Orrm spells his own name in two different ways on the manuscript (Orrm and Orrmin), so who knows how his name was pronounced at the time! But for other words, Orrm's manuscript, the Ormulum, has been enormously useful to linguists, who have used it to reconstruct Middle English pronunciation. Unfortunately for Orrm, his sticklerly system didn't stick. Only a portion of Orrm's original manuscript remains and there is no evidence that it was copied for widespread consumption after Orrm's death. Maybe Orrm's failure is due to the fact that the English language was changing very quickly at this time, which marks the transition period between Old and Middle English. Alternatively, it might also have something to do with the fact that even the contemporary scholars who choose to study and write about the Ormulum describe the text as "infinite tedium," which is a great name for a band, but a terrible blurb for a manuscript.[12]

Sticklerism really came into fashion in the fifteenth century when Johannes Guttenberg invented the printing press. Before the printing press, monks and scribes like Orrm aimed to write in ways that a particular client or audience would understand. This is why written language was largely phonetic, even to the point of spelling in accordance with regional dialects instead of settling on a single standard spelling for each word. Alas, as one scholar write, the mass production of texts "marked the beginning of the end for unbridled English orthographym"[13] (until now?!). As calls for standardization grew louder after the introduction of the printing press, so did resistance to standardization and calls for simplification. In the sixteenth century, Sir Thomas Smith published his reflections on English spelling, which proposed various spelling systems and at least 34 potential letters.[14] In the following centuries, spelling reformers continued to publish new proposals for standardization, often advocating for a phonetic system of spelling.[15]

By the eighteenth century, the printing press enabled spelling reformers like Noah Webster to distribute their spelling books en masse, successfully entrenching new orthographic standards in the emerging American primary education system. These standardized spellings were met with backlash in the nineteenth century, however, as reformers such as William James and Samuel Clemens advocated for simpler spelling systems. Brigham Young and the entire Mormon Church even got in on the game and proposed a new alphabet (the Deseret Alphabet) that purported to overcome the inconsistencies and limitations of the English alphabet.[16] Young's proposal didn't catch on, nor did other spelling reform proposals. By the early twentieth century, backed by Andrew Carnegie's philanthropic support, the simplified spelling movement scored a major victory when then President Theodore Roosevelt ordered the U.S. Government Printing Office to adopt simplified spelling rules in 1906.[17] Yet even the President's proposed reforms were met with swift backlash from Congress and members of the media, and he almost immediately rescinded his support for simplified spelling. Even the power of the purse couldn't overcome the power of pedants.

Even today, there are still simplified spelling reformers around who advocate for a simpler, more phonetic system. Some of these reformers advocate for spelling standardization, but they prefer a more phonetic approach to today's dominant system of spelling.[18] Others, like the English Language scholar Simon Horobin, argue that people should be more accepting of various ways of spelling words, insofar as readers are still capable of discerning the meaning of the words.[19] Horobin argues in favor of greater toleration for "personalized orthography" for proper nouns and a more relaxed attitude toward spelling and grammar in online communication.[20] On his view, language is always changing and the English language is flexible enough to accommodate multiple spellings (as it did during the Middle and Early Modern periods of English language development) as reformers and conservatives negotiate and advocate for their preferred orthographies.

4.2 FLEXIBLE LANGUAGE TODAY

In this section, I argue that linguistic prescriptivists should instead embrace a more FlExibLe approach to language because English speakers can get along: :just fine:: without all the fussy rules that the ☹ grammalitia ☹ enforce. English spelling has not always been bound by rules the way it is today, so we can imagine that English and other languages could become less spellbound going forward. The history of linguistic evolution reveals that languages can develop and function with only a minimal level of structure and consistency. Speakers can't throw out *all* rules, but they can throw out most of them. And in light of the harmful effects of language policing, there are moral reasons to trash the dictionaries in favor of a less structured, more flexible approach to communication.

Languages vary in the degree of flexibility they allow, but all languages have some very high-level conventions, which are very difficult to change, and which are probably necessary for any human language to function as a way of communicating. These cross-linguistic universal rules are wayyyy more abstract and basic than any of the rules peevish pedants favor though. They aren't even the kinds of conventions most people would notice. For example, all languages have certain structural features in common, such as a construction called 'dependency length minimization' (DLM). This means that all languages include grammatical rules that minimize the distance in a sentence between dependent words to a greater degree than random sentence constructions would.[21] For example, grammatical sentences group dependent terms together in orders like "John threw out the old trash sitting in the kitchen" rather than "John threw the old trash sitting in the kitchen out."[22] The second sentence requires more working memory to process, which explains why norms of speech and writing developed over time to favor the first construction. At the same time, some languages allow more space between dependent words than others.

If there are any good conventions about how to construct sentences, they are conventions like DLM, which account for speakers' and listeners' cognitive limitations. But even these kinds of high-level conventions vary between languages. Japanese and Turkish languages show much less minimization than Italian or Indonesian, for example. This doesn't make Turkish a less effective language than Italian though. DLM has advantages, but if a person said "John threw the old trash sitting in the kitchen out" a typical listener would know what this meant. Conventions like DLM arise due to the limits of humans' ability to infer context, attention, and working memory. Imagine a language with grammatical conventions that placed words in order of noun/verb/adjective would require a lot more memory and contextual knowledge for listeners to understand what a speaker was saying. Consider how a sentence like "John the trash the kitchen out threw sitting old" would require listeners to first remember all the nouns involved, then to assign the various verbs and nouns in order, and then guess which adjectives and verbs went with which nouns. The universal conventions that govern all languages have authority because these conventions make languages intelligible to listeners. And even for these conventions, there's still not a single 'right answer' to how people should construct sentences.

Languages also have auxiliary rules, which people uphold for the sake of consistency or as a matter of style. These are the rules that sticklers stick to. Most linguistic conventions are auxiliary—they are conventions that native speakers and listeners collectively uphold but they aren't strictly necessary for the language to function. Linguists use the term 'acceptability' to refer to whether a string of words is immediately comprehensible to a native speaker. They use the term 'grammaticality' to refer to the degree that someone's speech conforms to the norms of its use, as judged by a native speaker.[23] Core rules are important for acceptability. Auxiliary rules are important for grammaticality. My claim is that people should only value grammaticality for the sake of acceptability. As long as a person's speech or writing is acceptable, meaning that a native speaker can understand what they are saying, their use of the language functions as a tool for communication, which is the main thing that people should care about when it comes to linguistic conventions. In contrast, grammaticality often is not important for effective communication. When grammaticality is not needed for acceptability, people shouldn't care about it because people's intuitive judgments of grammaticality give undue weight to some native speakers' fussy preferences for their contingent and arbitrary auxiliary conventions.

Another reason to discount the importance of auxiliary language rules is that changes to speech that would strike a native speaker as ungrammatical could nevertheless be an improvement on the language. In the first chapter I mentioned the Golden Age phenomenon, wherein each generation upholds whatever normative standards for language that they happened to learn as children. There, I argued grammarians actually have good reasons to doubt that their linguistic standards are the best ones, in contrast to the rules that previous and future generations adopt. Adding to this argument against middle age grammarianism, I also argued in the previous chapter that some seemingly ungrammatical constructions, like the habitual be, can make language more precise as a communicative tool. Often, languages become more efficient as they evolve. For example, as languages evolve, pronunciations for words erode, meaning that people increasingly drop sounds from words. As John McWhorter writes,

> In real time, we process this kind of erosion as sloppy: to us, *Jeet yet?* is a barefoot version of *Did you eat yet?* as inevitable but formally unsavory as an unmade bed. But this very process was part of what turned Latin into French, and not 'sloppy' French but the toniest *formal* French.[24]

Over time, languages also evolve to become more uniform with fewer exceptions to rules.[25] Though these linguistic changes strike people as counter-normative at the time, they result in a language that is easier to say and easier to understand and predict.

Sticklers' excessive commitment to historically contingent and arbitrary linguistic conventions also prevents them from appreciating innovations from other languages and cultures. For example, English currently only has one spelling system. But English speakers can imagine borrowing an innovation in the Hebrew language which has two systems of spelling. One system, Niqqud, is used for children's stories, textbooks religious texts, and for non-native writers who are learning the language. This system includes dots to indicate vowel sounds.[26]

Another system, Ktiv Male, is more widely used. Ktiv Male is simpler, but it requires more context for readers to understand the text. Thinking back to Chapter 1's discussion of phonics education and schooling, an innovation like this might be helpful to English speakers and learners who would benefit from an alternative, phonetic approach to spelling.

To this, an orthographic authoritarian might reply that their sticklerism is itself a form of linguistic innovation that makes a language more functional because it's actually better to have only one system of spelling, just like it's better for a language to have some degree of DLM. Here I imagine a spelling stan saying that it would be too inefficient to have multiple spellings nowadays, even if orthographic anarchy was the norm hundreds of years ago, because people now communicate with a much wider audience where readers may lack the necessary context to decipher unorthodox orthographies. I imagine that someone making this argument is the type who is frustrated by the fact that Americans spell things differently than British writers too; orthographic authoritarians long for a spelling strongman to sort English writing out once and for all.

What orthographic authoritarians miss is that there have been spelling strongmen who attempted to standardize languages across cultural contexts, but they have not delivered on their promises of greater efficiency or clarity. For example, back in 1990, officials' representatives for all Portuguese-speaking countries adopted the Portuguese Language Orthographic Agreement, which created a unified orthography the language. Despite this agreement though, Portuguese spelling reform didn't stick.[27] Not all countries that initially adopted the agreement ratified it in their own countries, and to this very day Portuguese writers still don't use a global orthographic standard.

If anything, English speakers could benefit from even more linguistic openness and variation. An anarchic orthographic approach would enable English speakers to adopt helpful or interesting variations from any language that had something new to offer. For example, the Amazonian language Tuyuca has a convention of evidential marking on verbs, which denotes whether the speaker learned something second-hand or through their own experience.[28] Think how helpful linguistic innovation would be in all areas of communication, but especially in legal contexts and in academic writing. Evidential marking in English would enable writers to add helpful epistemic content to their sentences without cluttering up the page with qualifying statements and footnotes. Or consider the way that Korean and Japanese speakers can denote several varying layers of politeness through their verb conjugations.[29] If English speakers adopted this linguistic innovation, it could potentially make the language more expressive and exciting. The downside of this innovation is that it could also make speaker's verb choices more socially fraught. The best way to know if these would be useful innovations would be for some communicative entrepreneurs to try it out and see what sticks!

4.3 LINGUISTIC SOLIDARITY

Maybe some of the people who cling to existing linguistic conventions are worried that without a few grammarians keeping everyone in line, the deregulation of language would make it more difficult for people to understand each other across cultural divides. The Book of Genesis describes a time when all people spoke a single language. The vibes in this monolinguistic society were so good that they were all able to coordinate by building a city and a cool tower that touched heaven. God saw what they were up to and said, "Behold, the people is one, and they have all one language; and this they begin to do: and now nothing will be restrained from them, which they have imagined to do."[30] God then decided to put a stop to human's tower-building project by confusing everyone's languages and scattering people all over the earth. Other cultures have similar myths.[31] People have long acknowledged that linguistic variation divides people in ways that stifle peace and communication.

Philosophers take different lessons from the story. Michael Oakshot thinks the myth serves as a warning against the excessive pursuit of a single moral ideal.[32] If this is the lesson of the myth, then it serves as a warning against linguistic prescriptivism, like all other moralistic doctrines that demand universal conformity. Jacques Derrida reads the myth as a demonstration of the fact that words can never perfectly convey the true nature of whatever they signify, and in part for this reason, perfect translation between languages is impossible.[33] If this is the lesson of the myth, then it's also a case for anti-grammarianism, since every variation in vocabulary captures something true about the world that other languages miss.

But maybe the lesson of the myth is more pedestrian and pedantic. Maybe the myth just shows that linguistic variation divides us. And the more linguistic variation there is within a language, the more likely it is that new and different languages could branch off, further dividing people. Since linguistic disputes so often cause and exacerbate conflicts, grammarians may take this as a reason to try to maintain a unified approach to language as a way of keeping the peace, rebuilding the ruins of Babel. Might some pedants think that they're promoting intercultural solidarity and, dare I say, world peace through their rigid enforcement of the linguistic conventions that they learned in elementary school. Probably not, but the pervasiveness of the myth of Babel does indicate that people have long associated linguistic conformity with peace and prosperity, so maybe there's something to this view. Tbh idk what motivates sticklers, and this argument is as good as any other so let's consider it.

In part, I'm sympathetic to solidaristic arguments for sticklerism in that I agree languages function well to the extent that they enable effective communication. I just don't think that pedantic language policing is the way to achieve this goal. Linguistic similarity is necessary for communication, but linguistic diversity can make communication more precise, clearer, and more efficient.

Reflecting on the Babel myth, a solidaristic stickler might propose that people not only try to promote common linguistic standards, but also that people learn a single common language.[34] In a way, this is happening already. The tower of Babel is being rebuilt, due to the rise of English as an international lingua franca in business and in online spaces. As Gaston Dorren writes,

> Chinese schoolchildren begin to learn English before they have even mastered the art of writing in Mandarin. One in five books published worldwide is in English. Over 80 per cent of scholarly articles are written in English. Nearly all international blockbuster films and hit songs are in English. And about half the homepages of the most visited sites on the Internet are in English. The official language of non-military aviation is English. The lingua franca of Antarctica is English, and the only language ever spoken on the moon is English.... Linguistic diversity is still high ... but it's no longer an impregnable wall to communication with strangers. English is the gateway.[35]

This trend undercuts worries about lax linguistic standards causing cultural divides. Even if it's true that linguistic diversity divides people, the widespread adoption of English is likely to counteract whatever cultural divisions arise from a diversity of dialects and grammatical conventions. The recent development of universal translation technology provides people with another way to foster linguistic solidarity alongside linguistic diversity.[36] This kind of technology makes solidaristic sticklerism unnecessary, even if they have a point, because it would enable people to communicate across linguistic divides without changing their native modes of communication.

4.4 LINGUISTIC INNOVATION ¯_(ツ)_/¯

Grammarians generally lament deviant linguistic conventions, but in this section I argue that linguistic deviance is often a public service, even for grammarians. Emerging linguistic conventions make language more functional and precise. Pedants are prone to say that they *love* learning about languages, that they're 'word nerds' and that their snootiness is both an aesthetic commitment and a hobby. If they love language so much, though, they should take more delight in all the cool new conventions anti-grammarian innovators have created just in our lifetime.

As languages evolve, new generations of speakers and writers introduce innovative conventions that may strike old-school grammarians as wrongheaded, ugly, transgressive or unprofessional. Creative writers throughout history have enriched their languages by violating linguistic rules and spelling conventions. These violations enhanced their ability to communicate, rather than undermining it. For example, William Shakespeare invented hundreds of words, including 'sanctimonious,' 'critic,' and 'pious'—a few words that spelling sticklers might relate to! Luckily for English speakers everywhere, the earliest dictionaries were written during Shakespeare's lifetime and so they were not in wide circulation when Shakespeare wrote, so his work was spared the red-ink treatment of a sixteenth-century snoot.

As H.G. Wells once argued, the "tyranny of orthography" stands in in the way of self-expression and nuance. Wells writes,

> Let the reader take a pen in hand and sit down and write, 'My very dear wife.' Clean, cold, and correct this is, speaking of orderly affection, settled and stereotyped long ago. In such letters is butcher's meat also 'very dear.' Try now, 'Migh verrie deare Wyfe.' Is it not immediately infinitely more soft and tender? Is there not something exquisitely pleasant in lingering over those redundant letters, leaving each word, as it were, with a reluctant caress? Such spelling is a soft, domestic, lovingly wasteful use of material.[37]

Wells then wrote that he liked to add extra "tailey, twirley, loopey things" in his own romantic spelling and that men who refused to violate the rules of spelling for these expressive purposes was "neither more nor less than a prig." Other writers express similar sentiments. Mark Twain writes:

> Before the spelling-book came with its arbitrary forms, men unconsciously revealed shades of their characters and also added enlightening shades of expression to what they wrote by their spelling.[38]

Spelling standardization and grammar rules the enemies of self-expression. Charles Dickens and James Joyce wrote extraordinary run-on sentences. e.e. cummings shunned capital letters and invented new spellings for words. Emily Dickinson peppered her work with extraneous capitalizations, dashes, and exclamation marks. And William Faulkner barely punctuated his prose at all.

And so too, today, grammatical missteps and misspellings can also convey messages where the standard spelling, punctuation, or grammar falls short. In the last few decades, the rise of the internet and word processing has accelerated the pace of linguistic innovation, giving conservative language cops even more to complain about. For example, people have started using more cool fontz, non-standard spellings, Emoji ☺, internet slang, artistic innovations in writing, innovations in branding and marketing that make it easier for consumers to find and differentiate between products, and new technical jargon.

Consider, for example, the Irish writer Sally Rooney's naturalistic style of writing characters' dialogue, text messages, and emails, to reflect how the characters would actually communicate rather than adhering strictly to conventions for written grammar. Or Karl Ove Knausgaard's writing, which is somehow both fragmented and rambling—a chaotic prose style that effectively conveys the texture of the narrator's interior life. But with all due respect to these aforementioned luminaries, the author who has mastered intentional linguistic transgression is Dav Pilkey, the dyslexic author of DogMan and Captain Underpants.[39] Pilkey's prose is peppered with many intentional spellings to mirror the silliness and absurdity of his plots. It's clearly a deliberate stylistic choice, but to read parents' reviews of Pilkey's work you'd think his books included instructions for making meth, not speech bubbles where a character says 'laff' instead of 'laugh' or 'skool' instead of 'school.' Pilkey even spells his own first name, pronounced 'Dave' without the extraneous 'e' at the end. Pilkey's proof that not all heroes wear capes (though Captain Underpants definitely does).

Some readers might find these authors' stylistic choices gimmicky, tedious, or difficult to follow. About Pilkey, one parent writes, "This is a book written for kids, I don't want my kid reading books with so many spelling errors when they are at such an impressionable age."[40] But these authors' stylistic choices have also resonated with readers. Each have written bestselling novels that resonated with readers in part due to their innovative style.

Languages change, grow, adapt, and improve because people are willing to break the rules of language over the persistent objections of snoots and sticklers. As a general matter, systems of norms that can evolve organically without hierarchical rules are more likely to develop conventions and neologisms that are more informative or efficient. Consider the linguistic evolution of different ways of saying 'yes.' As Megan Garber writes,

> "Yes" is becoming outmoded in a world where out-of-context formality can be read as a sign of frustration or all-out hostility. Which is not, of course, an entirely new thing. We've long sought and found alternative ways—gentler ways, more nuanced ways—of offering affirmation to each other. "OK" and its cousin "okay," rumored to be an appropriation of a typo, have been in use since the mid-1800s as a means of giving casual consent. "Sure," an abbreviation of "sure thing," also came into use in the U.S. in the 1800s, and has remained part of our vernacular ever since. The 1980s saw the rise of "yeah"—a re-embrace of the centuries-old "yea"—with the term enjoying a steady upward trajectory since then. "Yep" has taken a similar path. So has "yup."[41]

Garber goes on to describe the explosion of yaaaaaas, yasssss, YAAASSSSS, and yiiisss in online spaces, along with mhmmmm and all manner of other alternative affirmatives to the standard old 'yes.'

More generally, the new grammar of the internet includes a range of innovations that make language more evocative and precise. The increased prevalence of Emoji has been one of the most noticeable linguistic innovations of this century. For the past decade or so, the Oxford Dictionary Online (ODO), which is has published a word of the year.[42] The authors of this dictionary intend for it to serve as a catalogue of English and uses including words like 'selfie' and 'vape.' In 2015, the word of the year was 😂, which can be written as "face with tears of joy emoji."[43] ODO chose the emoji on the grounds that it was the most used emoji in the world. At the time, Casper Grathwohl, the president of dictionaries at Oxford University Press, argued that emojis were emerging as a supplement to text-based communication. Text alone, Grathwohl argued, was unable to adequately accommodate cultural changes that demanded visual engagement, emotional expression, and immediate engagement.

Emoji makes online communication more accurate in several ways. First, emojis can provide conceptual content, such as cues about the emotional valance of a sentence, that text alone is unable to provide.[44] Additionally, emojis can in some cases function as a near-universal form of communication, transcending linguistic divides. Body language is nearly universal in this way too, and some linguists now understand emoji as a textual analog to gesture.[45] At the same time, emojis can also take on specific cultural meanings—the standard set of emoji characters includes both characters that have nearly universal meaning 😊 as well as characters with more culturally specific meanings 🍙.[46]

Most emoji users primarily use the symbols to supplement written communication when the old tools are insufficiently precise. When the earliest writers adopted phonetic characters and abandoned pictographic means of communication, they gained the ability to convey concepts and ideas that could never be drawn. But some of the emotional valance of written communication was lost in this transition, just as mathematical representations would have been lost if transition to a phonetic alphabet had not preserved the use of numerical symbols as well. Emojis revive these advantages of a pictographic writing system.

Despite the substantial communicative advantages of emojis, people still view the use of emojis as overly casual and unprofessional. Though it is common for authors to include charts, graphs, and diagrams in professional and academic writing, few papers, books, or newspaper articles include emojis, even when it could make the writing clearer and more precise. Hopefully, this prejudice against emojis as a mode of written communication is due to stickler's conservativism and more forms of text-based communication will embrace the benefits of emojis going forward.

Just as emojis make communication more accurate, so too do other mildly transgressive conventions that have developed in online communities.[47] A narrow allegiance to spelling and grammar rules impedes the development of personalized orthographies, which people develop in online spaces. As the internet linguist Gretchen McCulloch writes,

> The internet didn't create informal writing, but it did make it more common, changing some of our previously spoken interactions into near-real-time text exchanges. At the same time, keyboards took away some of our previous repertoire for expressive writing, like multiple

underlines, colored ink, fancy borders, silly doodles, and even subtle changes in someone's handwriting that might allow you to infer their mood.[48]

McCulloch then argues that new forms of online communication enable people to capture the nuance of personalized communication that would otherwise be lost in a world of text. Each writer can use line breaks, capitalization, repeated letters, and hundreds of other quirks and tricks to develop a personalized typography that expresses their communicative style over a screen. For example, people online often use abbreviations to communicate complex emotional states (lolol,;) ftw, jk, <3). Or people write in ALL CAPS to communicate AS IF THEY ARE SHOUTING, but in writing.[49]

Other internet innovations include neologisms and phrases such as 'Doge' and 'I can has cheeseburger.' These constructions are intentionally misspelled or ungrammatical. Yet these grammatical transgressions contribute to the message that is being communicated rather than undermining it. They convey a sense of informality or irony where a more grammatical sentence cannot. Some internet conventions emerged from what were initially spelling mistakes, but now serve a similar function. Words like 'pwned' and 'l44t' developed meanings that are distinctive from the words that writers initially were trying to communicate.

The linguistic changes associated with online communication are both homogenizing and niche. On one hand, everyone writing online is participating in a single monoculture where people new converge around new conventions such as putting ellipses at the end of sentences to indicate a long verbal pause, or the widespread adoption of !!!s in professional communication. On the other hand, everyone writing online is creating a bespoke lexicon for their own weird little corners of the internet—a secret code that only their friends can understand.

Considering innovation for the sake of specialization, tech companies also break spelling rules when they name their companies existing words with non-standard spellings. Consider names like Tumblr, Flickr, Lyft, Grindr, Digg and Reddit.[50] Other brands use strategic misspellings too. Names like Dunkin Donuts and Krispy Kreme makes me wonder if there is something about doughnut companies that makes them especially prone to orthographic chaos. Though, if so, Dunkin may be a victim of its own success as English speakers are increasingly adopting their spelling for Donuts![51] Here again, one generation's linguistic transgressions become the next's standard spelling, often because it is simpler and more efficient.

In each of these misspelled branding cases, a company's decision to violate spelling conventions enables their branding team to communicate more effectively and precisely. Companies that are named with existing words are easier to remember and they benefit from the association with the word they are named after. At the same time, spelling the word in a non-standard way makes it easier for the company to take advantage of trademark and copyright protections and to secure all the necessary domain names. These deliberate misspellings also enable users to easily find the company online.

Brands can also use non-standard spelling in advertising in order to convey a mood. Consider the contrast between an advertisement for 'X-treme Rawks Cliiiiiimbing!' versus 'Extreme Rock Climbing.' The former, more playful spelling suggests that the rock-climbing gym caters more to children and teenagers. The later, standard spelling, conveys a sense of serious, suggesting that the gym caters more to dedicated athletes and high-level climbers.

People who adopt non-standard spellings for the names of their children enjoy similar benefits (and drawbacks) associated with misspelling.[52] On the one hand, their children will not share their names with dozens of James's, Mohammeds, and Aaravs. On the other hand, their children may be stigmatized or discriminated against to the extent that having a name that is not spelled in the standard way is socially coded as lower status than having a name with a standard spelling.

Other forms of linguistic creativity can also facilitate useful innovations that make languages more useful for those who use them. For example, groups often develop specialized languages, such as jargon, which is tailored for the linguistic needs of the group. To an outsider, jargon can sound ridiculous or unnecessary. Critics of jargon argue that it is exclusionary, or that it obscures more than it illuminates when compared to plain language, or that it just sounds cheesy. For example, Molly Young calls the new language of the professional class Garbage Language, and argues that phrases like "Let's circle back to this" and words such as 'complexify' and 'replatform' mask the triviality of many corporate tasks and impede communication in ways that make people feel excluded or dominated.[53]

But, as Young's examples show, the meaning of these phrases and words is relatively easy to learn. If anything, it's actually Young who is being critical and dismissive of a particular (easy target) linguistic subcommunity. Moreover, as Mark Morgioni argues in response to Young, corporate jargon persists because, for people within an organization, specialized words and phrases, shorthand, and acronyms are more efficient and clearer for the people who use them.[54] Consider for example the idea of 'looping someone in' on an email or text conversation, which is a way of expressing that someone is 'in the loop' when previously they were not. The idea of 'the loop' can be difficult to articulate. A loop needn't correspond to any formal group or official role, and the boundaries are defined by who is included in an ongoing conversation. The metaphor of the loop enables people to navigate a complex web of affiliated subgroups within a large organization.

Jargon can also be an effective tool for clarifying the conceptual terrain. In philosophy, there are many specialized terms like 'Qualia' and 'Conciliatiationism,' which stand in for ideas that would otherwise take whole paragraphs to express. Or jargon can be used to respect people's privacy or to preserve a sense of decorum. For example, on film sets, people use the term '10-1' on walkie talkies to denote that someone is using the bathroom, and the bathroom trailer is called the 'honey wagon.' As the example of the honey wagon illustrates, people can also use jargon to introduce humor or irony into their everyday working environment.

Whatever the drawbacks of jargon as an exclusionary language, these hazards are often outweighed by its capacity to efficiently communicate complex ideas and its capacity to promote solidarity and a sense of community within a group.

4.5 LINGUISTIC CONSERVATIVISM

Predictably, some celebrity curmudgeons are unhappy with the linguistic changes wrought by online culture. Specifically, a few literary writers recently argued that the changing landscape of language is moving in the wrong direction. Here I have in mind, above all others, Jonathan Franzen, who has the best claim to serve as the spiritual executor of David Foster Wallace's SNOOTy Defense of Standards. Franzen hates the modern way that people communicate.⁵⁵ He hates the internet for destroying "the quiet and permanence of the printed word." He hates Twitter for inciting "Jennifer-Weinerish self-promotion." He hates e-books for the fact that they can so easily be modified. (Which is ironic, in a way, since his publisher once had to recall thousands of copies of one of his books because they accidentally printed an earlier draft that contained hundreds of typographical errors.)

To his credit, Franzen is remarkably self-aware of his prickly pedantry. In discussing his general displeasure with how things are going, literature-wise, Franzen writes, "the next thing you know, you're translating *The Last Days of Mankind* as *The Last Days of Privileging the Things I Personally Find Beautiful*."⁵⁶ He then considers that maybe this disposition is justifiable though, if only as one man's attempt to make his mark on the world by trying to preserve the things he values for as long as he possibly can. Here Franzen's grammatical grumpiness might be viewed as an effort at cultural preservation (more on this in the next chapter). And to Franzen the stakes feel high. He writes,

> The experience of each succeeding generation is so different from that of the previous one that there will *always* be people to whom it seems that any connection of the key values of the past have been lost. As long as modernity lasts, *all* days will feel to someone like the last days of humanity.⁵⁷

And Franzen isn't alone in his literary curmudgeonliness. Zadie Smith also frets that Kids These Days are Doing it Wrong when it comes to language. Smith worries that the way that people talk on social media flattens the human experience and prompts people to communicate in a fake, self-promotional, and falsely friendly way. Smith writes,

> I've noticed—and been ashamed of noticing—that when a teenager is murdered, at least in Britain, her Facebook wall will often fill with messages that seem to not quite comprehend the gravity of what has occurred. You know the type of thing: Sorry babes! Missin' you!!! Hopin' u iz with the Angles. I remember the jokes we used to have LOL! PEACE XXXXX.[58]

Franzen's and Smith's linguistic traditionalism echo Foster-Wallace's case for linguistic standards, while adding the specter of civilizational collapse. This is not a coincidence, in my view. Aesthetic preferences for linguistic conservatism appeal to people's inherent fear of change, and civilizational collapse. Language change is an omnipresent reminder of aging and death.

Samuel Scheffler provides a philosophical justification for Franzen's, Smith's, and all the other traditionalists' conservative takes on language. Scheffler argues that traditions can be normative, in the sense that they can give us reasons for action, and they can help us decide how to act.[59] On this view, our reasons and values are informed by where we stand in space and time. As members of intergenerational communities, we participate in a project that is bigger than ourselves, and participation in this long-term project is a way of infusing our lives with meaning that will persist after our deaths.

If Scheffler is right about the normativity of tradition and the significance of future generations for the meaning of our lives today, it's unsurprising that esteemed writers like Franzen and Smith are freaking out about the rapid changes in English communication today. After all, they have dedicated their lives to the written word and their literary projects are likely meaningful in part because they imagine that people will appreciate and learn from their work after they are gone. That assurance of meaning is threatened by teens on Facebook whose communicative styles are so drastically different from Franzen's and Smith's literary mode that it seems unlikely that they would ever pick up a copy of *The Corrections* or *White Teeth*, let alone that their future children would cherish these works.

In this way, Franzen's and Smith's concerns relate to a longstanding argument in favor of linguistic conservatism. Namely, that members of a linguistic communicate need a common language that enables them to communicate across generational divides, even to communicate with generations that are long gone. Some frame this concern as a worry that old literature will become inaccessible to newer generations. Others frame it as a broader concern about the durability of culture and tradition in the face of linguistic change.

Yet even granting that traditions can be an important source of reasons and values and granting that participating in an intergenerational cultural project gives meaning to many people's lives, it doesn't follow that linguistic changes are a threat to the intergenerational transmission of literature or culture. Consider how the Catholic Church has managed to uphold fairly consistent traditions for centuries, across the world, while managing substantial diachronic and synchronic linguistic diversity the whole time. Or, we can look to the many translations of Beowulf, some of which are translations to new languages but some of which are intergenerational translations that update the story for a new context.

Nevertheless, when faced with a threat to one's identity, self-image, or source of meaning in life, people are very prone to respond moralistically.[60] And language change definitely does threaten some in these ways. On the other hand, if the culture were entirely traditionalist and stagnant then there would be no new room for artists and writers in the first place. It's easy for traditionalists to forget that they were once the threatening young upstarts driving cultural change against the old literary guard.

Linguistic conservativism and traditionalism can also be counterproductive to the traditionalists' aims, insofar as they are worried that subsequent generations will fail to appreciate the cultural products of the current day. After all, there's no easier way to turn people off from taking an interest in classic books, movies, or songs than to moralistically criticize them for not appreciating it enough. Perhaps, paradoxically, traditionalists' best hope for preserving the most valuable parts of their communicative culture may be to quiet down about the importance of tradition and preservation and to encourage people to engage with historical cultural products on their own terms.

4.6 CONCLUSION

Lightening up about language doesn't spell out the end of civilization. If anything, it's the language police who are holding us all back. Communication continues to evolve in ways that are exciting and innovative. The way we all talk is becoming richer and ever-more efficient as people blend languages and dialects and use new technology to add humor, irony, and more accurate emotional valance to their speech. And antigrammarians are at the forefront of these innovations.

Yet I imagine that some members of the old guard are still unconvinced about the virtues of violating the rules of spelling and grammar. I concede that, in some cases, people do need to speak and write in ways that comport with the dominant standards for communication, if not in order to be clear then at least as a way of avoiding accusations of carelessness. Even in these contexts though, the self-appointed sticklery is unnecessary. Terminological trailblazers and grammatical groundbreakers don't need amateur syntacticians following them around and monitoring their every word. Instead, the orthographically unorthodox among us can call upon AI robot assistants and professional copyeditors to do the job far more efficiently and kindly.

Robot snoots are widely available to anyone who wants to use them. Translation apps can bridge linguistic divides. Spellchecking technology can clean up written communication. There's even software that can edit people's prose for grammar and tone. These technologies use artificial intelligence to craft recommendations and translations that reflect the prevailing usage, and in this sense, they are more adaptable than dusty old-style guides and dictionaries. If the robots fail, or if people are worried that they might fail, writers can always hire trained human copyeditors to ensure that their prose is sufficiently in line with professional standards. Human copyeditors have the virtue of offering advice and guidance only to people who actually asked them for it. And copyeditors and AI communication tools help writers in a non-judgmental way. All of which is to say, it's time for the moralistic language police to give up the beat. They can take desk jobs as software developers or copyeditors if they love the laws of language so much, but they are a menace to society when they take their sticklerism to the streets.

NOTES

1. Laurel Brehm, Carrie N. Jackson, and Karen L. Miller, "Speaker-Specific Processing of Anomalous Utterances," *Quarterly Journal of Experimental Psychology* 72, no. 4 (April 1, 2019): 764–78, https://doi.org/10.1177/1747021818765547.

2. On this point, a grammando may reply that "I seen you there" actually is unclear because it could be interpreted as "saw" or "have seen" and those two interpretations have different meanings. Three replies. First, people can typically use context clues to figure out which meaning of "I seen" is implicit in the sentence and many grammatically correct sentences are sensitive to context for their correct interpretation as well. Second, the kind of person who would make such a finicky point when clearly they do in fact know what a person who says "I seen you there" meant is exactly the kind of person I'm talking about here. And third, if you are the kind of person who would think this and then look at a footnote to see if I address it, I'm afraid that you are so far gone down the path of pedantry that I'm not even sure that this book can help you.
3. Hungarian, Russian, Arabic, and Hebrew omit verbs from sentences in some contexts. This was also common in ancient languages like ancient Greek, Latin, and Old Persian, where verbs could be inferred from context even if they were not stated explicitly in a sentence.
4. Daniel Everett, *How Language Began: The Story of Humanity's Greatest Invention* (Profile Books, 2017), p. xv.
5. Guy Deutscher, *The Unfolding of Language: An Evolutionary Tour of Mankind's Greatest Invention* (Macmillan, 2005), p. 56–8.
6. Gaston Dorren, *Babel: Around the World in Twenty Languages* (Atlantic Monthly Press, 2018), p. 229.
7. James Essinger, *Spellbound: The Surprising Origins and Astonishing Secrets of English Spelling* (Delta, 2007), p. 170.
8. Essinger.
9. Wolman, *Righting the Mother Tongue*, p. 22.
10. Wolman, p. 22.
11. A. Joseph McMullen, "Forr Þeȝȝre Sawle Need: The Ormulum, Vernacular Theology and a Tradition of Translation in Early England," *English Studies* 95, no. 3 (April 3, 2014): 256–77, https://doi.org/10.1080/0013838X.2014.897074.
12. Christopher Cannon, "Spelling Practice: The Ormulum and the Word," *Forum for Modern Language Studies* XXXIII, no. 3 (July 1, 1997): 229–44, https://doi.org/10.1093/fmls/XXXIII.3.229.
13. Wolman, *Righting the Mother Tongue*, p. 41.
14. Richard L. Venezky, *The American Way of Spelling: The Structure and Origins of American English Orthography*, 1st edition (New York: The Guilford Press, 1999). p. 214

15. Venezky.
16. Wolman, *Righting the Mother Tongue*, p. 103.
17. Venezky, *The American Way of Spelling*, p. 223; Wolman, *Righting the Mother Tongue*, p. 113.
18. See, e.g., The English Spelling Society spellingsociety.org
19. Horobin, *Does Spelling Matter?*
20. Horobin, pp. 225–8.
21. Richard Futrell, Kyle Mahowald, and Edward Gibson, "Large-Scale Evidence of Dependency Length Minimization in 37 Languages," *Proceedings of the National Academy of Sciences* 112, no. 33 (August 18, 2015): 10336–41, https://doi.org/10.1073/pnas.1502134112.
22. Michael Balter, "All Languages Have Evolved to Have This in Common," August 3, 2015, www.science.org/content/article/all-languages-have-evolved-have-common.
23. Noam Chomsky, "Some Methodological Remarks on Generative Grammar," *Word* 17, no. 2 (January 1961): 219–39, https://doi.org/10.1080/00437956.1961.11659755; Jon Sprouse, "Acceptability Judgments and Grammaticality, Prospects and Challenges," in *Syntactic Structures after 60 Years: The Impact of the Chomskyan Revolution in Linguistics*, ed. Norbert Hornstein et al. (De Gruyter Mouton, 2018), 195–224, https://doi.org/10.1515/9781501506925-199.
24. John McWhorter, *The Power of Babel: A Natural History of Language*, softcover edition (New York: Harper Perennial, 2003), p. 18.
25. McWhorter, p. 22.
26. Morris Alper, "UNIKUD: Adding Vowels to Hebrew Text with Deep Learning," *Medium*, May 8, 2022, https://towardsdatascience.com/unikud-adding-vowels-to-hebrew-text-with-deep-learning-powered-by-dagshub-56d238e22d3f.
27. Adrienne R. Washington, "Orthography Matters!: The Ideologies, Insecurities and Global Politics of the 1990 Portuguese Language Orthographic Agreement," *Journal of World Languages* 5, no. 3 (2018): 206–33.
28. Janet Barnes, "Evidentials in the Tuyuca Verb," *International Journal of American Linguistics* 50, no. 3 (1984): 255–71.
29. Chihon-GO!, "Korean and Japanese Particle and Grammar Similarities!," *Medium* (blog), October 10, 2019, https://medium.com/@nathanchinster/korean-and-japanese-particle-and-grammar-similarities-9ad0d9e48e71.

30. Genesis 11:1–9.
31. For accounts of similar Sumerian and Mexican myths that involve building a monument and a 'confusion of tounges" see e.g., Samuel Noah Kramer, "The 'Babel of Tongues': A Sumerian Version," *Journal of the American Oriental Society* 88, no. 1 (1968): 108–11, https://doi.org/10.2307/597903. and Geoffrey G. McCafferty, "Mountain of Heaven, Mountain of Earth: The Great Pyramid of Cholula as Sacred Landscape," in *Landscape and Power In Ancient Mesoamerica* (Routledge, 2001).
32. Michael Oakeshott, "The Tower of Babel," *Rationalism in Politics and Other Essays*, 1991, 465–87.
33. Christopher Norris, review of *Review of Difference in Translation*, by Joseph F. Graham, *Comparative Literature* 40, no. 1 (1988): 52–8, https://doi.org/10.2307/1770642.
34. This was an initial aspiration of the Esperanto movement.
35. Gaston Dorren, *Babel: Around the World in Twenty Languages* (Atlantic Monthly Press, 2018), p. 327.
36. For a discussion of how this may affect the dominance of English as a lingua franca see Dorren, p. 339; Kan, "Google Debuts Smart Glasses Built With Real-Time Language Translation," *PCMAG*, May 11, 2022, www.pcmag.com/news/google-debuts-smart-glasses-built-with-real-time-language-translation.
37. Herbert George Wells, *Certain Personal Matters: A Collection of Material, Mainly Autobiographical* (Lawrence & Bullen, Limited, 16, Henrietta Street, Covent Garden, WC, 1898),
38. Horobin, *Does Spelling Matter?* p. 225.
39. By and The Understood Team, "Dav Pilkey Sees ADHD and Dyslexia as His Superpowers," *Understood* (blog), October 16, 2019, www.understood.org/en/articles/dav-pilkey-adhd-dyslexia-superpowers.
40. Pam Gann, "The Book I Won't Let My Son Read," accessed May 12, 2023, www.pamgann.com/the-book/.
41. Megan Garber, "Why Everyone's Saying 'YAAAAAASSSSSS' Now," The Atlantic, April 10, 2015, www.theatlantic.com/technology/archive/2015/04/how-to-say-yes-by-not-saying-yes/390129/.
42. Oxford Dictionary Online is different from the Oxford English Dictionary, which is a historical record of the English language.
43. https://en.oxforddictionaries.com/word-of-the-year/word-of-the-year-2015

44. Marcel Danesi, *The Semiotics of Emoji: The Rise of Visual Language in the Age of the Internet* (Bloomsbury Publishing, 2016).
45. Gretchen McCulloch, *Because Internet: Understanding the New Rules of Language* (Penguin, 2019).
46. Danesi, *The Semiotics of Emoji*.
47. McCulloch, *Because Internet*.
48. McCulloch, p. 153.
49. The national weather service no longer writes in caps for just this reason! Jason Samenow, "All Caps off: Weather Service Will Stop SHOUTING AT US on May 11," *Washington Post*, December 4, 2021, www.washingtonpost.com/news/capital-weather-gang/wp/2016/04/12/all-caps-off-weather-service-will-stop-shouting-at-us-on-may-11/.
50. McCulloch, *Because Internet*, p. 225.
51. Denver Nicks, "'Donut' vs. 'Doughnut:' The Most Delicious Spelling Bee of All Time Rages On," *Time*, June 6, 2014, https://time.com/2837756/donut-or-doughnut/.
52. Horobin, *Does Spelling Matter?* p. 225.
53. Molly Young, "Why Do Corporations Speak the Way They Do?" *Vulture* (blog), February 20, 2020, www.vulture.com/2020/02/spread-of-corporate-speak.html.
54. Mark Morgioni, "Defending 'Garbage Language,' the Silly Corporate Terminology That Seriously Works," *Slate*, February 20, 2020, https://slate.com/human-interest/2020/02/garbage-language-business-speak-defense.html.
55. Jonathan Franzen, "What's Wrong with the Modern World," *The Guardian* 13 (2013), www.theguardian.com/books/2013/sep/13/jonathan-franzen-wrong-modern-world.
56. Franzen.
57. Franzen.
58. Zadie Smith, "Generation Why? | Zadie Smith," accessed May 12, 2023, www.nybooks.com/articles/2010/11/25/generation-why/.
59. Samuel Scheffler, *Equality and Tradition: Questions of Value in Moral and Political Theory* (Oxford University Press, 2010).
60. Alexander H. Jordan and Benoît Monin, "From Sucker to Saint: Moralization in Response to Self-Threat," *Psychological Science* 19 (2008): 809–15, https://doi.org/10.1111/j.1467-9280.2008.02161.x.

A World Without Word-Warriors

5

Let's pause to take stock. Sticklerism starts in grammar school where people are required to learn and comply with whatever arbitrary linguistic conventions are in fashion at the time. Complying with these conventions isn't important for literacy or for people's ability to communicate. But because so many people are sticklers, anti-grammarian kids who violate these rules face nontrivial social penalties at school, which persist into adulthood as they encounter pedants in all corners of public life. Sticklerism is harmful and regressive, so rather than asking anti-grammarians to change, the language police should hand in their badges. In a world without word-warriors, people might even adopt more cool and innovative linguistic reforms that further enrich our languages and our lives.

In this concluding chapter, I describe what it would take to achieve a world without sticklers. Given the anarchic and freewheeling history of the English language, we know that such an equilibrium is possible. One way to shift the social equilibrium away from the set of norms that sticklers have created today is to change the sticklers themselves. There is some evidence that people who have disagreeable personalities and people who are low on openness are more likely to be sticklers. To the extent that it's possible to meaningfully suppress these pedantic personality traits and intolerant attitudes, people should try to deter sticklerism and replace it with

DOI: 10.4324/9780429319198-6

more egalitarian dispositions. Researchers should explore educational, behavioral, and even pharmaceutical interventions that would make people more open and tolerant. These moral enhancements would, among other benefits, reduce the prevalence of snootiness in the population.

I then widen the lens to describe a vision of a stickler-free world. In such a world, the same arguments I've developed against linguistic prescriptivism also extend to sanctions that attach to other kinds of low-stakes non-compliance with social norms. Here I have in mind norms related to how people dress, their body language, and other non-linguistic elements of people's self-presentation. Rejecting sticklerism would create a freer and more tolerant society. Everyone should care a little less about the rules and go a little easier on the people who break them.

Another way to shift the social equilibrium away from the current tyranny of the snoots is for the poor spellers of the world to stand up for themselves a bit more by calling out pedantry. I recognize that the arguments in this book are sometimes a bit extra in drawing a parallel between sticklerism and other, much graver forms of oppression, and I don't want to overstate the case. But here again, philosophical accounts of oppression are helpful guides for the linguistically transgressive to overthrow the orthographic tyranny.

Specifically, I have in mind the philosopher Thomas Hill's arguments about victims' and bystanders' duties to resist oppression.[1] On Hill's account, people have reasons of self-respect that weigh in favor of acting in ways that recognize that they are morally equal to others. Hill describes a deferential wife as an example of someone whose servility is morally objectionable for this reason. Hill doesn't go so far as to say that victims of oppression have *duties* to assert their equality with others, but he does argue that bystanders have duties to resist where they can. More than that, Hill argues that bystanders to oppression have duties to cultivate their capacity to resist oppression in everyday contexts—to stand up to bullies and to scrutinize their motives for going along with the status quo.

Hill's work is an instructive guide to resisting grammarianism. Poor spellers, people with non-standard grammar, people who speak in dialect and non-native speakers are all victimized by snooty social sanctioning. These people have moral reasons to assert the equal worth of the way that they speak and write, because it's not wrong to speak and write in a non-standard way and because it is wrong to sanction or punish non-standard speakers and writers. At the same time, I recognize that it can often be costly for people to push back against spellocratic sanctioning. Resistance can come off as petty or defensive (though actually it's pettier to bring up someone else's spelling or grammar in the first place). People who are already at a social disadvantage for the way they talk and write are therefore not blameworthy if they choose not to incur the further social penalties they'd catch for calling sticklers out.

In contrast to Hill's claim that bystanders to oppression have duties to resist would imply that people do have an obligation to oppose the unfair enforcement of prescriptive linguistic standards whenever they can. In practice, this means that parents should question the weekly spelling test. People should publicly defend poor spellers and non-standard speakers when they witness language-based forms of discrimination. And bystanders can work proactively to reduce the salience of linguistic normativity in everyday life, e.g., by speaking up and informing would-be snoots that their language policing is unnecessary and unwelcome. Moreover, those who maintain the linguistic status quo should scrutinize their motives for doing so—how much of our complicity in snootiness can be explained by the fact that the current system benefits us? How many people go along with arbitrary linguistic norms because they have mastered those norms, and they enjoy the praise and inclusion that comes with their ability to comply.

Additionally, resisting linguistic normativity can also enable people to resist some of the other unfair inequalities and higher-stakes forms of oppression that Hill identifies. For example, resisting social practices that stigmatize poor spelling can also be a way of correcting for some of the disadvantages that people have due to unjust educational opportunities. Resisting the policing of women's speech, gay men's speech, and dialect, can be a way of resisting informal norms of exclusion and stigmatization against historically disadvantaged people and minority groups. So not only do bystanders have reason to resist grammarianism for its own sake, they also have reasons to resist grammarianism to the extent that grammarian enforcement aligns with broader oppressive practices.

5.1 DISPOSITIONS

Pedantry is not a virtuous disposition. Pedantic people uphold their preferred linguistic norms through social sanctioning, exclusion, or blame because they are really annoyed by linguistic deviance. These punitive social practices are harmful and inegalitarian. Earlier, in making the egalitarian case against the Gotcha Gang, I appealed to the idea of social egalitarianism, which is the view that people should structure their social relations in ways that reflect people's underlying moral equality. Social egalitarians also argue that people should be *disposed* to relate to each other as equals. By this they mean that it's not just morally important that everyone be treated with equal dignity and respect, people internalize a disposition to treat people in this way. In this section, I make the case that sticklerism is an inegalitarian disposition. Sticklers are likely to be more authoritarian and less open than people who take a more relaxed approach to linguistic conventions.

What does an egalitarian disposition require? The philosopher Sam Scheffler (who you may remember from the earlier discussion of tradition) defends this dispositional account of social egalitarianism.[2] According to Scheffler's version of the argument, the moral value of people relating as equals isn't that it's morally better if social status is distributed in a way that aligns with each person's equal moral worth. Rather, he argues that egalitarianism is better understood as an orientation. People should be disposed to forming egalitarian relationships across social divides and people should be averse to hierarchical or authoritarian relationships. Jim Wilson makes a similar point, arguing further that these egalitarian dispositions must be *robust* across surfaces.[3] It's not enough for people to be disposed to treat others as equals because their circumstances happen to be favorable to avoiding hierarchy, people must be disposed to treat others as equals even when it is costly. Both Scheffler and Wilson also argue that these dispositions aren't just instrumentally valuable as a way of encouraging people to avoid distributing resources or social status in unfair ways—it's also good for people to have these egalitarian dispositions for their own sake.

Say we accept this dispositional account of social egalitarianism. How do grammarians fare? As it happens, there is not much psychological research about the grammarian disposition. But as someone who's read the previous chapters of this book might predict, there is some reason to think that grammarian dispositions are inegalitarian and intolerant.

Grammarians are people who take joy in indicating that they are 'in the know' by accusing others of ignorance. They enjoy having the upper hand in social relationships, at least when they intervene to issue a correction. As Robert Kurzban says,

> When people, especially publicly, correct others' mistakes, a lot of that has to do with signaling to other people, "People are trying to signal their expertise, because being able to identify mistakes indicates that you know more about something than the person who committed the error."[4]

This signaling might not be a conscious choice. Often, people tell themselves stories that justify practices that are essentially just status seeking and signaling.[5] However, recalling the earlier discussion of Hill, people who are inclined to correct others' grammar should scrutinize their motives and ask themselves whether they are interjecting to correct someone's comma usage for the love of the grammar game, or if there are darker motives in play.

For just a moment, let's try to imagine what's going through a grammarian's mind when she decides to interject and correct someone's grammar. Say that she's talking to someone about the recent eclipse, and he says, "We was all stood at the lake when we seen it gone dark" and a tiny siren goes off somewhere in her hippocampus. She says, "You mean, 'we were all standing at the lake when we saw it get dark." What does this accomplish for her? From the fact that she was able to reconstruct her interlocutors' sentence, we can infer that she understood what he was saying. Does she think that the man who said the first sentence is interested in some free English tutoring? Does she think he will internalize her preferred linguistic conventions after hearing her timely interjection? In cases like these, I think pedantic people interject in these ways because, perhaps subconsciously, they want to make themselves look smart, sophisticated, and educated in contrast to the person they're talking to, who they portray as ignorant and wrong.

Some grammarians' sensitivity to linguistic error may be a symptom to a broader lack of agreeableness and openness. A few years ago, a group of psychologists studied the correlation between grammarianism and personality traits.[6] It was a small study, but it might offer a clue into the psychology of sticklerism. For this study, researchers asked participants to read email responses for a roommate ad that contained grammatical and typographic errors and then to evaluate the respondent based on what they read. They found that less agreeable people were more likely to negatively evaluate people who made grammatical errors and that people who were conscientious and not open were more likely to negatively evaluate people whose emails contained typos. Introverted people were more sensitive to both kinds of errors. These findings suggest that some people's grammarian disposition may not stem from inegalitarian attitudes *per se*, but to a resistance to deviation or error.

Happily, there is hope for the snoots who are willing to change. To the pedants who are motivated to signal their superior grasp of language rules, the solution is for bystanders and victims of pedantic correction to refuse to confer status on people for issuing corrections. For targets of correction, the current norm is to politely thank sticklers for clarifying that 'decimated' should only be used when something is reduced by 10 percent, and not as a synonym for 'destroyed.' But pedants who issue such corrections are liable to be corrected back and it is entirely permissible for anti-grammarians to reply to linguistic interventions by informing the snoots that languages are always changing and that the boundaries of words like 'decimate' needn't be defined by the word's etymology.

And to the pedants whose personalities dispose them to negatively judge people who commit typographic and grammatical errors, there is room for self-development on this score. Researchers find that with continued effort and habituation, people can sometimes change their personality traits (albeit only to a limited extent.)[7] And though it can be difficult at first, people may subsequently come to enjoy the personality changes they develop through habituation.[8]

The upshot here is that disagreeable and close-minded snoots may, with practice, be able to overcome the pedantic tendencies that undermine egalitarian sentiments and alienate them from their fellow citizens. Going forward, researchers might also consider investigating other ways of enhancing people's agreeableness, openness to experience, or whatever other traits make them more tolerant of linguistic diversity and other forms of difference too.[9]

5.2 STICKLERLESSNESS

Say the sticklers change their pedantic ways and give up on policing people's spelling and grammar through public policy and social sanctioning. What would a sticklerless world look like? In taking on the prescriptivist police, I am advocating for a linguistic landscape where thousands of dialects, accents, spelling conventions, and grammatical constructions can function together in communicative harmony. It's not contradictory to argue for a world where all ways of living and loving and speaking and writing and being are tolerated because criticizing people who stand in the way of understanding and open-mindedness is not contrary to the value of toleration.

Language is a subject of justice, and anti-grammarianism is just another step towards a progressive vision of acceptance, solidarity, and toleration.

Clearly, there is a broader lesson here about the benefits of a more permissive disposition. These arguments about language and justice are similar to other recent arguments against the excessive policing of people's private behavior in social groups and public life.[10] Grammarians aren't the only ones who seem to delight in public shaming, and the arguments against grammarianism serve as arguments against censoriousness and rigidity in social life more generally—though often this censoriousness aligns with language policing.

Another benefit of cultivating permissive dispositions towards language is that linguistic debates are often a distraction from the debates that really matter. Consider slogans on the left and right where people attempt to redefine terms and words in ways that are favorable to their political agenda. Here I have in mind phrases like "Love is Love" or "Marriage is Between a Man and a Woman." The first is an attempt to define love in a way that insinuates that all romantic relationships should have equal political status. The second is an attempt to define marriage in a way that explicitly excludes gay couples from being eligible for marriage. Both are attempts to use the tools of language policing to advance a political goal. And in both cases, the goal isn't that people use English words like 'love' or 'marriage' in a way that complies with the dictionary definition. Rather, each side fights a proxy battle about language when the real political conflict is about marriage policy.

In these cases, politically motivated language policing is generally counterproductive because language policing takes the place of genuine conversation about values. To take a few other examples, instead of talking about racial justice people talk about the definition of racism. Instead of talking about whether abortion should be allowed, people wear shirts that make seemingly definitional points like, "Women's rights are human rights." Instead of talking about whether a person was being unkind or insulting, people talk about whether they used language in a way that violated the prevailing social norms. Politically motivated language policing is also inegalitarian and harmful for all the reasons that other forms of language policing are. People who are not deliberately or culpably using language to minimize injustice, harm, or insult anyone are, nevertheless, subjected to the stigmatizing sting of having their speech corrected for moral and political reasons.

I raise these examples of the politics of definition in the service of a broader point about how language policing has negative social externalities beyond the harms of linguistic prescriptivism because language policing is so often a tool of social control. In contrast, imagine what a world without language policing would look like. On this point, we can distinguish three questions.

1. Should public officials regulate and police language?
2. Should people correct and criticize linguistic differences in social settings?
3. Should people comply with the dominant linguistic standards?

To the first question, I've argued that public officials should be very permissive of linguistic variation, transgressiveness, and even obscenity and offense. To the second, I've argued that people should also be permissive in their private lives. To the third question, I've suggested that people should comply with the dominant linguistic standards to the extent that they want to or to the extent that compliance is necessary for them to achieve their broader goals. However, if people were more permissive in social settings, then people would ideally have less reason to comply with the dominant linguistic standards.

Together, these three claims constitute a vision of linguistic toleration in government and in culture. A truly liberal society would be a sticklerless society. In such a society, people would still disagree about justice, people would disagree about matters of taste, and they may struggle to communicate across linguistic divides in some cases. Yet, in a sticklerless world, these disagreements would play out straightforwardly, not through the filters of grammarianism and pedantry. Sticklerism will not solve most of the problems that come with social change and transition, but a sticklerless society would be better than the status quo in at least two respects—people would be more tolerant of linguistic diversity and less punitive towards linguistic transgression.

5.3 IS THIS ARGUMENT SELF-DEFEATING?

At this point a proponent of grammarian gatekeeping may accuse me of a kind of hypocrisy. After all, I've argued that people should be far more tolerant of different forms of expression and far more reluctant to police the ways that people speak and write. But maybe sticklerism is just another way that people express themselves—just one approach to language among many. In defense of the word-nerds, a grammarian may argue that I'm the real language policer because I'm writing an entire book about how people should apply or uphold linguistic conventions while hypocritically blaming the sticklers who are doing the same.

Hypocrisy consists in someone criticizing other people for something that the hypocrite does as well.[11] Hypocritical criticism is presumptively inegalitarian for this reason, because the hypocritical critic exempts herself from her own standards of criticism. The charge here is that by criticizing sticklers for policing people's language, I'm hypocritically encouraging people to stigmatize and blame people (pedants) for their speech. If it is wrong for sticklers to criticize people for failing to comply with their preferred conventions, isn't it also wrong for me to criticize the sticklers for failing to be more orthographically open-minded? If successful, this objection would be very wounding to the argument in this book. Another version of this objection is that my argument against egalitarian language policing applies to my own egalitarian arguments. After all, I am saying that people have moral and political reasons not to tell other people that they have moral and political reasons not to speak in certain ways. Am I sanctioning speakers who sanction speakers for political reasons for political reasons?

Of course, my main goal is to destigmatize linguistic transgressiveness, not to make language policing another form of linguistic transgressiveness for people to stigmatize. I don't want the arguments for linguistic openness to be deployed against language policing in ways that were counterproductive, unfair, and ineffective. But I must admit that there is something to this objection. In a sense, I'm language policing the language police in this book. Nevertheless, the arguments in this book are not self-defeating insofar as language police are not justified in criticizing linguistic rebels whereas I am justified in criticizing language police.

A grammarian may reply that if semantic sanctioning is wrong, as I say it is, then sticklers also aren't liable to be reproached for their language. This argument would have to proceed in bad faith, since grammarians are people who do not seem to think that semantic sanctioning is wrong, but it accuses my argument of bad faith in turn. This objection misfires, however, because the arguments in this book are not an indictment of all forms of criticism. I'm arguing against people who excessively criticize the ways that their fellow citizens speak and write. It's not inconsistent to criticize people for language policing just as it is not inconsistent for a critic of police misconduct to say that some criminal officers should be arrested.

Additionally, my arguments in favor of greater linguistic openness are framed in response to an unfair status quo. If I'm correct that language policing mistreats people, then grammarians are liable to be criticized for sanctioning and stigmatizing speech. That doesn't mean that I support sanctioning and stigmatizing sticklers, but I do think that they are liable to be sanctioned and stigmatized in some cases. Consider an analogy with self-defense and defense of others. If a violent aggressor is assaulting a bystander, it is not hypocritical to physically interfere with the aggressor in order to defend the bystander. It's also not required. In a case like this, the aggressor would be liable to be interfered with because he forfeited his rights against interference when he committed violence.[12] At the same time, even if the aggressor does not have the standing to complain about being forcibly interfered with, it doesn't follow that interfering with him is the best response. In some cases, defensive interference is permissible, but it is also morally better for bystanders to protect victims in nonviolent ways, if those options are available.

Similarly, the case against grammarianism is defensive. Sticklers and snoots deploy social and sometimes legal sanctions to shape the social world in a way that disadvantages and shames the speakers or writers who violate their arbitrary standards. The people who are responsible for this pervasive pedantry are therefore liable to be socially discouraged from nitpicking nouns and criticizing commas. They lack the standing to complain about the promotion of anti-grammarian social norms because the promotion of anti-grammarianism is only necessary as a corrective response to their attempts to shape and control other people's linguistic practices. At the same time, if there are ways to effectively encourage pedants to change their ways without exposing them to social sanctions and stigma, there are also moral reasons to prefer this gentler approach.

5.4 POOR SPELLERS UNTIE!

I have argued that grammarianism is often political. People use linguistic sanctions to control people. Language instruction is often a way of indoctrinating children into a culture of compliance. People use language to police the boundaries of identity and class and to maintain social hierarchies. Anti-grammarians who reassert their dignity and resist pervasive pedantry not only make their languages more interesting, they make their communities more just and inclusive. Poor spellers and non-standard dialect speakers should not be shy about making anti-grammarians a political project, destigmatizing linguistic transgression and reclaiming their stigmatized identities as a source of pride.

Here I have in mind an analogy to the way that gay rights and disability pride advocates worked over the course of decades to destigmatize and normalize homosexuality and disability. I am *not* saying that the harm of grammarianism is comparable to the harms that gay people and disabled people have experienced throughout history. Though people often use language policing as socially acceptable cover for discrimination that would otherwise be socially unacceptable, sticklerism *per se* is not as much of as a social problem as other longstanding prejudices. I get that in the grand scheme of things, spelling is a small potato. Nevertheless, the analogies to gay rights and disability pride are instructive because advocates in these movements effectively changed people's minds about gender ideology, medical ideology, social norms, and stigma. Activists from these movements have written a useful script for subversive spellers and diction dissonants who aim to overturn the ideology of linguistic prescriptivism.

Throughout history, the legal system punished homosexuality and gay people were criticized, victimized, mocked, and excluded from social life. For this reason, many gay people were closeted. They concealed their gay identities to protect themselves from discrimination and embarrassment. Yet though closeting was understandable, the gay rights movement became more politically successful as more people openly identified as gay and homosexuality was normalized in popular culture and in people's communities. [13] As part of this social shift, gay rights advocates developed the concept of 'gay pride' which aimed to counteract the internalized shame and stigma that many gay people experienced. Gay pride activists chanted and displayed slogans such as "We're here, we're queer, get used to it!" and "Out of the closet and into the streets!" and "Two, Four, Six, Eight! How Do You Know Your Kids Are Straight?"

Anti-grammarians can also look to the disability rights and disability pride movements when envisioning a social change movement that aims to normalize non-standard ways of communicating. As I argued in the first chapter, dyslexic people face similar difficulties in educational and employment contexts as deaf speakers. Many of these difficulties are a result of social institutions that are unaccommodating and difficult for disabled people to navigate. As I said in the first chapter, this doesn't mean that being deaf or dyslexic is a deficit or a bad difference.[14] Rather, a mere difference in communicative abilities can be disadvantaged by social practices and discrimination. A similar argument extends, to a lesser extent, to people who are not dyslexic but who are nevertheless burdened by grammarian social practices.

These social movements are instructive because people who violate linguistic norms are similar to closeted gay people and disabled people in a few relevant ways. Again, I agree that the anti-grammarians' plight is lower stakes than either of these movements. But in all three cases, people's permissible behavior has historically been policed by socially powerful people who stigmatize deviance. The law entrenches these norms by punishing people who fail to comply with the dominant conventions. People who are different infer that they have something to be ashamed of, and they may try to pass. In each case, people change how they present themselves in order to avoid sanctions, even though those sanctions are unfair. Anti-grammarians could also align themselves with other pride movements, such as the fat acceptance, punk, and body neutrality communities. Each of these groups shares a common target, namely, people who unfairly wield the tools of social exclusion against those who are different.

Taking the lessons of the gay pride and disability rights movements seriously is therefore instructive for anti-grammarians. The first step towards language liberation is normalizing deviance. For example, people could just stop apologizing for their non-standard ways of talking and writing. This is a difficult step in the current circumstances, because pedantry is the norm in so many educational, political, and professional contexts. Outing oneself as a poor speller or as grammatically indifferent can have meaningful personal and professional penalties, as I described in previous chapters.

In the service of the movement then, it's good if people who are relatively secure take the first steps shifting the social equilibrium in favor of a more liberal approach to orthography, grammar, and speech. In an effort to do this, I'm including an unedited appendix in this book which contains many violations of spelling rules and grammatical conventions (though I'm sure the snoots will also find plenty of errors in the edited text of this book as well!). This appendix is partly an attempt to establish that errors are not a barrier to understanding. But it is also an effort to show that people from all walks of life are prone to linguistic error and all of us would benefit from social norms that were more tolerant of linguistic non-compliance.

Taking the program a step further, anti-grammarian advocates might also popularize slogans that call out orthographic tyranny and destigmatize linguistic transgressiveness. Surely, if linguistic toleration were to gain steam as a political project, then members of the movement could develop a few powerful and effective slogans for bumper stickers, signs, and T shirts, like:

- Stop your yammering about my grammaring!
- Better 2 mute if yr gonna SNOOT!
- Respect the dialect!
- It's never your job to be a word snob
- Please dont yell about the way I spell ☺
- Lets stop fighting about my wryting!
- Everyones a werk in progress
- Keep your corrections to yourself/Leave the stylebook on the shelf!
- ProudToSpeak and SoUnique ☺

These are just a few suggestions get the conversation started! I'm sure my fellow anti-grammarians can come up with much better catchphrases, since so many of them are already experts in creative linguistic innovation.

Additionally, to the extent that grammarianism is enforced through public institutions, including schools, anti-grammarians might consider engaging in political advocacy against politically mandated pedantry. In employment contexts, anti-grammarians might affix a note to their applications or email signatures clarifying that they are deliberately overlooking so-called errors and typos in an effort to promote greater linguistic toleration. Celebrities on social media have an excellent platform to transgress linguistic standards and to clapback at stuffy pedants who criticize them for it. Each of these tactics have the potential to destigmatize linguistic variation, thus liberating all speakers and writers to communicate without shame or sanction.

5.5 CONCLUSION

In this chapter I've sketched a vision of a sticklerless society, and I proposed some tentative next steps to bring about a better social equilibrium when it comes to grammar. Importantly, I am not arguing that public officials should intervene in the word wars on the side of anti-grammarians, or that pedantry should one day be stigmatized in the same way that linguistic transgressiveness is today. The problem with snoots is, in part, their authoritarian tendency to intervene when they identify perceived errors. The solution to this problem is not to call upon institutions with even more authoritarian tendencies on behalf of anti-grammarians. Rather, the anti-grammarian project is fundamentally a liberal endeavor. The anti-grammarian goal should be for people to give up the grammilitia, not to deploy a counterforce against them.

Nor am I arguing that people who like speaking and writing in a way that is compliant with the dominant linguistic standards are under any obligation to change. If people enjoy complying with existing spelling and grammar rules, I am not here to take that away from them. The only pleasures of pedantry they should quit are the pleasures of policing others' speech.

Of course, the destigmatization of linguistic transgressiveness is likely to be a slow process and it's not clear whether such a movement could succeed. Recall, as an analogy, nineteenth century spelling reformers' failure to get English speakers to adopt a phonetic alphabet. But there are reasons for hope that the pendulum of prescriptivism may be swinging back to the more permissive equilibrium of Early Modern English. As societies become more liberal, open, and tolerant, people's attitudes and dispositions are likely to change in ways that make them especially attuned to the pointlessness of pedantry. And as new technology emerges to facilitate communication across linguistic divides and within narrow cultural subgroups, we will all encounter new and exciting ways of speaking and writing which will further advance the case for linguistic openness. Languages are created by the people who use them every day. By rejecting the pedantry of the past, scrappy spellers and subversive stylists today have the power to make our languages more interesting, inclusive, and innovative for the speakers and writers of tomorrow.

NOTES

1. Thomas E. Hill, "Moral Responsibilities of Bystanders," *Journal of Social Philosophy* 41, no. 1 (2010): 28–39.
2. Samuel Scheffler, "The Practice of Equality," in *Social Equality: Essays on What It Means to Be Equals*, ed. Carina Fourie, Fabian Schuppert, and Ivo Wallimann-Helmer (Oxford University Press, 2015), 20–44, https://doi.org/10.1093/acprof:oso/9780199331109.003.0002.
3. James L. Wilson, "An Autonomy-Based Argument for Democracy," in *Oxford Studies in Political Philosophy Volume 7*, ed. David Sobel, Peter Vallentyne, and Steven Wall (Oxford University Press, 2021).

4. Matthew J. X. Malady, "Are You a Language Bully?" *Slate*, September 5, 2013, https://slate.com/human-interest/2013/09/language-bullies-pedants-and-grammar-nerds-who-correct-people-all-the-time-cut-it-out.html.
5. Kevin Simler and Robin Hanson, *The Elephant in the Brain: Hidden Motives in Everyday Life*, illustrated edition (New York: Oxford University Press, 2018).
6. Julie E. Boland and Robin Queen, "If You're House Is Still Available, Send Me an Email: Personality Influences Reactions to Written Errors in Email Messages," *PLOS ONE* 11, no. 3 (March 9, 2016): e0149885, https://doi.org/10.1371/journal.pone.0149885.
7. Marie Hennecke et al., "A Three-Part Framework for Self-Regulated Personality Development across Adulthood," *European Journal of Personality* 28, no. 3 (2014): 289–99, https://doi.org/10.1002/per.1945.
8. "If You Don't like Your Personality, You Can Change It," *Big Think* (blog), December 14, 2021, https://bigthink.com/neuropsych/big-five-personality-change/.
9. Javier Hidalgo, "Cosmopolitan Moral Enhancement," in *The Ethics of Ability and Enhancement*, ed. Jessica Flanigan and Terry L. Price, 1st edition (New York: Palgrave Macmillan, 2017).
10. Freddie deBoer, "Planet of Cops," Substack newsletter, *Freddie deBoer* (blog), August 25, 2021, https://freddiedeboer.substack.com/p/planet-of-cops.
11. R. Jay Wallace, "Hypocrisy, Moral Address, and the Equal Standing of Persons," *Philosophy & Public Affairs* 38, no. 4 (2010): 307–41.
12. David Rodin, "The Reciprocity Theory of Rights," *Law and Philosophy* 33, no. 3 (2014): 281–308.
13. For a review essay about visibility and gay rights see Melissa R. Michelson, "The Power of Visibility: Advances in LGBT Rights in the United States and Europe," *The Journal of Politics* 81, no. 1 (January 2019): e1–5, https://doi.org/10.1086/700591.
14. Barbara Riddick, "Dyslexia and inclusion: Time for a social model of disability perspective?" *International Studies in Sociology of Education* 11, no. 3 (2001): 223–36.

Appendix

This appendix serves as a proof of concept for my arguments about spelling and grammar. Here, I ll provide an unedited summary of the book which I havent autorcorrected for spelling or grammar. I have three goals for this appendix:

1. In this appendix, I show that writing that is ungrammatical and mispelled and somewhat informal can still be comprehensable to a reader.
2. I demonsrtate that there can be some virtues in writing in a more laid-back way.
3. I use this appendix as an opportunity to engage in linguistic transgressiveness—which I view as a kind of civil disobedience against the tyranny of grammarianism.

So ... on to the summary of the arguments!

In the first chapter i argued htat orthographic intolerance begins in elementary school. Evne that erely, widespread pedagogies like the weekly spelling tests and the use of spelling bees are useless at best and counerproductive at worst. As this appendix shows, many people have gone through years of education only to spell things incorrectly and/or to misplace commas and other allegedly crucial punctuation when left to their own devices. And as the rest of the book shows, it's basically fine that this happens becusae people can use automated spellcheckers and AI communication tools and professional copyeditors to bring thier writing up to professional standars when necessary. poor spelling is not an indicator of low intelligence. And a person's refusal to comply wiht gramattical standards reflects a praiseworthy anti-authoritarian disposition, which is an intellectual virtue, not a defect.

In the second chapter I argued that demands for lingusitic presccriptivism have bad consequences. to correct someone is to expose them to sanctions that theey are not liabl to experience. in this way it's harmful and insulting to correct someones' spelling or grammar (except in cases where advice was requestsed. In defesnese of curmudgenly sticklerism, on might argu that it's important to maintain some clear and consistent unified standards, either for aesthetic reasons or for reasons of national unity. But maintaining these standards is only worthwile if the standrds re maintained voluntarily, however, sticklers uphold grrammar and spelleing conventiosn by providing unsolicited feedback to innocent communicators, and sometimes, by using their political power to ennforce their prefered linguistic conventions.

In the third chapter i developed the egalitarian case against linguistic normativity. There I argue that linguistic presecritivism si especially harmful to peopel who are already sociallly disadvantaged or stigmatized. Additionally, language policing often serves as a socially acceptable cover for behavior that people would otherwise deem prejudiced or discriminatory. The fact thtat people engage in code switching shows that language policing has real costs to people who dont comply with the dominant linguistic conventions. These arguemnts showwthat egalitarian proponents of stickelrism cannot consistently claim that language policing is cnsistn with thier progressive political committments.

In the fourth chapter i talkd ab how t holding people to strict standards for spelling and grammar is a relatively new practice. And as it is enforced today this practice can prevent people from adopting useful innovations that would make their languages more expressive, more interesting, or more precise. There I discussed the linguistic innovations associated with internet and the promice of translation technology for making linguistic normativity even less necessary going foward

In the fifth chapter, I addressedthe broadeer phenomonon of language policing. there, i argued that there are often moral reasons to choose one's words carefully. but despite this fact there remain moral reaons that weigh against language policing as well. There, I envisioned a sticklerless world And I made the case that it would not be so bad! I also considered whether my anti-grammarian argument might be self defeatign, since in advocating against sticklerism i am also advocating for a kind of linguistic normativity. yet the arguemtns here are only self-defeating in the way that liberal arguemtns for toleraton are self-defeating. In this way, my linguistic liberalism will stand and fall with the more general case for liberalism, at least when it comes to self-defeatinness objections. To close, I sketched a vision for an antigrammarian polticial movement. Part of that vision involved poor spellers 'outing' themselves in an effort to destigmatize linguistic transgressiveness and to counteract the harmful and false narrative that poor spelling and grammar is necessarily associated with bad manners or low intelligence. This appendix is an effort to demonstrate what this political movement may look like in practice.

Nevertheless, as I am writing this appendix I find that the spectre of sticklerism still haunts me! Its been difficult to turn off the autocorrection and to self-consciouosly refrain from correcting all the spelling errors im introducing into the text. as I write this, I worry that readers may see what the text looks like and downgrade their judgments of my capacities afterseeing that my first-round prose is so sloppy and full of misspellings. And yet, That's The Whole Point! clearly the fact that i often forget to capitalize the letter i when i am usign it to refer to myself, or the fac tthat i so often reverse randomletters when typing or run some words together (apparently) isn't a reason to discount the ideas that i have. my failure to appropriately capitalize words isn't an indictment on the quality of my arguments. and yet (and yet!) writing this appendix somehow feels like I'm risking the credibility of the foregoing argument when in actuallity im just providing further evidence of my point :/ but we can only find freedom from faultfinders through small acts of resistance. Writers must silence the autocorrect once in a while and readers must silence their inner critics, embracing the idea that, in some contexts, it's ok to have 'bad' spelling and grammar ☺

Notes

INTRODUCTION

1. Lynne Truss, *Eats, Shoots & Leaves: The Zero Tolerance Approach to Punctuation*, 1st edition (New York: Avery, 2004).
2. Weird Al Yankovic, *Word Crimes*, Mandatory Fun (RCA Records, 2014).

CHAPTER 1

1. Harry Brighouse and Adam Swift, "Equality, Priority, and Positional Goods," *Ethics* 116, no. 3 (April 2006): 471–97, https://doi.org/10.1086/500524.
2. Gina Schouten, "Fair Educational Opportunity and the Distribution of Natural Ability: Toward a Prioritarian Principle of Educational Justice," *Journal of Philosophy of Education* 46, no. 3 (August 1, 2012): 472–91, https://doi.org/10.1111/j.1467-9752.2012.00863.x; Debra Satz, "Equality, Adequacy, and Education for Citizenship," *Ethics* 117, no. 4 (2007): 623–48, https://doi.org/10.1086/518805; Elizabeth Anderson, "Fair Opportunity in Education: A Democratic Equality Perspective," *Ethics* 117, no. 4 (2007): 595–622, https://doi.org/10.1086/518806.
3. Corey A. DeAngelis and Heidi Holmes Erickson, "What Leads to Successful School Choice Programs: A Review of the Theories and Evidence," *Cato Journal* 38, no. 1 (2018): 247–64.
4. Amy Gutmann, "Civic Education and Social Diversity," *Ethics* 105, no. 3 (1995): 557–79.
5. John R. Lott Jr, "Public Schooling, Indoctrination, and Totalitarianism," *Journal of Political Economy* 107, no. S6 (1999): S127–57, https://doi.org/10.1086/250106.
6. Rashawn Ray and Alexandra Gibbons, "Why Are States Banning Critical Race Theory?" *Brookings* (blog), July 2, 2021, www.brookings.edu/blog/fixgov/2021/07/02/why-are-states-banning-critical-race-theory/.

7. David Wolman, *Righting the Mother Tongue: From Olde English to Email, the Tangled Story of English Spelling*, reprint edition (Harper Perennial, 2010), p. 90.
8. E. D. Hirsch Jr, *Cultural Literacy: What Every American Needs to Know*, updated and expanded edition (New York: Vintage, 1988).
9. Walter Feinberg, "The Influential E.D. Hirsch," *Rethinking Schools* 13, no. 3 (Spring 1999), https://rethinkingschools.org/articles/the-influential-e-d-hirsch/.
10. For a critical analysis of this view, see Julie Hagemann and Melvin Wininger, "An Ideological Approach to Grammar Pedagogy in English Education Courses," *English Education* 31, no. 4 (1999): 265–94.
11. Private schools and homeschoolers are also required to teach spelling and grammar, at least in some jurisdictions.
12. Bryan Caplan, *The Case against Education: Why the Education System Is a Waste of Time and Money* (Princeton University Press, 2019); Fredrik deBoer, *The Cult of Smart: How Our Broken Education System Perpetuates Social Injustice* (St. Martin's Publishing Group, 2020).
13. See, e.g., the effectiveness of phonics instruction for students who were previously taught to read in other, less effective, ways. Sarah Mervosh, "In Memphis, the Phonics Movement Comes to High School," *The New York Times*, December 25, 2022, sec. U.S., www.nytimes.com/2022/12/25/us/reading-literacy-memphis-tennessee.html.
14. Joy Lin, "The Effects of Code-Based Literacy Interventions on Spelling Achievement: A Meta-Analysis" (The City University of New York, 2013), www.proquest.com/openview/e128610eabbb72a182f466cabc53a7ca/1?pq-origsite=gscholar&cbl=18750; Richard Andrews et al., "The Effect of Grammar Teaching on Writing Development," *British Educational Research Journal* 32, no. 1 (2006): 39–55, https://doi.org/10.1080/01411920500401997; Steve Graham and Dolores Perin, "A Meta-Analysis of Writing Instruction for Adolescent Students," *Journal of Educational Psychology* 99 (2007): 445–76, https://doi.org/10.1037/0022-0663.99.3.445; Steve Graham et al., "A Meta-Analysis of Writing Instruction for Students in the Elementary Grades," *Journal of Educational Psychology* 104 (2012): 879–96, https://doi.org/10.1037/a0029185.
15. "It's Time to Stop Debating How to Teach Kids to Read and Follow the Evidence," April 26, 2020, www.sciencenews.org/article/balanced-literacy-phonics-teaching-reading-evidence; William H. Jeynes, "A Meta-Analysis of the Relationship Between Phonics Instruction and Minority

Elementary School Student Academic Achievement," *Education and Urban Society* 40, no. 2 (January 1, 2008): 151–66, https://doi.org/10.1177/0013124507304128.

16. Mark Seidenberg, *Language at the Speed of Sight: How We Read, Why So Many Can't, and What Can Be Done About It* (Basic Books, 2017).

17. Hayley Glatter, "The Ignored Science That Could Help Close the Achievement Gap," *The Atlantic*, November 4, 2016, www.theatlantic.com/education/archive/2016/11/the-ignored-science-that-could-help-close-the-achievement-gap/506498/.

18. Kathryn Paige Harden, *The Genetic Lottery: Why DNA Matters for Social Equality* (Princeton University Press, 2022); Bryan Caplan, *The Case against Education: Why the Education System Is a Waste of Time and Money* (Princeton University Press, 2019); Fredrik deBoer, *The Cult of Smart: How Our Broken Education System Perpetuates Social Injustice* (St. Martin's Publishing Group, 2020).

19. Kristin Sayeski and David Hurford, "A Framework for Examining Reading-Related Education Research and The Curious Case of Orton-Gillingham," *Learning Disabilities* (Weston, MA) 27 (December 21, 2022), https://doi.org/10.18666/LDMJ-2022-V27-I2-11720.

20. In part, these approaches are ineffective because the effects of memorization quickly fade out. See, for example, Vickie Johnston, "Dyslexia: What Reading Teachers Need to Know," *The Reading Teacher* 73, no. 3 (2019): 339–46, https://doi.org/10.1002/trtr.1830.

21. Wolman, *Righting the Mother Tongue*, p. 146–8; Stanislas Dehaene, *Reading in the Brain: The New Science of How We Read*, reprint edition (New York, Toronto, Ontario London Dublin: Penguin Books, 2010), p. 247.

22. James Essinger, *Spellbound: The Surprising Origins and Astonishing Secrets of English Spelling* (Random House Publishing Group, 2007), p. 74.

23. Wolman, *Righting the Mother Tongue*, p. 147.

24. Barbara Riddick, "Dyslexia and Inclusion: Time for a Social Model of Disability Perspective?" *International Studies in Sociology of Education* 11, no. 3 (November 1, 2001): 223–36, https://doi.org/10.1080/09620210100200078.

25. For a clear overview of these arguments (albeit in the service of a different conclusion) see Jacqueline Mae Wallis, "Is It Ever Morally Permissible to Select for Deafness in One's Child?" *Medicine, Health Care and Philosophy* 23, no. 1 (March 1, 2020): 3–15, https://doi.org/10.1007/s11019-019-09922-6.

26. Simon Horobin, *Does Spelling Matter?* (OUP Oxford, 2013), p. 227.
27. Though the good news is that dyslexia alone doesn't seem to undermine kids' overall social wellbeing. Julie-Ann Jordan and Kevin Dyer, "Psychological Well-Being Trajectories of Individuals with Dyslexia Aged 3–11 Years," *Dyslexia* 23, no. 2 (2017): 161–80, https://doi.org/10.1002/dys.1555.
28. Peter Johnston and Donna Scanlon, "An Examination of Dyslexia Research and Instruction with Policy Implications," *Literacy Research: Theory, Method, and Practice* 70, no. 1 (2021): 107–28.
29. Kristin L. Sayeski et al., "Orton Gillingham: Who, What, and How," *Teaching Exceptional Children* 51, no. 3 (2019): 240–9.
30. Elizabeth A. Stevens et al., "Current State of the Evidence: Examining the Effects of Orton-Gillingham Reading Interventions for Students with or at Risk for Word-Level Reading Disabilities," *Exceptional Children* 87, no. 4 (July 2021): 397–417, https://doi.org/10.1177/0014402921993406.
31. In a recent meta-analysis of OG, the authors found no statistically significant effect of OG interventions. One issue is that OG is time-consuming, so it's difficult to implement in large classes. Also, despite certification programs and materials for direct instruction, instructional quality varies a lot. Stevens et al.
32. "Spelling – International Dyslexia Association," October 11, 2014, https://dyslexiaida.org/spelling/.
33. Douglas C. Baynton, *Forbidden Signs: American Culture and the Campaign against Sign Language* (Chicago, IL: University of Chicago Press, 1998), https://press.uchicago.edu/ucp/books/book/chicago/F/bo3683567.html.
34. Susan Burch, "Capturing a Movement: Sign Language Preservation," *Sign Language Studies* 4, no. 3 (2004): 293–304.
35. Burch.
36. Johnston and Scanlon, "An Examination of Dyslexia Research and Instruction with Policy Implications."
37. For this reason, dyslexic students may benefit from additional instructional resources as well, such as the use of spellchecking software for writing assignments. Kara Dawson et al., "Assistive Technologies to Support Students with Dyslexia," *Teaching Exceptional Children* 51, no. 3 (2019): 226–39.
38. Though the good news is that dyslexia alone doesn't seem to undermine kids' overall social wellbeing. Jordan and Dyer, "Psychological Well-Being Trajectories of Individuals with Dyslexia Aged 3–11 Years."

39. Anna Maria Re et al., "Spelling Errors among Children with ADHD Symptoms: The Role of Working Memory," *Research in Developmental Disabilities* 35, no. 9 (2014): 2199–204; Darina Czamara et al., "Children with ADHD Symptoms Have a Higher Risk for Reading, Spelling and Math Difficulties in the GINIplus and LISAplus Cohort Studies," *PloS One* 8, no. 5 (2013): e63859.
40. Flint Simonsen and L. E. E. Gunter, "Best Practices in Spelling Instruction: A Research Summary," *Journal of Direct Instruction* 1, no. 2 (2001): 97–105.
41. Misty Adoniou, *Spelling It Out: How Words Work and How to Teach Them* (Cambridge University Press, 2016), p. 12.
42. Rebecca Putman, "Using Research to Make Informed Decisions about the Spelling Curriculum," *Texas Journal of Literacy Education* 5, no. 1 (2017): 24–32.
43. Linnea C. Ehri et al., "The Roots of Learning to Read and Write: Acquisition of Letters and Phonemic Awareness," *Handbook of Early Literacy Research* 2 (2006): 113–34; Rebecca Treiman and Brett Kessler, "Spelling as Statistical Learning: Using Consonantal Context to Spell Vowels," *Journal of Educational Psychology* 98, no. 3 (2006): 642; Barbara R. Foorman et al., "The Impact of Instructional Practices in Grades 1 and 2 on Reading and Spelling Achievement in High Poverty Schools," *Contemporary Educational Psychology* 31, no. 1 (2006): 1–29; Louisa Moats, "What Teachers Don't Know and Why They Aren't Learning It: Addressing the Need for Content and Pedagogy in Teacher Education," *Australian Journal of Learning Difficulties* 19, no. 2 (2014): 75–91.
44. Belinda Luscombe, "The Massive Effort to Change the Way Kids Are Taught to Read," *Time*, August 11, 2022, https://time.com/6205084/phonics-science-of-reading-teachers/.
45. As scholars note, however, it is difficult to establish a causal link between parental investment and achievement. Frances Van Voorhis et al., "The Impact of Family Involvement on the Education of Children Ages 3 to 8 A Focus on Literacy and Math Achievement Outcomes and Social-Emotional Skills" (MDRC, October 2013), https://files.eric.ed.gov/fulltext/ED545474.pdf.
46. Ericka Mellon, "Some Schools Ditch Traditional Spelling Tests," *Houston Chronicle*, December 25, 2009, sec. Houston & Texas, www.chron.com/news/houston-texas/article/Some-schools-ditch-traditional-spelling-tests-1729815.php.
47. Mellon.

48. Mellon.
49. "Why Is English so Weirdly Different from Other Languages? – John McWhorter | Aeon Essays," Aeon, accessed September 30, 2020, https://aeon.co/essays/why-is-english-so-weirdly-different-from-other-languages.
50. Emily Stagg, "Opinion | Definition, D-E-F-I-N-I-T-I-O-N, Definition," *The New York Times*, May 31, 2006, sec. Opinion, www.nytimes.com/2006/05/31/opinion/31stagg.html.
51. Stagg.
52. William Strunk Jr and E. B. White, *The Elements of Style*, 4th edition (Independently published, 2022).
53. Geoffrey K. Pullum, "The Land of the Free and The Elements of Style," *English Today* 26, no. 2 (June 2010): 34–44, https://doi.org/10.1017/S0266078410000076.
54. Pullum.
55. Ian Jack, "So You Want to Write Better Sentences than Jane Austen? Take Some Lessons," *The Guardian*, May 27, 2017, sec. Opinion, www.theguardian.com/commentisfree/2017/may/27/write-better-sentences-jane-austen-lessons; Jim Holt, "The Value and Virtue of Good Writing (Rule No. 7: Don't Be a Bore)," *The New York Times*, May 17, 2017, sec. Books, www.nytimes.com/2017/05/17/books/review/do-i-make-myself-clear-harold-evans.html.
56. Steven Pinker, *The Sense of Style: The Thinking Person's Guide to Writing in the 21st Century* (Penguin, 2014).
57. David Foster Wallace, "Tense Present: Democracy, English, and the Wars over Usage," *Harper's Magazine* 302, no. 1811 (2001): 39–58.
58. Pullum, "The Land of the Free and The Elements of Style."
59. Kirk Hazen, *An Introduction to Language*, 1st edition (Malden, MA: Wiley-Blackwell, 2014), p. 333. See also James Milroy and Lesley Milroy, *Authority in Language: Investigating Standard English* (Routledge, 2012); Nils Langer and Agnete Nesse, "Linguistic Purism," *The Handbook of Historical Sociolinguistics*, 2012, 607–25.
60. David Marsh, "The Golden Age of Grammar Is a Myth," *The New Republic*, October 22, 2013, https://newrepublic.com/article/115280/golden-age-grammar-myth. David Marsh, "Why the "Golden Age" When Everyone Knew Their Grammar Is a Myth," *New Statesman* (blog), June 10, 2021, www.newstatesman.com/uncategorized/2013/10/forget-bad-

grammar-and-greengrocers-real-enemies-language-are-politicians-and-businesspeople.
61. Langer and Nesse, "Linguistic Purism," p. 617.
62. James Milroy, "Children Can't Speak or Write Properly Anymore," in *Language Myths*, ed. Laurie Bauer and Peter Trudgill, 0 edition (London; New York: Penguin Books, 1999), pp. 58–67.
63. James Milroy, "Variability, Language Change and the History of English," *International Journal of English Studies* 5, no. 1 (2005): 1–11.
64. Nick Bostrom and Toby Ord, "The Reversal Test: Eliminating Status Quo Bias in Applied Ethics," *Ethics* 116, no. 4 (2006): 656–79.
65. Rick Marin, "Grunge: A Success Story," *The New York Times*, November 15, 1992, sec. Style, www.nytimes.com/1992/11/15/style/grunge-a-success-story.html.

CHAPTER 2

1. Will Kymlicka and Alan Patten, "1. Language Rights and Political Theory," *Annual Review of Applied Linguistics* 23 (2003): 3–21.
2. *Meyer v. Nebraska* ruled in 1923 that these laws were unconstitutional, as were mandates for English-only education. For more on this see, e.g., John C. Maher, *Multilingualism: A Very Short Introduction* (Oxford University Press, 2017).
3. Alan Patten, *Equal Recognition: The Moral Foundations of Minority Rights* (Princeton University Press, 2014), p. 186.
4. And this process can reinforce itself as nationalist identities grow more salient. See, e.g., Eugen Weber, *Peasants into Frenchmen: The Modernization of Rural France, 1870-1914* (Stanford University Press, 1976), p. 89.
5. Paul Gomberg, "Patriotism Is Like Racism," *Ethics* 101, no. 1 (1990): 144–50.
6. Ken Hale, "Endangered Languages: On Endangered Languages and the Safeguarding of Diversity," *Language* 68, no. 1 (1992): 1–42; Anthony Woodbury, "Documenting Rhetorical Aesthetic and Expressive Loss in Language Shift," in *Endangered Languages: Language Loss and Community Response*, ed. Lenore A. Grenoble and Lindsay J. Whaley (Cambridge University Press, 1998).
7. Sue Wright, *Language Policy and Language Planning: From Nationalism to Globalisation* (Springer, 2016).

8. Daniel Nettle and Suzanne Romaine, *Vanishing Voices: The Extinction of the World's Languages* (Oxford: Oxford University Press, 2000).
9. Will Kymlicka, *Politics in the Vernacular: Nationalism, Multiculturalism, and Citizenship* (Oxford University Press, 2001), p. 41.
10. Suzanne Romaine, "Preserving Endangered Languages," *Language and Linguistics Compass* 1, no. 1–2 (2007): 115–32, https://doi.org/10.1111/j.1749-818X.2007.00004.x.
11. Catrin Fflur Huws, "The Welsh Language Act 1993: A Measure of Success?" *Language Policy* 5, no. 2 (June 1, 2006): 141–60, https://doi.org/10.1007/s10993-006-9000-0.
12. Heather Horn, "Assessing the Value of Dying Languages," *The Atlantic* (blog), December 19, 2009, www.theatlantic.com/national/archive/2009/12/assessing-the-value-of-dying-languages/347198/.
13. John Edwards, "Language Revitalization and Its Discontents: An Essay and Review of Saving Languages: An Introduction to Language Revitalization," 2007, https://journals.lib.unb.ca/index.php/CJAL/article/download/19736/21414.
14. Heather Horn, "Assessing the Value of Dying Languages."
15. These four arguments appear in Sue Wright's defense of language preservation Wright, *Language Policy and Language Planning*.
16. David Crystal, *Language Death*, Canto (Cambridge: Cambridge University Press, 2002), https://doi.org/10.1017/CBO9781139871549.
17. Patten, *Equal Recognition*, p. 203.
18. For a further argument to this effect see, Brian Barry, *Culture and Equality: An Egalitarian Critique of Multiculturalism* (John Wiley & Sons, 2013).
19. Patten, *Equal Recognition*, p. 208.
20. Patten, p. 6.
21. Wright, *Language Policy and Language Planning*, p. 272.
22. Consequentialists who claim that standards of blaming should simply promote overall wellbeing are a notable exception here.
23. For a helpful overview of how these categories matter for applied ethics, see Rae Langton, "Speech Acts and Unspeakable Acts," *Philosophy & Public Affairs* 22, no. 4 (1993): 293–330.
24. Daniela Dover, "The Walk and the Talk," *Philosophical Review* 128, no. 4 (2019): 387–422.
25. Kyle Wiens, "I Won't Hire People Who Use Poor Grammar. Here's Why," *Harvard Business Review*, July 20, 2012, https://hbr.org/2012/07/i-wont-hire-people-who-use-poo.

26. Simon Jeffery, "Rarely Is the Question Asked, Is Our Children Learning?" *The Guardian*, April 13, 2010, sec. Politics, www.theguardian.com/politics/blog/2010/apr/13/labour-spelling-mistake.
27. Steven Nelson, "Biden Misspells Number 8 as 'E-I-G-H' in Maryland Speech," NY Post, April 19, 2023, https://nypost.com/2023/04/19/biden-misspells-number-8-as-e-i-g-h-in-maryland-speech/.
28. Farhad Manjoo, "So Trump Makes Spelling Errors. In the Twitter Age, Whoo Doesn't?" *The New York Times*, August 27, 2017, sec. Technology, www.nytimes.com/2017/08/27/technology/donald-trump-twitter-spelling.html.
29. Susan Moller Okin, *Justice, Gender, and the Family*, 50843rd edition (New York: Basic Books, 1991).
30. Elizabeth Anderson, "Equality and Freedom in the Workplace: Recovering Republican Insights," *Social Philosophy & Policy* 31, no. 2 (2015): 48. Anca Gheaus, "Child-Rearing with Minimal Domination: A Republican Account," *Political Studies* 69, no. 3 (August 1, 2021): 748–66, https://doi.org/10.1177/0032321720906768.
31. Philip Pettit, Republicanism: A Theory of Freedom and Government (Clarendon Press, 1997).
32. Aaron James, "Power in Social Organization as the Subject of Justice," *Pacific Philosophical Quarterly* 86, no. 1 (2005): 25–49, https://doi.org/10.1111/j.1468-0114.2005.00213.x.
33. Laura Valentini, "Respect for Persons and the Moral Force of Socially Constructed Norms," *Noûs* 55, no. 2 (2021): 385–408, https://doi.org/10.1111/nous.12319.
34. Justin Tosi, "Relational Sufficientarianism and Basic Income," in *The Future of Work, Technology, and Basic Income* (Routledge, 2019). One might make a similar case in favor of free migration, free speech, free association, or economic freedom—protections which would blunt the harmful effects of violating norms in communities that would otherwise demand compliance.
35. Darwall, e.g., argues that advice is merely informative and that it is not disrespectful *per se* to either give nor to ignore advice. Rather, advice giving and receiving can convey appraisal of someone's epistemic authority while not taking a stand on their authority to decide for themselves. Stephen Darwall, "Respect and the Second-Person Standpoint," *Proceedings and Addresses of the American Philosophical Association* 78, no. 2 (2004): 43–59, https://doi.org/10.2307/3219724.

36. Horobin, *Does Spelling Matter?* p. 229.
37. In making this point in a more general way, Sarah Buss argues that "all else being equal, people have a basic moral obligation to make themselves agreeable to others." Sarah Buss, "Appearing Respectful: The Moral Significance of Manners," *Ethics* 109, no. 4 (1999): 795–826.
38. Max Plenke, "This Is What Bad Grammar Does to You're Brain," *Mic* (blog), October 21, 2015, www.mic.com/articles/127144/this-is-what-bad-grammar-does-to-youre-brain.
39. Bri Williams, "Why Misspelling a Name Is More of a Problem than You Realise," *SmartCompany*, July 30, 2018, www.smartcompany.com.au/marketing/networking/why-misspelling-name-more-problem-than-you-realise/.
40. Philippa Foot, "Morality as a System of Hypothetical Imperatives," *The Philosophical Review* 81, no. 3 (1972): 305–16.
41. Karen Stohr, for example, argues that impoliteness can be a sign that someone lacks a moral imagination, that they are insensitive to others, or that they have a deficient grasp of moral concepts. Karen Stohr, "Manners, Morals, and Practical Wisdom," in *Values and Virtues: Aristotelianism in Contemporary Ethics*, ed. Timothy Chappell (Clarendon Press, 2006).
42. Foot, "Morality as a System of Hypothetical Imperatives."
43. On this view, gaslighting is wrong because it causes someone to have a false view of their capacities. See, e.g., Cameron Domenico Kirk-Giannini, "Dilemmatic Gaslighting," *Philosophical Studies* 180, no. 3 (2022): 745–72, https://doi.org/10.1007/s11098-022-01872-9.
44. Abramson advances an account of the wrongfulness of gaslighting that emphasizes manipulation. Kate Abramson, "Turning up the Lights on Gaslighting," *Philosophical Perspectives* 28, no. 1 (2014): 1–30, https://doi.org/10.1111/phpe.12046.
45. Nora Berenstain, "White Feminist Gaslighting," *Hypatia* 35, no. 4 (2020): 733–58, https://doi.org/10.1017/hyp.2020.31.
46. Eric Beerbohm and Ryan W. Davis, "Gaslighting Citizens," *American Journal of Political Science* n/a, no. n/a, accessed May 5, 2023, https://doi.org/10.1111/ajps.12678.
47. Tell Harry Frankfurt that the word bullshit is unprofessional! Harry G. Frankfurt, *On Bullshit* (Princeton University Press, 2009), https://doi.org/10.1515/9781400826537.

48. Though, as an aside, people seem to swear nowadays more than ever! See Jean M. Twenge, Hannah VanLandingham, and W. Keith Campbell, "The Seven Words You Can Never Say on Television: Increases in the Use of Swear Words in American Books, 1950–2008," *SAGE* Open 7, no. 3 (July 1, 2017): 2158244017723689, https://doi.org/10.1177/2158244017723689.
49. Rebecca Roache, "Where Does Swearing Get Its Power – and How Should We Use It?" *Aeon*, n.d., https://aeon.co/essays/where-does-swearing-get-its-power-and-how-should-we-use-it.
50. Roache, "Where Does Swearing Get Its Power – and How Should We Use It?"
51. See, e.g., Chang Liu, "Slurs as Illocutionary Force Indicators," *Philosophia* 49, no. 3 (2020): 1051–65, https://doi.org/10.1007/s11406-020-00289-0; Cameron Domenico Kirk-Giannini, "Slurs Are Directives," Philosophers' Imprint 19 (2019): 1–28.
52. Roache, "Where Does Swearing Get Its Power – and How Should We Use It?"
53. Luvell Anderson and Ernie Lepore, "Slurring Words," *Noûs* 47, no. 1 (2013): 25–48.
54. Alec Greven and I expand on this point elsewhere. Jessica Flanigan and Alec Greven, "Speech and Campus Inclusivity," *Public Affairs Quarterly* 35, no. 3 (July 1, 2021): 178–203, https://doi.org/10.2307/48628247.
55. Joel Feinberg, *Offense to Others* (Oxford University Press, 1984).
56. Robert M. O'Neil, "Hate Speech, Fighting Words, and Beyond – Why American Law Is Unique Symposium: What Are We Saying – Violence, Vulgarity, Lies and the Importance of 21st Century Free Speech," *Albany Law Review* 76, no. 1 (2013 2012): 467–98.
57. *Street v. New York*, 394 US 576 (Supreme Court 1969).
58. *Terminiello v. Chicago*, 337 US 1 (Supreme Court 1949).

CHAPTER 3

1. Or at least that people should be disposed to relate as equals. For an overview of this view, see Carina Fourie, Fabian Schuppert, and Ivo Wallimann-Helmer, *Social Equality: On What It Means to Be Equals* (Oxford University Press, 2015).

2. Sophia Moreau, "What Is Discrimination?" *Philosophy & Public Affairs* 38, no. 2 (2010): 143–79, https://doi.org/10.1111/j.1088-4963.2010.01181.x.
3. Niko Kolodny, "Rule Over None II: Social Equality and the Justification of Democracy," *Philosophy & Public Affairs* 42, no. 4 (September 1, 2014): 287–336, https://doi.org/10.1111/papa.12037.
4. Anderson, "Equality and Freedom in the Workplace."
5. Charles R. Beitz, *Political Equality: An Essay in Democratic Theory* (Princeton University Press, 1989), p. 190.
6. James Wilson, for example, develops an instrumentalist argument for reforming existing institutions with an eye to establishing social equality in the service of creating a well-functioning democracy, which is then instrumental to further promoting social equality. *Democratic Equality*, 2019, https://press.princeton.edu/books/hardcover/9780691190914/democratic-equality.
7. Paul Fussell, *Class: A Guide through the American Status System* (Simon and Schuster, 1992), p. 151.
8. Jonathon Green, *Slang: A Very Short Introduction* (Oxford University Press, 2016), p. 71.
9. Cheryl J. Boucher et al., "Perceptions of Competency as a Function of Accent," *Psi Chi Journal of Psychological Research* 18, no. 1 (2013).
10. Fussell, *Class*, p. 168.
11. Amanda Montell, *Wordslut: A Feminist Guide to Taking Back the English Language* (HarperCollins, 2019), p. 137.
12. Brad Hoover, "Good Grammar Should Be Everyone's Business," *Harvard Business Review*, March 4, 2013, https://hbr.org/2013/03/good-grammar-should-be-everyon.
13. Kathleen Doheny, "When a Worker's Grammar and Spelling Are Embarrassing," SHRM, September 15, 2020, www.shrm.org/resourcesandtools/hr-topics/people-managers/pages/poor-grammar-and-spelling-.aspx.
14. Doheny, "When a Worker's Grammar and Spelling Are Embarrassing"; Catherine Rampell, "With Positions to Fill, Employers Wait for Perfection," *The New York Times*, March 6, 2013, sec. Business, www.nytimes.com/2013/03/07/business/economy/despite-job-vacancies-employers-shy-away-from-hiring.html; "Spelling Skill Test | Online Skills Test for Employment," *Skillsarena* (blog), accessed January 4, 2021, https://skillsarena.com/skills-tests/english/spelling/.

15. John Sullivan, "Rejecting Resumes with Spelling Errors: A Silly and Costly Hiring Mistake," ERE, February 10, 2020, www.ere.net/rejecting-resumes-with-spelling-errors-a-silly-and-costly-hiring-mistake/.
16. Quentin Fottrell, "3 Ways Bad Spelling Could Alter the Course of Your Life," MarketWatch, April 9, 2016, www.marketwatch.com/story/3-ways-bad-spelling-could-alter-the-course-of-your-life-2015-08-20.
17. Christelle Martin-Lacroux and Alain Lacroux, "Do Employers Forgive Applicants' Bad Spelling in Résumés?" Business and Professional Communication Quarterly 80, no. 3 (2017): 321–35.
18. Sullivan, "Rejecting Resumes with Spelling Errors."
19. Sullivan.
20. Jim Saksa, "What 'Your' vs. 'You're' Says about Congress Right Now," Roll Call, December 2, 2021, https://rollcall.com/2021/12/02/what-your-vs-youre-says-about-congress-right-now/.
21. Annie Linskey- Reporter, "Does Donald Trump Write His Own Tweets? Sometimes – The Boston Globe," BostonGlobe.Com, May 22, 2018, www.bostonglobe.com/news/nation/2018/05/21/trump-tweets-include-grammatical-errors-and-some-them-are-purpose/JeL7AtKLPevJDIIOMG7TrN/story.html.
22. Swift reaffirms her commitment to linguistic prescriptivism in the song "Me" where she exclaims "Hey kids, spelling is fun!" This line operates on two levels. On one hand she recognizes the absurdity of it and means it to read somewhat ironically. On the other hand, she then engages in a recitation of how to spell words, in an (unsuccessful) attempt to cast spelling as genuinely fun.
23. Montell, Wordslut, p. 80.
24. Jennifer Coates, Women, Men and Language: A Sociolinguistic Account of Gender Differences in Language, 3rd edition (Harlow; New York: Routledge, 2004).
25. Laura M. Ahearn, Living Language: An Introduction to Linguistic Anthropology (John Wiley & Sons, 2021), p. 223.
26. Liana Van Nostrand, "Sounding Like a Reporter—And a Real Person, Too," NPR, August 7, 2019, sec. Language, www.npr.org/sections/publiceditor/2019/08/07/749060986/sounding-like-a-reporter-and-a-real-person-too.
27. Lesley Wolk, Nassima B. Abdelli-Beruh, and Dianne Slavin, "Habitual Use of Vocal Fry in Young Adult Female Speakers," Journal of Voice 26, no. 3 (May 1, 2012): e111–16, https://doi.org/10.1016/j.jvoice.2011.04.007.

28. "From Upspeak to Vocal Fry: Are We 'Policing' Young Women's Voices?" *FreshAir* (NPR, July 23, 2015), www.npr.org/2015/07/23/425608745/from-upspeak-to-vocal-fry-are-we-policing-young-womens-voices.
29. "From Upspeak to Vocal Fry."
30. Andrea Scheuringer, Ramona Wittig, and Belinda Pletzer, "Sex Differences in Verbal Fluency: The Role of Strategies and Instructions," *Cognitive Processing* 18, no. 4 (2017): 407–17, https://doi.org/10.1007/s10339-017-0801-1.
31. For a critical overview see Kristina Sommerlund, "Critical Overview: Gender and Tentative Language," *Leviathan: Interdisciplinary Journal in English*, no. 1 (2017).
32. Jennifer Coates, *Women, Men and Language: A Sociolinguistic Account of Gender Differences in Language* (Routledge, 2015), pp. 89–91.
33. John McWhorter, "The Linguistic Evolution of 'Like,'" *The Atlantic*, November 25, 2016, www.theatlantic.com/entertainment/archive/2016/11/the-evolution-of-like/507614/.
34. Rudolf P. Gaudio, "Sounding Gay: Pitch Properties in the Speech of Gay and Straight Men," *American Speech* 69, no. 1 (1994): 30–57, https://doi.org/10.2307/455948.
35. Arianne E. Miller, "Searching for Gaydar: Blind Spots in the Study of Sexual Orientation Perception," *Psychology & Sexuality* 9, no. 3 (July 3, 2018): 188–203, https://doi.org/10.1080/19419899.2018.1468353.
36. "What Does It Mean to Sound Gay?" *The New Republic*, accessed August 19, 2024, https://newrepublic.com/article/122287/what-does-it-mean-sound-gay.
37. *Do I Sound Gay?* (IFC/Sundance, 2014), www.doisoundgay.com.
38. "Stigmatization of 'Gay-sounding' Voices: The Role of Heterosexual, Lesbian, and Gay Individuals' Essentialist Beliefs - Fasoli - 2021 - British Journal of Social Psychology - Wiley Online Library," accessed July 7, 2022, https://bpspsychub.onlinelibrary.wiley.com/doi/full/10.1111/bjso.12442.
39. See, e.g., Ana Beatriz Gomes Fontenele, Luana Elayne Cunha de Souza, and Fabio Fasoli, "Who Does Discriminate Against Gay-Sounding Speakers? The Role of Prejudice on Voice-Based Hiring Decisions in Brazil," *Journal of Language and Social Psychology*, June 30, 2022, 0261927X221077243, https://doi.org/10.1177/0261927X221077243.

40. Ana Swanson, "What It Means to 'Sound Gay,'" *Washington Post*, November 25, 2021, www.washingtonpost.com/news/wonk/wp/2015/07/28/what-it-means-to-sound-gay/.
41. David Thorpe, "Video: Opinion | Who Sounds Gay?" *The New York Times*, June 23, 2015, sec. Opinion, www.nytimes.com/video/opinion/100000003757238/who-sounds-gay.html.
42. *Do I Sound Gay?*
43. Kelly Servick, "Where Did the 'Gay Lisp' Stereotype Come From?" November 9, 2015, www.science.org/content/article/where-did-gay-lisp-stereotype-come.
44. David Sedaris, "Go Carolina," *Me Talk Pretty One Day* (New York: Little, Brown and Company, 2000).
45. Guy Branum, "Opinion | My Gay Voice," *The New York Times*, July 28, 2018, sec. Opinion, www.nytimes.com/2018/07/28/opinion/sunday/my-gay-voice.html.
46. *Do I Sound Gay?*
47. *Do I Sound Gay?*; Branum, "Opinion | My Gay Voice."
48. Jeff Gordinier, "Hollywood's Secret Weapon for Losing the Gay Accent," *Details*, May 19, 2019, www.corffvoice.com/wp-content/uploads/Details-Bob-Corff-Article-5-2010.pdf.
49. David Adger, *Language Unlimited: The Science Behind Our Most Creative Power* (Oxford: Oxford University Press, 2019), pp. 234–6.
50. Paul Baker, "A Brief History of Polari: The Curious after-Life of the Dead Language for Gay Men," *The Conversation*, February 8, 2017, http://theconversation.com/a-brief-history-of-polari-the-curious-after-life-of-the-dead-language-for-gay-men-72599.
51. Salina Cuddy, "Can Women 'Sound Gay'?: A Sociophonetic Study of /s/ and Pitch of Gay and Straight British-English Speaking Women" (PhD Thesis, University of York, 2019), https://etheses.whiterose.ac.uk/27430/; Simone Sulpizio et al., "Auditory Gaydar: Perception of Sexual Orientation Based on Female Voice," *Language and Speech* 63, no. 1 (March 2020): 184–206, https://doi.org/10.1177/0023830919828201; John Van Borsel, Jana Vandaele, and Paul Corthals, "Pitch and Pitch Variation in Lesbian Women," *Journal of Voice: Official Journal of the Voice Foundation* 27, no. 5 (September 2013): 656.e13–16, https://doi.org/10.1016/j.jvoice.2013.04.008.

52. Chloe Willis, "Bisexuality and/s/Production," *Proceedings of the Linguistic Society of America* 6, no. 1 (2021): 69–81; Mariya Yoshovska, "Understanding the Speech Cues to Bisexuals," *The Journal of the Acoustical Society of America* 143, no. 3_Supplement (March 1, 2018): 1970, https://doi.org/10.1121/1.5036491; James S. Morandini et al., "BIDAR: Can Listeners Detect If a Man Is Bisexual from His Voice Alone?," *The Journal of Sex Research* 60, no. 5 (June 13, 2023): 611–23, https://doi.org/10.1080/00224499.2023.2182267.

53. Servick, "Where Did the 'Gay Lisp' Stereotype Come From?"

54. Hyung-Tae Kim, "Vocal Feminization for Transgender Women: Current Strategies and Patient Perspectives," International Journal of General Medicine 13 (February 12, 2020): 43–52, https://doi.org/10.2147/IJGM.S205102.

55. "English with an Accent: Language, Ideology and Discrimination in the United States," Routledge & CRC Press, accessed July 15, 2022, www.routledge.com/English-with-an-Accent-Language-Ideology-and-Discrimination-in-the-United/Lippi-Green/p/book/9780415559119.

56. Faye K. Cocchiara, Myrtle P. Bell, and Wendy J. Casper, "Sounding 'Different': The Role of Sociolinguistic Cues in Evaluating Job Candidates," *Human Resource Management* 55, no. 3 (2016): 463–77, https://doi.org/10.1002/hrm.21675.

57. https://cdn.ncte.org/nctefiles/groups/cccc/newsrtol.pdf

58. *Martin Luther King Jr., etc. v. Ann Arbor Sch. Dist.*, 473 F. Supp. 1371 (Dist. Court, ED Michigan 1979).

59. "Full Text of 'Ebonics' Resolution Adopted by Oakland Board," *Education Week*, January 15, 1997, sec. Equity & Diversity, www.edweek.org/leadership/full-text-of-ebonics-resolution-adopted-by-oakland-board/1997/01.

60. Walt Wolfram, "Language Ideology and Dialect: Understanding the Oakland Ebonics Controversy," *Journal of English Linguistics* 26, no. 2 (June 1, 1998): 108–21, https://doi.org/10.1177/007542429802600203.

61. John McWhorter, *What Language Is* (New York: Gotham, 2011), p. 128.

62. McWhorter, p. 131.

63. McWhorter, pp. 163–6.

64. Katherine D. Kinzler and Jasmine M. DeJesus, "Northern = Smart and Southern = Nice: The Development of Accent Attitudes in the United

States," *Quarterly Journal of Experimental Psychology* 66, no. 6 (June 1, 2013): 1146–58, https://doi.org/10.1080/17470218.2012.731695.

65. Devyani Sharma, "British People Still Think Some Accents Are Smarter than Others – What That Means in the Workplace," *The Conversation*, accessed July 14, 2022, http://theconversation.com/british-people-still-think-some-accents-are-smarter-than-others-what-that-means-in-the-workplace-126964.

66. Kate Cooper, "The English Obsession with Accents is Bad for Business," *Forbes*, accessed May 5, 2023, www.forbes.com/sites/katecooper/2020/02/04/the-english-obsession-with-accents-is-bad-for-business/.

67. Jennifer M. Morton, "Cultural Code-Switching: Straddling the Achievement Gap," *Journal of Political Philosophy* 22, no. 3 (2014): 259–81, https://doi.org/10.1111/jopp.12019.

68. For a further discussion of this issue see Jamelle Bouie, "Talking White," *Slate*, October 1, 2014, https://slate.com/news-and-politics/2014/10/talking-white-black-peoples-disdain-for-proper-english-and-academic-achievement-is-a-myth.html.

69. Adger, *Language Unlimited*, p. 238; Jennifer Smith, "'You Ø Na Hear o' That Kind o' Things': Negative Do in Buckie Scots," *English World-Wide* 21, no. 2 (January 1, 2000): 231–59, https://doi.org/10.1075/eww.21.2.04smi.

70. Jennifer Jenkins, "Global Intelligibility and Local Diversity: Possibility or Poroolox," in *English in the World: Global Rules, Global Roles*, ed. Rani Rubdy and Mario Saraceni (Bloomsbury Publishing, 2006).

71. Gerrit B. Smith, "I Want to Speak Like a Native Speaker: The Case for Lowering the Plaintiff's Burden of Proof in Title VII Accent Discrimination Cases Note," *Ohio State Law Journal* 66, no. 1 (2005): 231–68.

72. Erich Hatala Matthes, "Cultural Appropriation and Oppression," *Philosophical Studies* 176 (2019): 1003–13.

73. C. Thi Nguyen and Matthew Strohl, "Cultural Appropriation and the Intimacy of Groups," *Philosophical Studies* 176, no. 4 (April 1, 2019): 981–1002, https://doi.org/10.1007/s11098-018-1223-3.

74. Richard A. Rogers, "From Cultural Exchange to Transculturation: A Review and Reconceptualization of Cultural Appropriation," *Communication Theory* 16, no. 4 (2006): 474–503.

75. Laura M. Ahearn, *Living Language: An Introduction to Linguistic Anthropology*, 3rd edition (Hoboken, NJ: Wiley-Blackwell, 2021), pp. 252–3.

76. C. A. Cutler, "Crossing over: White Youth, Hip-Hop and African American English," 2003, 1, p. 213.
77. Jeff Guo, "How Iggy Azalea Mastered Her 'Blaccent,'" *Washington Post*, November 25, 2021, www.washingtonpost.com/news/wonk/wp/2016/01/04/how-a-white-australian-rapper-mastered-her-blaccent/.
78. CNN Staff, "What a 'blaccent' Is, and Why It's Wrong," CNN, February 8, 2022, www.cnn.com/2022/02/08/entertainment/blaccent-explainer-cec/index.html.
79. Steffi Cao, "Awkwafina's Statement Finally Addressing Her 'Blaccent' Controversy Is Drawing More Backlash," *BuzzFeed News* (blog), February 6, 2022, www.buzzfeed.com/stefficao/awkwafina-blaccent-appropriation-backlash.
80. For a further argument about the complexities involving making claims of collective ownership over culture, see James O. Young, *Cultural Appropriation and the Arts*, 1st edition (Chichester: Wiley-Blackwell, 2010).
81. For a compelling counterpoint to this claim, see C. Thi Nguyen and Matthew Strohl, "Cultural Appropriation and the Intimacy of Groups," *Philosophical Studies* 176, no. 4 (April 1, 2019): 981–1002, https://doi.org/10.1007/s11098-018-1223-3.
82. Lisa Green and Thomas Roeper, "The Acquisition Path for Tense-Aspect: Remote Past and Habitual in Child African American English," *Language Acquisition* 14, no. 3 (2007): 269–313; Janice E. Jackson and Lisa Green, "Tense and Aspectual Be in Child African American English," *Perspectives on Aspect* (2005): 233–50.
83. Adger, *Language Unlimited*, p. 246.
84. Adger, p. 246.
85. Montell, *Wordslut*, p. 85.
86. James O. Young, "Profound Offense and Cultural Appropriation," *The Journal of Aesthetics and Art Criticism* 63, no. 2 (2005): 135–46.
87. For an example of pronoun debates in another language (Swedish) see Nathalie Rothschild, "Sweden's New Gender-Neutral Pronoun: Hen," *Slate*, April 11, 2012, https://slate.com/human-interest/2012/04/hen-swedens-new-gender-neutral-pronoun-causes-controversy.html.
88. See, e.g., David McConnell who was initially fined for publicly misgendering someone in the UK before his sentence was overturned. "Leeds Preacher's Sentence for Trans Woman's Harassment Quashed," March 9, 2023, www.bbc.com/news/uk-england-leeds-64905216.

89. "Opinion | Gender-Neutral Pronouns: The Singular 'They' and Alternatives," *The New York Times*, October 9, 2021, sec. Opinion, www.nytimes.com/2021/10/09/opinion/letters/gender-neutral-pronouns.html.
90. Jessica A. Clarke, "They, Them, and Theirs," *Harvard Law Review* 132, no. 3 (2019 2018): 894–991.
91. For a further discussion of this aspect of the ethics of pronouns see Cameron Domenico Kirk-Giannini and Michael Glanzberg, "Pronouns and Gender," in *The Oxford Handbook of Applied Philosophy of Language*, ed. Luvell Anderson and Ernie LePore (Oxford University Press, n.d.).
92. Paul Sacca, "Matt Walsh Joins Gender Pronoun Debate on Dr Phil," *TheBlaze* (blog), January 20, 2022, www.theblaze.com/news/matt-walsh-dr-phil-gender-pronoun-debate.
93. Robin Dembroff and Daniel Wodak, "He/She/They/Ze," *Ergo: An Open Access Journal of Philosophy* 5 (2018), https://doi.org/10.3998/ergo.12405314.0005.014.
94. "Why I'm Done with 'Preferred Pronouns,'" *National Review* (blog), June 5, 2023, www.nationalreview.com/2023/06/why-im-done-with-preferred-pronouns/.
95. In this way, the argument against pronoun requirements is similar to the complicity-based arguments against using slurs that I discussed in the previous section on offense.
96. Jonathan Franklin, "A University Pays $400K to Professor Who Refused to Use a Student's Pronouns," NPR, April 20, 2022, sec. Education, www.npr.org/2022/04/20/1093601721/shawnee-state-university-lawsuit-pronouns.
97. "Why I Don't Have Pronouns In My Bio. | Practical Ethics," October 2, 2023, https://blog.practicalethics.ox.ac.uk/2023/10/why-i-dont-have-pronouns-in-my-bio/.
98. Colin Wright, "When Asked 'What Are Your Pronouns,' Don't Answer," *Reality's Last Stand* (blog), February 1, 2021, www.realityslaststand.com/p/when-asked-what-are-your-pronouns.
99. Wright.
100. Jason McBride, "A Professor's Refusal to Use Gender-Neutral Pronouns, and the Vicious Campus War That Followed," *Toronto Life* (blog), January 25, 2017, https://torontolife.com/city/u-t-professor-sparked-vicious-battle-gender-neutral-pronouns/.
101. Dembroff and Wodak, "He/She/They/Ze."

102. Nina Dragicevic, "Canada's Gender Identity Rights Bill C-16 Explained," CBC, 2018, www.cbc.ca/cbcdocspov/features/canadas-gender-identity-rights-bill-c-16-explained; Matt Gonzales, "LGBTQ Inclusion: Using Pronouns at Work," *Society for Human Resource Management* (blog), September 9, 2022, www.shrm.org/resourcesandtools/hr-topics/behavioral-competencies/global-and-cultural-effectiveness/pages/lgbtq-inclusion-using-pronouns-at-work.aspx.

103. McBride, "A Professor's Refusal to Use Gender-Neutral Pronouns, and the Vicious Campus War That Followed."

104. "How Gender Stereotypes Are Built into Mandarin," *The Economist*, accessed May 2, 2023, www.economist.com/the-economist-explains/2018/09/06/how-gender-stereotypes-are-built-into-mandarin.

105. Ives Goddard, "Grammatical Gender in Algonquian," *Algonquian Papers-Archive* 33 (2002).

106. Francesca Di Garbo and Yvonne Agbetsoamedo, "Non-Canonical Gender in African Languages: A Typological Survey of Interactions between Gender and Number, and between Gender and Evaluative Morphology," in *Non-Canonical Gender Systems*, ed. Sebastian Fedden, Jenny Audring, and Greville G. Corbett (Oxford University Press, 2018), 0, https://doi.org/10.1093/oso/9780198795438.003.0008.

107. P. J.L. Frankl, "The Indifference to Gender in Swahili and Other Bantu Languages: Part 2 in Consultation with Yahya Ali Omar," *South African Journal of African Languages* 13, no. 3 (January 1993): 85–9, https://doi.org/10.1080/02572117.1993.10586970.

108. Victor Mair, "Misogyny as Reflected in Chinese Characters," *Language Log* (blog), December 25, 2015, https://languagelog.ldc.upenn.edu/nll/?p=23043.

109. Montel, *Wordslut*, p. 145.

110. Webb Phillips, "Can Quirks of Grammar Affect the Way You Think? Grammatical Gender and Object Concepts," January 1, 2003.

111. Lera Boroditsky, Lauren Schmidt, and Phillips Webb, "Sex, Syntax, and Semantics," in *Language in Mind: Advances in the Study of Language and Thought*, ed. Dedre Gentner and Susan Goldin-Meadow, vol. 22 (MIT Press, 2003), pp. 61–79.

112. Grigorios Petsos, "(Gender) Stars in Their Eyes," kontextor, August 31, 2021, www.kontextor.org/en/blog/gender-stars/.

113. Christopher F. Schuetze, "'Gender Star' Stirs Linguistic Conservatives to Battle in Germany," *The New York Times*, March 7, 2019, sec. World, www.nytimes.com/2019/03/07/world/europe/germany-language-gender.html.
114. Marc Caputo and Sabrina Rodriguez, "Democrats Fall Flat with 'Latinx' Language," *Politico*, December 6, 2021, www.politico.com/news/2021/12/06/hispanic-voters-latinx-term-523776.
115. Montell, *Wordslut*, p. 17.
116. Brian D. Earp, "The Extinction of Masculine Generics," *Journal for Communication and Culture* 2, no. 1 (2012): 4–19.
117. Blocked and Reported, "Episode 136: How The Left Can Fight Cancel Culture (With Clementine Morrigan)," October 22, 2022, www.blockedandreported.org/p/episode-136-how-the-left-can-fight.
118. Joe Pinsker, "The Problem With 'Hey Guys,'" *The Atlantic*, August 23, 2018, www.theatlantic.com/family/archive/2018/08/guys-gender-neutral/568231/.
119. Steven Pinker, "Opinion | The Game of the Name," *The New York Times*, April 5, 1994, sec. Opinion, www.nytimes.com/1994/04/05/opinion/the-game-of-the-name.html.
120. Pinker.
121. Elizabeth Anderson, "The Problem of Equality from a Political Economy Perspective: The Long View of History," in *Oxford Studies in Political Philosophy*, Volume 3, ed. David Sobel, Peter Vallentyne, and Steven Wall (Oxford University Press, 2017), 0, https://doi.org/10.1093/oso/9780198801221.003.0003.
122. R. I. M. Dunbar, "Structure and Function in Human and Primate Social Networks: Implications for Diffusion, Network Stability and Health," *Proceedings of the Royal Society A: Mathematical, Physical and Engineering Sciences* 476, no. 2240 (August 26, 2020): 20200446, https://doi.org/10.1098/rspa.2020.0446.
123. Katherine D. Kinzler and Jocelyn B. Dautel, "Children's Essentialist Reasoning about Language and Race," *Developmental Science* 15, no. 1 (2012): 131–38, https://doi.org/10.1111/j.1467-7687.2011.01101.x.
124. Daniel L. Everett, *How Language Began: The Story of Humanity's Greatest Invention* (Liveright Publishing, 2017), p. 102–3.

CHAPTER 4

1. Laurel Brehm, Carrie N. Jackson, and Karen L. Miller, "Speaker-Specific Processing of Anomalous Utterances," *Quarterly Journal of Experimental Psychology* 72, no. 4 (April 1, 2019): 764–78, https://doi.org/10.1177/1747021818765547.
2. On this point, a grammando may reply that "I seen you there" actually is unclear because it could be interpreted as "saw" or "have seen" and those two interpretations have different meanings. Three replies. First, people can typically use context clues to figure out which meaning of "I seen" is implicit in the sentence and many grammatically correct sentences are sensitive to context for their correct interpretation as well. Second, the kind of person who would make such a finicky point when, clearly, they do in fact know what a person who says "I seen you there" meant is exactly the kind of person I'm talking about here. And third, if you are the kind of person who would think this and then look at a footnote to see if I address it, I'm afraid that you are so far gone down the path of pedantry that I'm not even sure that this book can help you.
3. Hungarian, Russian, Arabic, and Hebrew omit verbs from sentences in some contexts. This was also common in ancient languages like ancient Greek, Latin, and Old Persian, where verbs could be inferred from context even if they were not stated explicitly in a sentence.
4. Daniel Everett, *How Language Began: The Story of Humanity's Greatest Invention* (Profile Books, 2017), p. xv.
5. Guy Deutscher, *The Unfolding of Language: An Evolutionary Tour of Mankind's Greatest Invention* (Macmillan, 2005), p. 56–8.
6. Gaston Dorren, *Babel: Around the World in Twenty Languages* (Atlantic Monthly Press, 2018), p. 229.
7. James Essinger, *Spellbound: The Surprising Origins and Astonishing Secrets of English Spelling* (Delta, 2007), p. 170.
8. Essinger.
9. Wolman, *Righting the Mother Tongue*, p. 22.
10. Wolman, p. 22.
11. A. Joseph McMullen, "Forr Þeȝȝre Sawle Need: The Ormulum, Vernacular Theology and a Tradition of Translation in Early England," *English Studies* 95, no. 3 (April 3, 2014): 256–77, https://doi.org/10.1080/0013838X.2014.897074.

12. Christopher Cannon, "Spelling Practice: The Ormulum and the Word," *Forum for Modern Language Studies* XXXIII, no. 3 (July 1, 1997): 229–44, https://doi.org/10.1093/fmls/XXXIII.3.229.
13. Wolman, *Righting the Mother Tongue*, p. 41.
14. Richard L. Venezky, *The American Way of Spelling: The Structure and Origins of American English Orthography*, 1st edition (New York: The Guilford Press, 1999), p. 214.
15. Venezky.
16. Wolman, *Righting the Mother Tongue*, p. 103.
17. Venezky, The American Way of Spelling, p. 223; Wolman, *Righting the Mother Tongue*, p. 113.
18. See, e.g., The English Spelling Society spellingsociety.org
19. Horobin, *Does Spelling Matter?*
20. Horobin, pp. 225–8.
21. Richard Futrell, Kyle Mahowald, and Edward Gibson, "Large-Scale Evidence of Dependency Length Minimization in 37 Languages," *Proceedings of the National Academy of Sciences* 112, no. 33 (August 18, 2015): 10336–41, https://doi.org/10.1073/pnas.1502134112.
22. Michael Balter, "All Languages Have Evolved to Have This in Common," August 3, 2015, www.science.org/content/article/all-languages-have-evolved-have-common.
23. Noam Chomsky, "Some Methodological Remarks on Generative Grammar," *Word* 17, no. 2 (January 1961): 219–39, https://doi.org/10.1080/00437956.1961.11659755; Jon Sprouse, "Acceptability Judgments and Grammaticality, Prospects and Challenges," in *Syntactic Structures after 60 Years: The Impact of the Chomskyan Revolution in Linguistics*, ed. Norbert Hornstein et al. (De Gruyter Mouton, 2018), pp. 195–224, https://doi.org/10.1515/9781501506925-199.
24. John McWhorter, The Power of Babel: A Natural History of Language, softcover edition (New York: Harper Perennial, 2003), p. 18.
25. McWhorter, p. 22.
26. Morris Alper, "UNIKUD: Adding Vowels to Hebrew Text with Deep Learning," *Medium*, May 8, 2022, https://towardsdatascience.com/unikud-adding-vowels-to-hebrew-text-with-deep-learning-powered-by-dagshub-56d238e22d3f.
27. Adrienne R. Washington, "Orthography Matters!: The Ideologies, Insecurities and Global Politics of the 1990 Portuguese Language

Orthographic Agreement," *Journal of World Languages* 5, no. 3 (2018): 206–33.
28. Janet Barnes, "Evidentials in the Tuyuca Verb," *International Journal of American Linguistics* 50, no. 3 (1984): 255–71.
29. Chihon-GO!, "Korean and Japanese Particle and Grammar Similarities!," Medium (blog), October 10, 2019, https://medium.com/@nathanchinster/korean-and-japanese-particle-and-grammar-similarities-9ad0d9e48e71.
30. Genesis 11:1–9.
31. For accounts of similar Sumerian and Mexican myths that involve building a monument and a 'confusion of tounges" see e.g., Samuel Noah Kramer, "The 'Babel of Tongues': A Sumerian Version," *Journal of the American Oriental Society* 88, no. 1 (1968): 108–11, https://doi.org/10.2307/597903. and Geoffrey G. McCafferty, "Mountain of Heaven, Mountain of Earth: The Great Pyramid of Cholula as Sacred Landscape," in *Landscape and Power in Ancient Mesoamerica* (Routledge, 2001).
32. Michael Oakeshott, "The Tower of Babel," *Rationalism in Politics and Other Essays*, 1991, 465–87.
33. Christopher Norris, Review of Difference in Translation, by Joseph F. Graham, *Comparative Literature* 40, no. 1 (1988): 52–8, https://doi.org/10.2307/1770642.
34. This was an initial aspiration of the Esperanto movement.
35. Gaston Dorren, *Babel: Around the World in Twenty Languages* (Atlantic Monthly Press, 2018), p. 327.
36. For a discussion of how this may affect the dominance of English as a lingua franca see Dorren, p. 339; Kan, "Google Debuts Smart Glasses Built with Real-Time Language Translation," *PCMAG*, May 11, 2022, www.pcmag.com/news/google-debuts-smart-glasses-built-with-real-time-language-translation.
37. Herbert George Wells, *Certain Personal Matters: A Collection of Material, Mainly Autobiographical* (Lawrence & Bullen, Limited, 16, Henrietta Street, Covent Garden, WC, 1898),
38. Horobin, *Does Spelling Matter?* p. 225.
39. By and The Understood Team, "Dav Pilkey Sees ADHD and Dyslexia as His Superpowers," *Understood* (blog), October 16, 2019, www.understood.org/en/articles/dav-pilkey-adhd-dyslexia-superpowers.
40. Pam Gann, "The Book I Won't Let My Son Read," accessed May 12, 2023, www.pamgann.com/the-book/.

41. Megan Garber, "Why Everyone's Saying 'YAAAAAASSSSSS' Now," *The Atlantic*, April 10, 2015, www.theatlantic.com/technology/archive/2015/04/how-to-say-yes-by-not-saying-yes/390129/.
42. Oxford Dictionary Online is different from the Oxford English Dictionary, which is a historical record of the English language.
43. https://en.oxforddictionaries.com/word-of-the-year/word-of-the-year-2015
44. Marcel Danesi, *The Semiotics of Emoji: The Rise of Visual Language in the Age of the Internet* (Bloomsbury Publishing, 2016).
45. Gretchen McCulloch, *Because Internet: Understanding the New Rules of Language* (Penguin, 2019).
46. Danesi, *The Semiotics of Emoji*.
47. McCulloch, *Because Internet*.
48. McCulloch, p. 153.
49. The national weather service no longer writes in caps for just this reason! Jason Samenow, "All Caps off: Weather Service Will Stop SHOUTING AT US on May 11," *Washington Post*, December 4, 2021, www.washingtonpost.com/news/capital-weather-gang/wp/2016/04/12/all-caps-off-weather-service-will-stop-shouting-at-us-on-may-11/.
50. McCulloch, *Because Internet*, p. 225.
51. Denver Nicks, "'Donut' vs. 'Doughnut:' The Most Delicious Spelling Bee of All Time Rages On," *Time*, June 6, 2014, https://time.com/2837756/donut-or-doughnut/.
52. Horobin, *Does Spelling Matter?* p. 225.
53. Molly Young, "Why Do Corporations Speak the Way They Do?" *Vulture* (blog), February 20, 2020, www.vulture.com/2020/02/spread-of-corporate-speak.html.
54. Mark Morgioni, "Defending 'Garbage Language,' the Silly Corporate Terminology That Seriously Works," *Slate*, February 20, 2020, https://slate.com/human-interest/2020/02/garbage-language-business-speak-defense.html.
55. Jonathan Franzen, "What's Wrong with the Modern World," *The Guardian* 13 (2013), www.theguardian.com/books/2013/sep/13/jonathan-franzen-wrong-modern-world.
56. Franzen.
57. Franzen.
58. Zadie Smith, "Generation Why? | Zadie Smith," accessed May 12, 2023, www.nybooks.com/articles/2010/11/25/generation-why/.

59. Samuel Scheffler, *Equality and Tradition: Questions of Value in Moral and Political Theory* (Oxford University Press, 2010).
60. Alexander H. Jordan and Benoît Monin, "From Sucker to Saint: Moralization in Response to Self-Threat," *Psychological Science* 19 (2008): 809–15, https://doi.org/10.1111/j.1467-9280.2008.02161.x.

CHAPTER 5

1. Thomas E. Hill, "Moral Responsibilities of Bystanders," *Journal of Social Philosophy* 41, no. 1 (2010): 28–39.
2. Samuel Scheffler, "The Practice of Equality," in *Social Equality: Essays on What It Means to Be Equals*, ed. Carina Fourie, Fabian Schuppert, and Ivo Wallimann-Helmer (Oxford University Press, 2015), 20–44, https://doi.org/10.1093/acprof:oso/9780199331109.003.0002.
3. James L. Wilson, "An Autonomy-Based Argument for Democracy," in *Oxford Studies in Political Philosophy* Volume 7, ed. David Sobel, Peter Vallentyne, and Steven Wall (Oxford University Press, 2021).
4. Matthew J. X. Malady, "Are You a Language Bully?" *Slate*, September 5, 2013, https://slate.com/human-interest/2013/09/language-bullies-pedants-and-grammar-nerds-who-correct-people-all-the-time-cut-it-out.html.
5. Kevin Simler and Robin Hanson, *The Elephant in the Brain: Hidden Motives in Everyday Life*, illustrated edition (New York: Oxford University Press, 2018).
6. Julie E. Boland and Robin Queen, "If You're House Is Still Available, Send Me an Email: Personality Influences Reactions to Written Errors in Email Messages," *PLOS ONE* 11, no. 3 (March 9, 2016): e0149885, https://doi.org/10.1371/journal.pone.0149885.
7. Marie Hennecke et al., "A Three-Part Framework for Self-Regulated Personality Development across Adulthood," *European Journal of Personality* 28, no. 3 (2014): 289–99, https://doi.org/10.1002/per.1945.
8. "If You Don't like Your Personality, You Can Change It," *Big Think* (blog), December 14, 2021, https://bigthink.com/neuropsych/big-five-personality-change/.
9. Javier Hidalgo, "Cosmopolitan Moral Enhancement," in *The Ethics of Ability and Enhancement*, ed. Jessica Flanigan and Terry L. Price, 1st edition (New York: Palgrave Macmillan, 2017).

10. Freddie deBoer, "Planet of Cops," Substack newsletter, *Freddie deBoer* (blog), August 25, 2021, https://freddiedeboer.substack.com/p/planet-of-cops.
11. R. Jay Wallace, "Hypocrisy, Moral Address, and the Equal Standing of Persons," *Philosophy & Public Affairs* 38, no. 4 (2010): 307–41.
12. David Rodin, "The Reciprocity Theory of Rights," *Law and Philosophy* 33, no. 3 (2014): 281–308.
13. For a review essay about visibility and gay rights see Melissa R. Michelson, "The Power of Visibility: Advances in LGBT Rights in the United States and Europe," *The Journal of Politics* 81, no. 1 (January 2019): e1–5, https://doi.org/10.1086/700591.
14. Barbara Riddick, "Dyslexia and inclusion: Time for a social model of disability perspective?" *International Studies in Sociology of Education* 11, no. 3 (2001): 223–36.

Index

AAVE *see* African American Vernacular English
abbreviations 190
academic ability 27
academic bullying 36
Académie Française 167
accents: Indian 133; northern 127; perception of 127–8; southern 108, 120, 127
acceptability 178
achievement gaps 14, 17, 26
active listening 135
advertising 92, 191
advice 50, 75–81; ethics of 77–8; public 78; and social control 80–1; unsolicited 79
aesthetic quality 81, 82
affirmations 135
African Americans 125; *see also* Black Americans
African American Vernacular English (AAVE) 124–7, 129, 131–2, 134
African languages 148
agreeableness 203, 209, 210
Ahearn, Laura 125
Alfred the Great (King) 172
Algonquian languages 147
alphabetic languages 19
alphabets 172, 175, 189, 221
Anderson, Elizabeth 154
Angles 171
Anglo-Saxons 172; language 172–3
annunciation 108

anti-grammarianism 40, 63, 127, 168, 182, 184, 211, 216–20
Arabic 170
argument mapping 16
artificial intelligence (AI) 198
Asian Americans 131–2
ASL translations 19, 23
assistive technologies 21, 23, 24, 169; *see also* software; spellchecking technology
audio formats 22
Austen, Jane 34
Awkwafina 132
Ayaucuho Quechua 134
Azaria, Hank 133

Babel myth 182–3
behavioral disorders 25
Berenstain, Nora 90
Biden, Joe 68
bilingualism 22, 53, 57, 60, 69
bimodal approach 22–4
Blaccent 131–2; *see also* African American Vernacular English (AAVE)
Black Americans 132; *see also* African Americans; Black children; Black women
Black children 134
Black Lives Matter movement 127
Blackfeet Nation 57
BlacKkKlansman 129
Black women 135
blame 64–6, 71

bonding 93
brands 186, 191–2
Branum, Guy 121
Brown, Brookes 63
Bruce, Lenny 92
Buckie 129
Bush, George W. 68
bystanders 204–6, 215

Canada 53
Captain Underpants 186–7
captioning 22, 23
Carlin, George 92
Carnegie, Andrew 175
catechism 31
Catholic Church 196
children 4–5; Black 134; with disabilities 15, 18–27; dyslexic 15, 18–24; gay 120–1; and social status 154–5; spelling and grammar instructions for 9–10; White 134
China 54
Chinese language 19, 147, 148
Christianity 26–7
civic participation 13
civics education 11–12
civic solidarity 12, 13, 51
civic virtue 11, 12
civilizational collapse 195
class hierarchy 107, 113, 114
classism 113
Clemens, Samuel 175
club rules 86
Coates, Jennifer 117
code-switching 128–9
cognitive disorders 25
colonialization 171
common language 12, 183–4
common law 12
communicative styles 115–19
community-building 135
compliance 5, 14–15, 30, 37, 216; *see also* linguistic non-compliance

comprehension 5, 40
conscientiousness 14, 25, 111
conversational hedges 117
copyeditors 35, 65, 77, 172, 198
Cordelli, Chiara 63
Corff, Bob 122
credibility 66, 90, 113
critical grammar 127
critical thinking 5, 40
crosstalk 135
cultural appropriation 104, 131
cultural minorities 55; *see also* minority groups
cultural preservation 194
culture: of compliance 216; dominant 57, 95, 122, 131; educational 16–17; heterosexist 121–2, 130; intergenerational transmission of 196; oralist 19
curriculum 11, 13, 16–17

Danish 147
dating 70, 73
deaf education 21–3
deafness 19–20, 24–5
decency standards 92
deception 89
democratic participation 13
dependency length minimization (DLM) 176–7, 180
Derrida, Jacques 182
Deseret Alphabet 175
deviance: linguistic 78, 123–4, 184, 206; normalizing 218; social 140
dialects 12, 15, 25–6, 51; Buckie 129; and economic classes 107–8; in fiction 133; Polari 122; and race 124–7; regional 124, 127–30; Scottish 129
Dickens, Charles 185
Dickinson, Emily 186
dictation software 21, 22, 24
Digg 191

disabilities 6, 15, 18–27, 216–18
disability pride 216–18
disadvantage 70; economic 26, 112; social 17, 26, 62, 104, 130–1, 152–3, 205; socioeconomic 124
discrimination 69, 124, 127–8
disempowerment 90–1
dispositions 206–10
diversity 54, 55, 58, 183–4, 196, 210
DLM *see* dependency length minimization
DogMan 186
Dorren, Gaston 183
Dover, Daniella 66
drafts 16
Dunkin Donuts 191
dyslexia 186; bimodal approach 22–4; children with 15, 18–24; and deafness 19; as a disability 18, 19; and literacy instruction 18, 20–3

Ebonics 125; *see also* African American Vernacular English (AAVE)
e-books 194
economic disadvantage 26, 112
economic equality 13
economic mobility 12–13
editing software 198
education 5, 11–14; civics 11–12; deaf 21–3; and indoctrination 11; and justice 11; K-12 12; *see also* schools
educational culture 16–17
educational policy 124–5
educational standards 12
egalitarian disposition 204, 206–7
"egalitarian impulse" 154
egalitarianism 38, 72, 89; and language policing 104–6, 130, 134, 143–6, 150–5; relational 105; social 103–7, 154–5, 206–7; *see also* egalitarian disposition; "egalitarian impulse"
Ekert, Penny 116
Elements of Style, The 32, 35
emojis 168, 186, 188–189
employment 69, 111, 124, 128, 130, 220
England 122, 127–8
English 19, 56, 167; Black 125–6; in Canada 53; evidential marking in 181; grammatical genders in 146–7, 150; history of 171–6; as an international language 183–4; Middle 174, 176; Old 172, 173; spelling system 179–80; during WWI 52; *see also* African American Vernacular English (AAVE); Standard American English (SAE); Standard Written English (SWE)
equality 11, 13; economic 13; social 4, 13, 105–6, 116, 155; *see also* inequality
Essinger, James 172
esteem 71, 103; *see also* self-esteem
ethics: of advice-giving 77–8; of curriculum 11; of language policy 53; of legal sanctions 50; of linguistic communication 134; of social life 6; of social norms 72–5, 85; of social sanctions 50, 60–75
ethnicity 124–30
etiquette 73, 81–6; *see also* manners
euphemisms 152, 154
Evans, Sir Harold 34
Everett, Daniel 170
evidence-based approach 16–17, 19–21, 28
evidential marking 181
exclamation marks 118–19
exclusion 63–4, 70, 72, 206, 218

Faulkner, William 186
Feinberg, Joel 96–97
feminism 71
"fighting words" 96–7
filler words 116–17
Flickr 191
Foot, Philippa 83–4, 86
France 52–3
Franzen, Jonathan 193–6
freedom 106
French 52–3, 147, 148, 167, 173, 179
"Friday test, Monday miss" 28
Fussell, Paul 108, 109

Gaelic 56
Garbage Language 192
Garber, Megan 187–8
gaslighting 88–91
gay children 120–1
gay men 119–22, 124; see also homosexuality
gay rights 122, 216–18
gay voice 119–23
gender 114–19; and communicative styles 115–19; grammatical 146–51; identity 123, 136–40, 142; inequalities 71; stereotypes 141, 142, 148–9, 150; see also men; trans people; women
German 147, 148, 149
Germanic tribes 171
Golden Age 37–40, 178
golf 86–8
Google 111
grammar errors 110–11, 209, 210; see also spelling errors
grammarianism 2, 4, 7, 50, 61, 69, 75, 78, 81, 82, 168, 211, 215; and class divides 109–10; as a form of gaslighting 88–91; and personality traits 209; and women's social equality 116; political 216; resisting 205–6; see also anti-grammarianism; sticklerism
Grammarly 110
grammatical genders, 146–51
grammaticality 178
Grathwohl, Casper 188
Greek 147
Grindr 191
group-cohesion 93
grunge slang 39
Guttenberg, Johannes 174

"habitual be" 134, 179
hand tremors 23
handwriting 23
health workers 77
Hebrew 179
heterosexism 74, 120, 121, 122
Hill, Fiona 127–8
Hill, Thomas 204–6, 208
Hindi 147
hip-hop 132
Hirsch, E.D. 12
Holywhitemountain, Sterling 57
homework 26, 30
Homo erectus 170
homophobia 120, 121, 122
homosexuality 119, 122, 124, 216
Hoover, Brad 110
Horobin, Simon 175
house rules 87
human capital 17
hypercorrection 109
hypocrisy 66, 213–14

identity-based groups 133–4
iFixit 67
illiteracy 14
immigrants 26, 55, 130; see also non-native speakers
impulse control 25
Indian people 133
indigenous people 55, 57–58

indoctrination 9, 11, 216
Indonesian 177
inequality: gender 71; social 4, 90, 106, 124, 130, 151, 156; *see also* equality
insults 64, 65
intelligence 5, 14, 111; *see also* artificial intelligence (AI); IQ
intergenerational injustice 38
internet 194; linguistic innovation 186, 188–91; slang 168, 186
IQ 19; *see also* intelligence
Ireland 56
Italian 147, 177

James, Aaron 72
James, William 175
Japanese 134, 177, 181
jargon 168, 192–3; *see also* slang
Jepperson, Otto 115
Joyce, James 185
justice 11, 53, 72
Jutes 171

K–12 education 12
Kinzinger, Adam 113
Knausgaard, Karl Ove 186
Korean 181
Krispy Kreme 191
Ktiv Male 179
Kurzban, Robert 208
Kymlicka, Will 51, 55

labor market 108, 110
Lakhota 134
Lakoff, Robin 117
"Land of the Free and The Elements of Style, The" 33
Lanehart, Sonja 135
Langton, Rae 65
language: alphabetic 19; auxiliary rules 178; and civics education 12; common 12, 183–4; death 58; endangered 57–8; evolution of 170–1; flexible approach to 176–81; and grammatical genders 146–51; and law 51–61; minority 51–60; native 12, 49; offensive 91–7, 153; patterns 28; preservation 52, 56–8; rights 55; sign 21–2, 134–5; universal conventions 176–8; *see also* language policies; language policing
Language Act of 1993 56
Language Arts instruction 21, 26, 28
language policies 51–52; bilingual 53; ethics of 53; national 49, 51, 53–5, 58–60
language policing 6, 15, 27, 52, 53, 62, 65–6, 73–4, 82, 88, 92, 97; and class 107, 112; egalitarian 104–6, 130, 134, 143–6, 150–5; and gender 114, 116, 118; politically motivated 211–12; and pronouns 136–8; and race 124; and sexuality 122
Latin 147
Latinx 149
law: common 12; and language 51–61; and social norms 70–1
leadership 68–9
legal codes 172
legally protected speech 95
legal sanctions 49–52
lesbians 123
LGBT rights 113
liberalism 51, 72, 144, 151, 213, 220, 221, 225
libertarianism 60
lingua franca 183
linguistic anarchism 6
linguistic appropriation 131–6
linguistic authoritarianism 4, 51, 52
linguistic competency 12, 13, 68–70, 106, 110–11

linguistic compliance 3, 10, 50, 52, 78, 90, 110; *see also* linguistic non-compliance
linguistic conservatism 193–7
linguistic disobedience 5
linguistic diversity 54, 55, 58, 183–4, 196, 210
linguistic guidelines 10
linguistic innovation 6, 168, 179–180, 184–193
linguistic non-compliance 7, 9, 50, 70, 76, 84, 111, 138–9, 143, 219; *see also* linguistic compliance
linguistic normativity 128, 135, 143, 224–225; and dyslexia education 18; enforcement of 5–6, 39, 50; and gender 114–115; and labor market 110; and race 124; and regional dialects 127; resisting 205–206; and respect 82–3; in school education 9–10; and style guides 32, 37
linguistic prescriptivism 34–5, 37, 127, 142–3, 168, 176, 182, 217
linguistic reform 149–51
linguistic rules 3, 5, 6, 9, 14, 49–50, 79, 168, 169, 184
linguistic variation 53–4, 70, 87–8, 124, 135, 172–3, 182, 212
LinkedIn 110
lipreading 22
lisp 119, 120–1, 123
literacy 9, 10; markers 14; promoting 9, 15, 21; *see also* literacy instruction
literacy instruction 14–18, 23, 28, 40; and dyslexic children 18, 20–1, 23
logographic writing systems 19
lower class 108–10, 113–14, 127
lower-status groups 106, 152, 154
Lum, Nora 132
Lyft 191

Mace, Nancy 112–13
Madagascar 115
Mandarin 54
manipulation 89–90
manners 81–8
manualism 21–2
marginalized groups 105, 130–1, 133
McCullogh, Gretchen 189–90
McWhorter, John 179, 125–6
medical advice 76–7
men: bisexual 123; gay 119–22; straight 120–1; *see also* gender
Meriwether, Nicholas 141, 142
metal songs 95
middle class 108
Middle English 174, 176
minority groups 6, 55, 152, 206
minority languages 51–60
misspellings 64, 65, 72, 113, 186; of names 83, 85, 92; in online communication 190–2
Mitchell, David 80
morality 54, 81–5, 94, 113, 133, 141; *see also* ethics
moral obligations 73
moral standards 82–3
moral status 106
Morgioni, Mark 192
Mormon Church 175
Morrigan, Clementine 150
multi-sensory learning 20
music 95
myths 182

names 83, 85, 92; non-standard spellings 192; trade 168
National Council of Teachers of English 124
national identity 54
national language policies 49, 51, 53–5, 58–60
national pride 13

nation-building 12
Native Americans 12
native languages 12, 49
neologisms 190
neuroticism 5
New York Times 39
Niqqud 179
non-binary people 136–40, 142–3, 145–6, 149
non-native speakers 6, 15, 25–6, 129–30
non-standard spellings 113, 186, 191–2; *see also* misspellings
nuance 185, 187, 190

Oakshot, Michael 182
obscenity 93–6
Ocasio-Cortez, Alexandria 114
ODO *see* Oxford Dictionary Online
Offense to Others 96
offensive language 91–7, 153
Official Languages Act of 2003 56
Old English 172, 173
older generations 39–40
Oliver, Jamie 19
online communication 176, 188–91; *see also* internet
oppression 56, 90, 131, 204–6
oralism 22–3
oralist culture 19
Orrm 173–4
orthographic anarchy 169, 180, 181
orthographic standards 175, 180
Orton–Gillingham (OG) approach 20–1
ostracization 62, 70, 103
Oxford Dictionary Online (ODO) 188
Oxford University Press 188

parental investment 14, 28
parents' preferences 27–32
Patten, Alan 51, 59–60

pedantry 208–10
personality traits 209–10
"personalized orthographies" 175, 189
personalized typography 190
Peterson, Jordan 143, 145
Pettit, Philip 71
philosophy 193
phonetic symbols 19
phonics 16, 20–1
pictographic writing system 189
Pilkey, Dav 186–7
Pinker, Steven 34–5, 152
Polari 122
Polish 147
politeness 181
political leadership 68–9
Portuguese 180
poverty 17
power asymmetry 89
praise 2, 9, 71, 206
prejudice 10, 70, 152, 189, 216, 224
printing press 174–5
profanity 92–6
professional communication 118–19, 190
professional success 110–11
pronoun refusers 136–46; pedantic 138–40, 144; political 138, 143–4; principled 138, 141–4; punitive 138, 140–1, 144–6
pronouns 136–7; gender-specific 139; non-binary 139, 140, 143; rituals 142; *see also* pronoun refusers
pronunciation 108
public life 53, 60, 91, 203, 211
public service 55
Pullman 36
Pullum, Geoffrey K. 33
punctuation 10, 23, 118, 119, 186, 223
punk 95

Quayle, Dan 68
Quebec 53

race 70, 124–30
racial hierarchy 125
racism 93, 126, 127, 153
radicals 148
radio 115–16
rap 95
reading 9, 12; comprehension 14, 16, 21, 22; skills 14; *see also* reading instruction
reading instruction: and children with dyslexia 20–3; outdated strategies 16–17; phonics-based approach 16, 20–1; whole-word approach 16
Reddit 191
regional dialects 124, 127–30
reinforcement 135
relationships 71
religious convictions 141
republicanism 71
reputation 64, 65
respect 82–3
resume screening software 111
Roman alphabet 172
Rooney, Sally 186
Roosevelt, Theodore 175
rote memorization 28
Runic writing system 172
Russian 147
Rutgers 126–7

SAE *see* Standard American English
Savage, Dan 121
Saxons 171
Scheffler, Samuel 195, 207
schools 4–5, 9–41; and linguistic normativity 9–10; private 11, 21; public 13, 15, 21, 31, 49, 52, 60, 91, 107, 110; use of dialects by students 125; *see also* education

Scottish dialect 129
screening software 111, 112
Scripps National Spelling Bee 30
Sedaris, David 120–1
Seidenberg, Mark 16–17
self-censorship 153–4
self-esteem 58, 65, 80
self-expression 185
self-respect 204
Sense of Style, The 34
sexual identity 119–24
sexuality 119–24
Shakespeare, William 184–5
sign language 21–2, 134–5
silencing 66
skill deficit 111
slang: grunge 39; internet 168, 186; as a working-class phenomenon 108; *see also* jargon
slurs 92–4
Smith, Jennifer 129
Smith, Sir Thomas 174
Smith, Zadie 194–6
snoots 36–7, 64, 78, 85, 104, 135–6, 205, 209–10
social change 151, 213, 217
social class 107–14; lower 108–10, 113–14, 127; middle 108; and sticklerism 109–10, 114; and stigmatization 113–14; upper 109; working 107–8, 112, 113, 128
social control 5, 31, 80–1, 146, 153, 212
social disadvantage 17, 26, 62, 104, 130–1, 152–3, 205
social dominance 4, 5, 88, 90, 106
social egalitarianism 103–7, 154–5, 206–7
social equality 4, 13, 105–6, 116, 155
social hierarchy 4, 62, 71, 73, 103–6, 114, 151, 154

social identity 54–5, 58, 103–5, 183–4, 196, 210; linguistic appropriation 130–3
social inequality 4, 90, 106, 124, 130, 151, 156
social justice 72
social life 6
social media 194–5
social mobility 12, 27, 60
social norms 7, 61–3, 71–5; for communicators 91–2; disrespectful 73; ethics of 72–5, 85; and law 70–1; and moral obligations 73; and profanity 93
social power 72, 93–4, 107
social practices 72–4, 91, 106, 107, 116, 206, 218
social pressure 71
social sanctions 4, 5, 7, 49–50, 81, 94, 96, 105, 117, 137, 206; ethics of 50, 60–75; and pronoun refusal 136–8, 140, 142–6
social standing 71–2, 106, 145
social status 62, 80, 90, 103, 105–7, 154–5, 207; *see also* lower-status groups; social hierarchy
socioeconomic disadvantage 124
socioeconomic status 6
software 110, 198; dictation 21, 22, 24; editing 198; screening 111, 112
Sorry to Bother You 129
southern accents 108, 120, 127
Spain 60
Spanish language 147, 149–50
speech: act theory 65–6; freedom of 143; gendered differences 115–17, 123; lesbians 123; political 143; trans people 123; *see also* gay voice
spellchecking technology 21, 24, 198
spelling bees 10, 30–2, 37, 223

spelling books 175
spelling competitions 30–1; *see also* spelling bees
spelling conventions 21, 30, 85, 147, 184, 191
spelling errors 49, 111, 187, 226; *see also* spelling mistakes
spelling grades 14
spelling homework 30
spelling instruction 27
spelling mistakes 83, 111–12, 190; *see also* spelling errors
spelling reform 173
spelling rituals 27–32
spelling tests 5, 10, 28–30; pre-employment 111–12
Stagg, Emily 30
Standard American English (SAE) 124, 125, 129, 132
Standard Written English (SWE) 36
static ideology 11
St. Felix, Doreen 129
sticklerism 2–5, 9, 32, 37–8; and gaslighting 90–1; as an inegalitarian disposition 207; harmful effects of 69–70; informal 50; justifications for 75–8, 80–1, 85; legal, 49–50; origins of 172–4; psychology of 209; rejecting 204, 213; and social class 109–10, 114; and social norms 61–3, 65–7, 73; and social sanctions 49–50; solidaristic 182–3; *see also* grammarianism
sticklerlessness 210–13
stigmatization 4, 18, 63, 65, 73, 93, 95, 103–4, 106, 130; and class 113–14; and gender 114–15; and pronoun refusal 137–8, 140–2, 145–6; and sexual identity 119–21, 137, 140–2, 217
Strunk Jr, William 32–4, 67

style guides 10, 32–7
Sullivan, John 111–12
Supyire 148
Swahili 148
Swedish 147
Swift, Taylor 113
Switzerland 60

taboo words 92–4, 153
taste 81
Taylor-Greene, Marjorie 112–14
teaching instruction 16–17
text-based communication 188–9
Thrope, David 120
Tibet 54
Topics 134–5
traditions 73, 195
translation 182, 184, 194, 198
trans people: pronouns 137–40, 142–6, 149; speech 123
translation apps 198
Trump, Donald 112–14, 128
Truss, Lynne 2, 3
Tumblr 191
Turkish 177
Tuyuca 181
Twain, Mark 185
Twitter 194

United Kingdom 92, 116, 153
United States 113:
communicative styles 115; indigenous communities 57–8; offensive speech 95, 96, 153; official language 12, 51, 53; regional accents 127–8; use of profanity 92–3
universal basic income (UBI) 73–4
upper class 109
up-speak 115

Valentini, Laura 73
verbal communication 126; *see also* speech

verbs 169–70, 181
violence 96–7
vocabularies 28, 108, 115, 186
vocal fry 115, 116
vocal training 123

Wallace, David Foster 36, 193, 195
Webster, Noah 175
Wells, H.G. 185
Welsh 56
White, E. B. 32–4, 67
White children 134
Wiens, Kyle 67
William the Conqueror 173
Wilson, Jim 207
Wolman, David 173
women: bisexual 123; Black 135; communicative styles 114–19, 135; *see also* gender; lesbians
word study 28
working class 107–8, 112, 113, 128
World War I 52
Wright, Colin 141–2
Wright, Sue 55
writers 10, 32–6
writing 12, 14–15; *see also* writing instruction
writing instruction 16; dyslexic students 20–4; evidence-based approach 16–17; outdated strategies 16–17
written communication 14; shift in formality and standardization 126; and students with dyslexia 20–4; and use of emojis 189; and women 118; *see also* text-based communication

"yes" 187–8
Young, Brigham 175
Young, Molly 192
young people 6, 39–40

For Product Safety Concerns and Information please contact our EU representative GPSR@taylorandfrancis.com
Taylor & Francis Verlag GmbH, Kaufingerstraße 24, 80331 München, Germany

www.ingramcontent.com/pod-product-compliance
Lightning Source LLC
Chambersburg PA
CBHW050519170426
43201CB00013B/2013